Return on or before the
last date stamped below.

Learning Resources
Centre

Kingston College
Kingston Hall Road
Kingston upon Thames
KT1 2AQ

THE
INNISKILLING
DIARIES
1899-1903

THE INNISKILLING DIARIES 1899-1903

1st Battalion, 27th Royal Inniskilling Fusiliers in South Africa

by

MARTIN CASSIDY

Foreword by

BRIGADIER W. J. HILES CBE

LEO COOPER

First published in Great Britain in 2001 by
LEO COOPER
an imprint of
Pen & Sword Books
47 Church Street,
Barnsley,
South Yorkshire,
S70 2AS

A catalogue record for this book
Is available from the British Library

Typeset by S. S. & R. S. Cassidy
Printed in the United Kingdom by
CPI UK

Dedication

*For my wife Penny
and children Simon, Ruth and Stephanie.
Also my son and friend Steven,
a very brave, courageous and truly remarkable young man
whom we all deeply love and miss.*

Contents

Foreword

Since the inception of the Regiment in 1689 the history of the Royal Inniskilling Fusiliers has been a catalogue of outstanding valour and unstinting courage. The Regiment's impressive list of Battle Honours bear ample testimony to the exemplary conduct and sacrifice of its men, of all ranks, throughout the centuries. One such Battle Honour, the Relief of Ladysmith, like so many others now, bears silent witness to the valour of a bygone age, an age which witnessed the last great Victorian campaign of the nineteenth century and marked one of the Regiment's most glorious, if costly, engagements of its long, illustrious history.

This book rekindles the memory of those halcyon days and acknowledges the participation of both officers and enlisted men alike, on an equal footing. However, to appreciate this book fully one must realize that a Regiment is more than a name on a banner or an anonymous collection of individuals. It is an amalgam of the deeds and aspirations of those who now serve and those who have gone before. It is the embodiment of all that a nation holds to be just and right in a world that all too often fails to respect and honour creed, colour or caste. It is therefore only fitting that this book endeavours to awaken long-forgotten memories, to bring to the fore once more the deeds of Inniskilling Hill and acknowledge the ultimate sacrifice paid by so many. Rightful credit is given to Lieutenant Colonel Thackeray and the men of the 1st Battalion for their gallant charge on that late February day in 1900, which brought about the relief of the beleaguered Ladysmith and a reversal in the fortunes of the British Army, which until then had been less than glorious.

However, it must also be stated that this book, while celebrating the valour of the Royal Inniskilling Fusiliers, is not in itself a glorification of war. One only has to examine the content of the diaries and the lengthy casualty index to appreciate the full horror of warfare. War in itself is never glorious but the deeds men are often called upon to perform most certainly can be and as such deserve our lasting admiration and gratitude.

Moreover we are brought face to face, metaphorically speaking, with those long since dead individuals who, in their time, added yet another glorious chapter to the annals of the Regiment and in so doing create an atmosphere in which we can appreciate the individual, rather than simply impartially viewing the overall conduct of the war. History books, on the whole, concentrate on facts, statistics, ideologies and the main participants to an event to the exclusion of all else, especially the common individual. Seldom if ever do they lend credence to the smaller 'bit players,' so to speak. This work tries to rectify this and give existing family members the chance to have the participation of a relative rightfully acknowledged and honoured. Without them there would be no Royal Inniskilling Fusiliers. A Regiment is only as honourable and glorious as those who constitute it. It is only right and fitting that this work gives deserved credit where credit is due and most certainly credit is due to Mr. Martin Cassidy. Driven by family links with the Regiment, he set out to chronicle its, and by association their, movements during the 2nd Boer War. By skilful use of three contemporary diaries held by the Regimental Museum he has managed to put together a fascinating and immensely readable story. This has been a true labour of love, which Inniskillings, and all those who cherish the memory of our forbears who fought in South Africa a century ago, will appreciate and treasure.

Bill Hiles

Brigadier W. J. Hiles CBE
Chairman of Trustees
Royal Inniskilling Fusiliers

Acknowledgements

It is not my intention here to delve into the rights and wrongs, whys and wherefores, causes or effects of the Boer War 1899-1902. My intention is to trace and highlight the contribution of the 1st Battalion the Royal Inniskilling Fusiliers, from mobilization to repatriation, to detail their movements, achievements and casualties over the same period in such a manner as will allow the reader a more human, less statistical, approach. To this end I am gratefully indebted to Major G. Stephens MBE, lately curator of the Royal Inniskilling Fusiliers Regimental Museum, Enniskillen Castle, and his staff, especially Margaret Mulligan, for their kind assistance and permission to make use of their archive material. In more recent times I would like to thank Major Jack Dunlop and Captain Dick Thompson for their invaluable assistance. I would also like to thank Mr David Hall of Enniskillen, the Derry City Council and The Honourable The Irish Society for their assistance in this venture.

I would like to thank my wife Penny and children Simon, Ruth and Stephanie for their support and encouragement throughout this entire project. A very special debt of thanks is owed to my late son and friend Steven, a graduate in Applied Computing at the University of Ulster, for his invaluable assistance, encouragement and above all, counsel, which I now so sadly miss. Also I am indebted to my son Simon, a computer whiz in his own right, without whose expertise this book would never have been possible. I would also like to thank my daughter Ruth, an A Level history student, for aiding my research, and my daughter Stephanie for her keen knowledge of photography and scanning. Without them my task would have been much more difficult.

I would like to express my thanks to Brigadier W. J. Hiles CBE and the Trustees of the Royal Inniskilling Fusiliers for their support and permission to use Private L. J. Bryant's and Lieutenant D. G. Auchinleck's diaries of which they hold copyright. In the case of Captain Jeffcoat, I would like to thank the Museum of Ladysmith, South Africa, for their kind permission to use his diary, of which they hold both the original manuscript and copyright.

Thanks is also extended to Colonel James Condon, Royal Inniskilling Fusiliers Retd., who proof read my manuscript and assisted in the clarification of several points contained within the diaries.

However, undoubtedly the lion's share of my appreciation must fall to the three diarists, Captain A. C. Jeffcoat DSO, Lieutenant D. G. Auchinleck, and 4445 Private L. J. Bryant. Without their invaluable insight in recording such accounts this book would not have been possible. However, of these, Private Bryant stands head and shoulders above the rest, his being the most comprehensive. His account of the movements of the Regiment, from its departure from Mullingar until his return to the United Kingdom is highly informative but above all human, written I might add in a manner one would seldom expect of an enlisted soldier at the turn of the century.

Unpretentious, his diary does not attempt to analyse any aspect of the war. Such niceties were of no major significance to the ordinary soldier in the field. It was simply his task to follow orders and hope for a speedy and, above all, safe outcome. His diary is all the more remarkable, in that even through all his duties and fatigues he still found time to keep such an informative account. Although possibly not always recorded on the actual day, his account of certain dates may differ from the other two diaries, which is quite excusable under the circumstances.

The diaries of the two officers of the Regiment, on the other hand, are extremely brief, especially that of Captain A. C. Jeffcoat. Nevertheless, they are equally informative and allow us a brief insight into their lives and personal thoughts. By comparing these diaries I hope I have produced a book, which whilst informative, is also entertaining.

As a great deal centres on the diary accounts of three vastly differing individuals I have kept to their personal script as much as possible. To interfere with this would be to alter the reader's perception of the writer. To this end I have endeavoured to retain the spelling and grammar as originally intended, even though they may fall far short of today's standards. Also, as can be clearly recognized, many of the place names differ in spelling from individual to individual because the writers were often spelling them as they heard them pronounced, possibly writing in haste depending upon the circumstances in which they found themselves at the time.

As might be expected, dates and circumstance may also differ for a variety of reasons. Captain Jeffcoat and Lieutenant Auchinleck were not always with the main body of the Battalion, which resulted in differing accounts recorded on particular dates. Likewise, what was important to one individual may not necessarily have been as significant to the next. What is clear, however, is, whether on detachment, convoy or column, a common strain links their individual accounts.

It is also clearly evident from the diaries of Captain Jeffcoat, Lieutenant Auchinleck and Private Bryant that, whilst belonging to the same Regiment and engaged in the same conflict, their preferences differ quite significantly. Whereas the entries of both officers are scant and brief, terminating quite abruptly in the case of Captain Jeffcoat, those of Private Bryant span from embarkation to repatriation. He has the ability to capture the every-day mood of a private soldier whilst charting the movement of the Regiment throughout the campaign.

It is quite understandable to expect the diary account of an officer to concentrate on the more logistical side of the conflict, yet this is not the case. Both officers demonstrate a preference for the more mundane, relating their personal social experiences rather than cataloguing strategies.

However, be that as it may, the combination of all three diaries give us a wonderful insight into what it must have been like to be a soldier at the turn of the century. Uppermost, all three diarists record what it was like to be involved in the last great Victorian campaign of the nineteenth century before the stagnated trench warfare of World War I, a war which would claim the lives of many of those selfsame troops. In all I hope these diaries are both informative and entertaining, providing the reader with as much enjoyment reading their accounts as I have had compiling them

I wish also to acknowledge the assistance and support of Tom Hartman and Barbara Bramall, Production Manager Pen & Sword throughout this venture. My thanks are also extended to Mary Campbell for her unstinting energy upon my behalf.

Finally I would like to express my thanks to Brigadier Henry Wilson and my publisher Pen & Sword for giving me this opportunity to bring to light diaries which hitherto, for the most part, have remained dormant and unappreciated.

Biographies

The following are brief biographies of the three Diarists.
Of the three, two lost their lives in the Great War 1914-1919.

Lieutenant D. G. H. Auchinleck

Lieutenant Daniel George Harold Auchinleck was the son of Major Thomas Auchinleck of Crevenagh, Omagh, Co. Tyrone and the husband of Madoline Auchinleck. Having served with the 1st Battalion during the Boer War 1899-1903, he served as a Captain with the 2nd Battalion the Royal Inniskilling Fusiliers during World War I. He was killed in action after just a few months at the Front on 20 October 1914 at the age of 37. He is interred in the Strand Military Cemetery, Colines-Warneton, Hainaut, Belgium, 13 km South of Ieper, Grave Ref. VIII. Q. 6. Originally located near an Advanced Dressing Station, the cemetery was extended when plots VII to X were added after the Armistice. These rows contain soldiers who lost their lives in battlefields between Wytschaete and Armentières.

Captain A. C. Jeffcoat, DSO

For his service in the Boer War 1899-1902 Captain A. C. Jeffcoat was Mentioned in Despatches on 13 September 1900 and also awarded the Distinguished Service Order during the Boer War 1899-1903. During World War I he served as a full Colonel in the Royal Fusiliers. He was appointed a CB and CMC and died on 10 December 1963.

4445 Private L. J. Bryant

Born at Leytonstone, Essex, he received a Mention in Despatches on 4 September 1901 during the Boer War. A member of the Regimental Band he served as a sergeant with the 2nd Battalion Royal Inniskilling Fusiliers during World War I. He died at home on Saturday 6 July 1919 and is interred in the Brookwood Military Cemetery, Woking Surrey, Grave Ref. VI. H. 8A. Brookwood is situated 30 miles from London near the village of Pirbright.

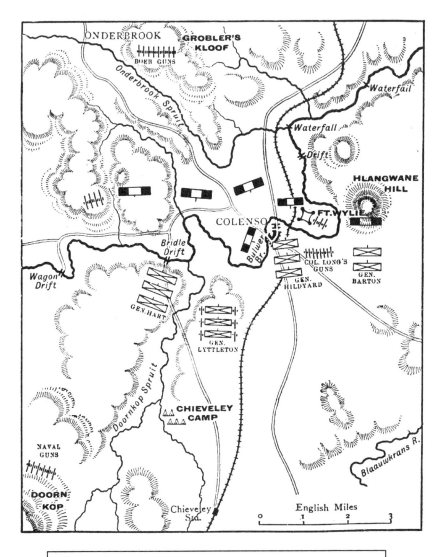

Map of the Battle of Colenso 15 December 1899

Map showing Buller's three unsuccessful and final successful attempt to drive the Boers from their position on the Tugela

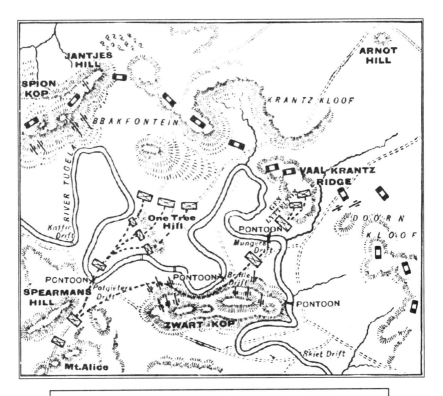

Map showing the terrain and displacement of forces at the
Battle of Vaal Krantz.

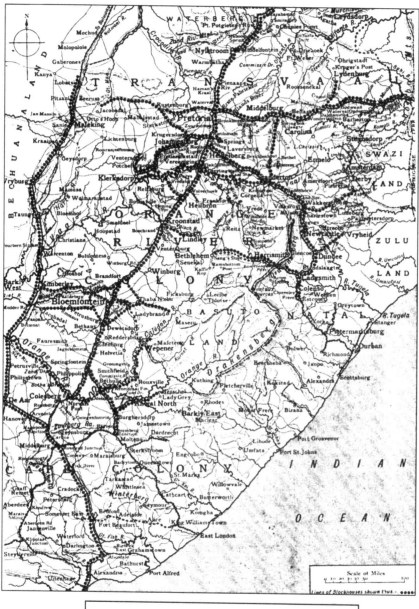

Map of South Africa depicting Blockhouse lines.

Chapter One

Declaration of War
Mobilization-Transportation

October the 11th 1899 saw the British Empire drawn deeper into a conflict in South Africa which had been brewing for decades. Reckless indifference and political apathy resulted in what many observers, both at home and abroad, had been predicting since the 1st Boer War of the early 1880s.

Rearmament in the Transvaal, ever-growing hostility to British interests in the region and racially motivated tensions had gone unchecked by a British government whose policy of softly, softly and appeasement was interpreted by many as nothing less than moral cowardice. Such political indifference lent credence to a Boer manifesto that promised to sweep the British from South Africa once and for all. The quasi-independent states of Transvaal and Orange Free State, geographically dependent on such close relations with their British neighbours, harboured a scarcely concealed desire to see a united Dutch Free State that would encompass the British-dominated regions of Natal and Cape Colony.

A century which had witnessed the abolition of slavery, the annexation of Natal in 1834, the Great Trek[1] of 1837, the annexation of the Orange Free State in 1848 and the prohibition of the Dutch language in all official documents and court proceedings, combined to heighten growing fear amongst the Boers of British domination and the loss of their Dutch cultural identity.

However, as previously stated in the introduction, it is not my intention to delve into the rights and wrongs of the Boer War. Whether Britain had any moral right to take the stance which it found itself adopting at the turn of the century, or for that matter whether it was justifiably right for a section of the Boer populace to take upon itself the task of enforcing its ideology upon the remainder, is not my objective in this book. Suffice to say that the past nine decades have more than amply tested and found wanting a Boer policy of short-sighted isolation and racially motivated apartheid.

The first inkling the people of Britain received that the government was about to take action against the Boers was the issue of a proclamation on 9 October 1899 calling upon army reservists to report to their regiments in preparation for the impending conflict. In the case of the Royal Inniskilling Fusiliers four hundred and sixty eight reservists were notified, of which all but four duly reported for duty within a few days. The whole process of mobilization progressed quite swiftly and was completed by 19th of the month.

At first mobilization and the impending prospect of all-out hostilities was greeted with mixed feelings, especially at governmental level. Whilst one faction accused the British government of immorally using the plight of the Outlanders[2] to annex the rich goldfields of the Rand, government supporters declared it was acting justly in defence of the civil rights of not only the Outlanders but also the local native population. It was also widely believed that, should the government ignore their cause, it would signal a capitulation to the Boers, which would demean and erode the very fabric of the Empire.

After months of lengthy negotiations between London and Pretoria, aimed at securing a compromise acceptable to all, the prospect of all-out war still loomed on the horizon. In a final attempt to avert hostilities a message was dispatched to President Kruger[3] in which the British Government laid down a series of final demands which had to be acceptable to the government of the Transvaal if war was not to be inevitable. The British ultimatum demanded a franchise attainable after five year's residence, a greater representation for the Outlander majority in the Volksraad, the Transvaal parliament, and equality of the Dutch and English languages within that Parliament.

Although Britain wished to avoid hostilities by inciting the Boers into all-out conflict, it took steps to reinforce the small detachment of around 7000 troops already in South Africa by despatching 5000 from England and recalling a further 5000 from India. It was hoped such a move would strengthen their hand and force an early reply to their ultimatum.

Unfortunately the response from the Volksraad took the form of a flat, all-out refusal. It seemed there was no room for manoeuvre. The Boer refusal not only slammed the door upon any further negotiations, it was accompanied by a stepping-up of military preparation in defiance of Britain.

Yet the British Government held off and waited. Its failure to move positively to a state of mobilization and readiness was seized upon by the Boers. It was only on 7 October, after a delay of approximately three weeks, that mobilization in England was finally ordered. By 9 October the Boers had handed the British a counter ultimatum.

The Boers not only demanded the withdrawal of all troops who had landed in South Africa since 1 June 1899, but also that no further troops be sent. In issuing such an ultimatum the Volksraad left Britain little or no room to manoeuvre. However Kruger had misinterpreted Britain's dalliance and banked on her reluctance to engage in hostilities. On the contrary not only did his ill-conceived ultimatum unite a previously divided England, it left the British Government with no alternative but to put the Empire on a war footing. As a consequence, mobilization and the stepping-up of preparations for war was inevitable.

Mobilization, out of necessity, was a hasty affair. Delay resulted in inadequate arrangements hastily prepared. Nevertheless, had mobilization been completed in May or June, as some had wished, it might in fact only have delayed the inevitable. Britain wasn't ready to engage in a conflict of the size envisaged, preparations for which would be lengthy and inevitably delayed to facilitate time for all avenues, of a political settlement, to be investigated.

However, as events unfolded the order to mobilize was issued on 7 October, but mobilization did not officially begin until the 9th. Indeed there could be no great haste, as transport on the scale required simply could not be assembled at such short notice.

The following is a facsimile of the official telegram that gave notice of the declaration of war.

Natal Government Telegraphs.[4]
Handed in at PIETERMARITZBURG, 9:10a.m.
Received LADYSMITH, 9:25 A.M. 12TH Oct. 1899.

FROM: General, Communications.

TO: (Col: W. Knox C.B.), Commandant, Ladysmith.

12th Octr. 1899. No. 662. South African Republic have declared war against Great Britain Stop. British Agent left Pretoria last evening. Durban, Estcourt, Glencoe & Ladysmith informed.

When preparations had finally been completed the force to be despatched was comprised as follows.[5]

Nominal Strength

• 1Cavalry Divisions	5,500	Troops
• 3 Infantry Divisions	30,000	Troops
• Corps Troops	5,000	Troops
• Line of Communications and Reserves	11,000	Troops
Total number	51,500	Troops

Actual Fighting Strength

Manpower	Artillery pieces
• 4,820 (1Cavalry Divisions)	12
• 26,430 (3 Infantry Divisions)	54
• 3,450 (Corps Troops)	48
• 11,000 (Lineof Communications And Reserves)	----
Total	114

When examining these figures it must be realized, however, that the fighting strength of this force included only cavalry, artillery and infantry. It excluded engineers, army service corps and ammunition columns. Thus it must be noted that from the outset the Army Service Corps was theoretically below strength. The overall figure of 46,000 troops belies the fact that the force was seriously ill-prepared. Out of the 46,000 men only 5,600 were either cavalry or mounted infantry, which when we realize the Boers were mounted almost to a man placed the Army Corps at a serious disadvantage.

The ratio of troops to artillery field pieces was also well below standard. Normally a force of such magnitude would have had five more batteries of artillery or thirty more guns. As it was, it became necessary to remove the guns from battleships such as HMS *Powerful* to supplement the lack of artillery on the ground. Under the direction of

Captain Percy Scott CB of HMS *Terrible* a number of 45-pounder naval guns were rapidly acquired to act as makeshift heavy artillery. Captain Scott was also responsible for the design of a railway truck which allowed for greater mobility and from which they could be fired.

These improvised artillery pieces, mounted on makeshift limbers, which were to become known as Scott carriages, played a significant role throughout the course of the war. Though their huge bulk could prove quite a transport problem, movement of such guns was further hampered by the climatic conditions that often dictated the speed of the campaign. The veldt is a dry arid landscape which rain can transform in a matter of hours into an impassable quagmire.

Besides the use of the naval guns, sailors were also widely used to redress a lack of army personnel. Not only were they used to man the 4.7 inch naval guns and to operate as maxim gun detachments, they were also used at the front to support and supplement the infantry. Known as Bluejackets, because the sailors disliked wearing khaki jackets which unlike their loose- fitting naval jackets fitted too closely around the neck, these men together with detachments of Royal Marines saw action in various battle including Belmont, Enslin or Graspan, Modder River and Magersfontein to mention but a few. Together they made up a small naval brigade under Flag-Captain Prothero of HMS *Doris*.

From the outset a catalogue of errors, misjudgements, miscalculations and botched opportunities on both sides dogged the course of the war. The abortive Jameson Raid did little but draw Kruger's attention to the inadequate defence of the Transvaal thus affording him the opportunity to bolster its armaments. When again, having learnt of the proposed reinforcement of the British military presence in South Africa, his ill-conceived, ill-timed ultimatum simply added weight to Sir Alfred Milner's[6] efforts to precipitate hostilities. A highly intelligent but unbending Imperial Administrator, his appointment by the Conservative Colonial Secretary Joseph Chamberlain[7] was a clear indication of the Government's intention to follow a course of federation for the Transvaal, and should all else fail, Kruger was to be portrayed as the aggressor.

Once hostilities had begun, however, both factions demonstrated an almost uncanny similarity in their ability to opt for the wrong strategy. The Boers for their part, rather than learning from the mistakes encountered during the 1st Boer war of 1881 and seizing upon their crushing victory at Majuba Hill,[8] set about a policy of investment. Having taken the British forces by surprise at Dundee resulting in the death of Major-General Sir Penn-Symons and the near annihilation and capture of his troops, the Boers rather than following up their success, set about investing Ladysmith, Kimberley and Mafeking. Of little strategic importance, this only served to tie up a vital mobile guerrilla force for an indefinite period. Such an act of investment rather than forcing the British to the negotiating table only served to strengthen their resolve. It placed the government in such a position that the overwhelming strength of public opinion, which had hitherto been indifferent if not opposed to a military solution, now actually demanded it.

On the part of the British, General Sir George White having bungled his attempt to halt the advance of the Boers after Dundee, allowed his Natal Field Force to become cut off and trapped within the besieged Ladysmith. However, this was just the first in a series of blunders British forces would suffer a series of mostly self-induced, morale-crushing defeats that would become known in the press as Black Week.

Poor intelligence, a lack of thorough reconnoitring and a military policy of near suicidal frontal attacks resulted in a series of ignominious defeats inflicted by the Boers. The defeat of General Gatacre's troops at Stormberg on 10 December, followed closely by the defeat of the Guards and Highlanders at Magersfontein on the 11th, culminating in Buller's abortive attempt to cross the Tugela and the disastrous consequences of Colenso on the 15th, convinced many opponents of the war that the South African campaign was going to be more than a punitive expedition against a handful of farmers. The war was now viewed in a different light. It became a matter of honour to restore the good name of the Empire and the British Army.

The announcement that the 27th had been called up and would soon embark for South Africa was greeted, on the whole, with enthusiasm. In the best Victorian tradition, the Royal Inniskilling Fusiliers were given a rousing send-off by crowds of well-wishers as they vacated their barracks and entrained at Mullingar bound for Queenstown[9] in County Cork on 30 October 1899.

An air of expectation was prevalent among the troops as they travelled south. Such was the enthusiasm of the local people as they passed through the various small towns and villages en route that crowds gathered at every opportunity along the way to cheer them on. After a pleasant if uneventful trip the Inniskilling Fusiliers were greeted once more by enthusiastic flag-waving crowds as they reached Queenstown. Hundreds of well-meaning residents turned out to wish the departing regiments good luck as they embarked for South Africa aboard the steamship SS *Catalonia*. In all, a total compliment of twenty-nine

Officers and 971 other ranks embarked with the battalion at 4pm on 5 November 1899.

5th Nov. 99 L. J. Bryant
"Send Off," from Ireland.

We appeared in Battalion Orders to proceed to Queenstown, to embark on the S S Catalonia, en route for South Africa. The left Hand Battalion & the Band, fell in on the Barrack Square, Mullingar, Ireland at 12.30 a.m. to march off to the Railway Station.

(The Right Half Battalion & the Drums fell in at 11.30 p.m. 4.12.1899) We (the Left Half Bn.) marched off to the Station at 12.45 a.m. to catch the 1.30 train for Queenstown, the Band played the usual Farewell Tunes. We received a hearty send off from the townspeople [Mullingar] some of whom formed a torchlight procession and formed up in front of us!........A large crowd of people, from all parts of Ireland, assembled on the Quay to watch our Embarkation.

Our band played a few patriotic airs to while away the time whilst everything was being got on board the ship before she sailed. We left Queenstown about 4 p.m. amid loud cheering and waving of handkerchiefs from the crowd assembled on the Quay and from the Blue Jackets on board Her Majesty's Training Ship Black Prince. We passed very close to their ships, & their band played "Soldiers of the Queen," "Rule Britannia" & other patriotic airs as we sailed by.

Many of the people of Queenstown had their houses beautifully illuminated with coloured lights etc., which they displayed as we steamed out of the harbour. We then made ourselves as comfortable as the circumstances would permit.

Little did the cheering crowds realize, nor for that matter did the departing troops, just how difficult and protracted the road ahead would prove to be, a course of events which would keep the Regiment in South Africa for nigh on three years and from which many of those who readily answered the call to mobilize would never return.

Eleven days previous to their departure the assembled Fusiliers were reviewed by Field Marshal Lord Roberts[10] VC of Kandahar and Waterford, Commander of the British Imperial Forces in Ireland since 1895 and soon to be Commander-in-Chief of the British Expeditionary Forces in South Africa. At that time the regimental strength of the 1st Battalion Inniskilling Fusiliers numbered thirty-one Officers and 1,215 NCOs & ORs.

First day out a storm arose which persisted for several days as they made their way south through the Bay of Biscay. Not having long to get accustomed to their new surroundings, seasickness was rife and there was a general air of relief when the storm finally subsided on the 10th after a continuous five days confined below decks.

6th Nov. L. J. Bryant
" Sea Voyage"

We encountered very rough weather.

7th Nov.

The Storm has not abated yet, so we have to stay below deck, as it is too rough for any of us to be above deck.

8th Nov.

The Storm is still raging. I, with many other, fell a victim of Sea Sickness.

9th Nov.

The Storm is not over yet, tho' its not as rough as on the proceeding days.

10th Nov.

The Storm is over at last. All hands at once scrambled up on deck to get a taste of fresh air, and to have a look around to see if there was any damage done to the boat by the storm.

A little wooden building which had been rigged up on deck to serve as a wash house for the troops was blown down during the storm. We had five horses on board ship when we started on our voyage but two were drowned during the storm and two more were so knocked about that they had to be shot.

Life on board ship was certainly anything but pleasant. The further they proceeded south, the more the stifling heat forced the men to remain on deck under awnings specially erected to provide shelter from the fierce sun. Time passed slowly and, as in all such cases the troops had plenty of time to examine their surroundings, especially the uncomfortable, cramped conditions in which they were billeted.

By the time the SS *Catalonia* docked at Las Palmas in the Grand Canary to take on fuel for the remainder of the trip south the ship was rife with rumours. Everything abounded, from the Siege of Ladysmith having been lifted to the near total cessation of hostilities. So keyed up for the impending conflicts were the Inniskillings that for the rest of the trip a sense of disappointment prevailed. However, the feeling that they would arrive too late quickly evaporated when they eventually dropped anchor in Table Bay on 30 November as news filtered through that the war was still very much ongoing.

11th Nov. L. J. Bryant

We arrived in Las Palmas about 7 p.m. & anchored for the night, as we have to get some more coal on board.

12th Nov.

The natives of Las Palmas came out very early this morning in their small boats, & surrounded the ship. They did a roaring trade by selling us Fruit, Tabacco, Cigarettes, Cigars, etc. dirt-cheap. The youngsters also reaped a good harvest by diving into the water for coppers. We left Las Palmas again at 3 p.m. amid loud cheers from the Blue Jackets on board H.M.S. "Hermione", which was anchored just outside Las Palmas, our band playing "A Life on the Ocean Wave," & other similar airs as we sailed away.

14th Nov. L. J. Bryant

Turned out very hot to day. The ship is now covered with awnings to protect us from the fierce heat from the sun. We had to remain on deck all day to make ourselves anyway comfortable, as it is too stifling to stay down below.

15 November 1899 witnessed a demoralizing setback for those British troops already in South Africa, the derailment of the armoured train at Chieveley, Natal. Having left Estcourt with a company of the Dublin Fusiliers, half a company of the Durban Light Infantry and a contingent of Bluejackets, the train passed Frere, south of Chieveley, only to discover that a large number of Boers held a section of high ground further up the line. Ordered to return, the armoured train headed back but was once more cut off by a party of Boers before it could reach Frere. Derailed by a boulder placed across the track, the Boers pinned the troops down until forced to surrender. However, the driver did manage to break the locomotive free of the wreckage and escape carrying several of the wounded and a section of the troops back to Frere. In doing so, those left behind were soon made captive, including Winston Churchill, who was there in his capacity as a newspaper correspondent. His capture and eventual escape would be closely followed by the world press in the weeks that followed.

15th Nov. L. J. Bryant

This was another very hot day. We started doing Gymnastics, in slippers, Three Coys. at a time.

16th Nov.

Another very hot day. The Orderly Sergeants came round the Battalion looking for Volunteers to be Bakers, as the ships Bakers were all sick, one having heat apoplexy.

17th Nov.

It was very cool all this day. The wind sprang up during the morning, which made the boat rock & pitch like a piece of cork in the water, but it turned out fine & calm afterwards. We got up a singsong amongst ourselves to pass away the time, & we are going to continue the practice every night if possible.

18th Nov.

A lot of the Troops got inoculated today, as it is supposed to be a preventative against Enteric Fever.

As the days passed slowly, the troops whiled away the time reading out-of- date magazines, playing House (Bingo), and occasionally taking part in target practice which constituted firing at bottles and boxes thrown overboard and trailed by ropes behind the ship. Bryant's account of the trip gives a brief insight into life on board ship, the hardships, deprivations and boredom but more especially how the troops coped with an alien environment on board ship for four long weeks.

21st Nov. L. J. Bryant

Firing Practice was started to day. A lot of Bottles & Boxes are thrown overboard, or pulled through the water by a piece of string & the men fire at the Bottles. One or two Companies fire each day.

23rd Nov.

We got served out with Magazines & other periodicals to read, which was a luxury to us, altho' the papers were somewhat out of date. We can also get a book to read out of the Library, but must return it within 7 days or pay for the same. We can then get it out for another week if we haven't finished with it.

25th Nov.

The Drums played a few tunes this evening from 6 to 8 p.m. for the benefit of the Troops, which was greatly enjoyed.

27th Nov.

We got orders to get our things ready for disembarkation at Cape Town on the morrow.

29th Nov.

We sighted Cape Town at 9 p.m. but anchored for the night in Table Bay.

30th Nov.

We steamed into Cape Town Harbour about 9 a.m. & had to await further orders. We received orders soon afterwards that we were to proceed to Durban as soon as possible, but as more coal was wanted on board we anchored for the night.

The Transport Ship "Englishman" which sailed from Queenstown the day after us, arrived her at 2 p.m. & left for East London. The Troops on both boats exchanging cheers etc.

Whilst anchored in the bay, General Hart[11], who was also on board and in whose 5th Irish Brigade the Inniskillings would serve with such distinction, ordered a route march through Cape Town, in order to give the native levies time to refuel and stock the ship for the remainder of the journey.

1st Dec. L. J. Bryant

All the Troops on board the "Catalonia" went for a Short Route March through Cape Town under General Harte, whilst the Natives were putting coal on board the boat.

We fell in at 9 a.m. in Khaki & started on our march, the Band & Drums playing alternatively on the March. We marched by Greenpoint way. It was a very hot day & as we had no water bottles with us we found it very hard to march, owing to the excessive heat & through having no water with us.

We marched about 8 miles or so & returned to the Ship again about 1 p.m. very thirsty & tired. We found everything below deck black with coal dust.

Natives came on the Quay to sell us food stuffs, which we needed badly, as we were half starved, but directly the officers saw the men buying the food, they made them stop it & posted Sentries on the sides of the boat, so as to stop the men from buying anything. They themselves went into the town during the evening & could buy what they wanted.

We left Cape Town for Durban about 8 p.m. The Band played a few Marches etc. before we left.

2nd Dec.

Very Calm all day. We saw a few whales & porpoises swimming about.

5th Dec.

We arrived at Durban at 4 a.m. & got off the boat at 10 a.m. and left our kits etc. in the Station to be sent to our Base at Pieter-Maritz-

Burg; we then had to go on board the Ship once more & stay there until 2 p.m. when we were for disembarking.

We got our dinner on board ship, it consisted of Bully Beef & Rice with no Sugar in it. We were not sorry when two o'clock came round, for we were glad to get off the boat as we were half starved on it.

Our fare for the whole voyage consisted as follows:-

viz.- for breakfast, we got Bread one day, and Biscuits the next day. The Bread was black and sour, but it was called Brown Bread and as for the biscuits, they were that hard that we couldn't get our teeth through them, and one of the sailors hung one up in his cabin as a Curio, and put a piece of blue ribbon round it as a frame, just to show what a Tommy got, when going to Fight for his Country.

The Biscuits were as old as Adam too, and often in my mess of ten men, we would only draw a dozen biscuits, to last us the whole day....

We also had Black Tea without milk, and with very little sugar in it.

We got no Jam or Butter to spread on our Bread or Biscuits, but had to eat them dry, or else buy Butter from the canteen out of our own pockets.

Even then it was very seldom that we could buy anything out of the canteen as the man in charge of it used to open it when he liked & sometimes we had to wait an hour, sometimes more before we could get near the place, and then 9 cases out of ten there would be nothing in the place worth buying, and the man in charge would be too lazy to go down to the stores and get more eatables etc. For Dinner we would get a few changes of meat, but we only got Fresh Meat once or twice during the whole voyage.

Our Fare on other days consisted of either Salt Junk or Bully Beef, (Tinned Meat). Once or twice a week we would get a Tea Spoon full of preserved potatoes, and sometimes a little rice or pickles. Every Sunday we had plum pudding, which was made by our own Mess Orderlies on a Saturday, and then given to the ships cooks to boil. The pudding tho' hard, was the best thing we got to eat, whilst on board the boat. For tea we got Black Tea as mentioned, and to eat we got our leavings from breakfast, which wasn't much, especially on a Biscuit day.

There were three Trains to take us to Frere, our destination, & only one train had closed carriages, which of course were for the poor officers; the other trains were composed of Cattle Trucks, with wooden seats in them for the occasion; & the Soot & Dirt from the

Engine blew in our eyes and down our backs, so that we were soon transformed into sweeps.

We were very kindly treated by the people of Durban who gave us fruit, Tobacco etc. We arrived at P.M. Burg at 9.30 p.m. & had two slices of Bread & Butter & a canteen of Tea given to us which we greatly relished. We then resumed our journey. We had to sleep in the train all night, as we could not reach Frere until the next day.

It was raining all night & we got drenched to the skin, & half frozen with the cold, as we only had our big Coats on us, we also had our Blankets with us but we were that packed up, that we couldn't move to put them over us, or even lay down, so we didn't get much sleep.

5th Dec. Capt. A. C. Jeffcoat DSO

Arrived Durban 4 AM unloaded all the morning, spent several hours in the hold trying to find Maxim gun. Went for a run on shore and had some Rickshaw races. Inspected an armoured train standing in the wharf. Left Durban by train at 5.30 with men in open trucks. Splendid scenery, wonderful railway, all sharp curves in and out of gorges. Reached PMB about 10 PM and waited half an hour for Sir Redvers Buller then set off to the front.

Chapter Two

Battle of Colenso
"Our Doings in Natal"

A period of inactivity followed the Royal Inniskilling Fusiliers' arrival at Frere on 6 December 1899. For the following six days they were occupied on outpost duties whilst awaiting orders to march. These dutifully arrived on the morning of the 13th when Hart's Irish Brigade was ordered to break camp and advance northward and position themselves north of Chieveley Railway Station.

6th Dec. L. J. Bryant
We arrived at Frere at 6 a.m. looking like so many Sweeps & we marched about 2 miles from the Station to where we were to Camp. As our tents had not arrived we had to knock about all day under a very hot sun. We had a few Biscuits given to us but half of them were mouldy. We were just in time to witness the Burial of six men belonging to the D. L. I. Regt. who fell victim in the Armoured Train Affair in November, we also saw two of the Carriages that belonged to the Armoured Train, they were off the line & just near our Camp & as a lot of tommies were knocking pieces off the Carriages to keep as curios, most of us too went & done likewise. We pitched our Camp at 6 p.m.

6th Dec. Capt. A. C. Jeffcoat DSO
On the 6th we trained on through Estcourt to Frere camp and marched 2 miles to camping ground by wrecked armoured train and waited all day for our tents. C went out on picket and I went to station and

brought up the Maxim Gun fastened behind a bullock wagon. Very hot.

9th Dec.

On duty Jim arrived with transport mules. Had my two out for trial on machine gun. They will take some handling especially under fire.

10th Dec.

Church parade. Splendid bathe in deep waterhole with Stewart. Struck camp and packed everything onto wagons and pitched it again. One of the pack mules broke loose and scattered a box of ammunition over the veldt.

13th Dec. L. J. Bryant

We were on Commanding Officers parade, at 10a.m. and we were just going to practice the Attack, when an Orderly came up to our C.O. with a message, and our C.O. told us that we were for the Front at once, and dismissed us off parade. We then struck Camp at once and then had our dinner. We fell in on parade again at 12-30 p.m. and marched to Chieveley (8 miles). We had our Great Coats rolled on our belts, and the following articles were rolled up in the Great Coats; viz:- 1 Shirt, 1 Suit of Khaki, 1 pair of Slippers, 1 Brush, 1 Cap, and 1 tin of Dubbin.

Besides this the men had 250 rounds of ammunition, and a rifle, and their equipment to carry.

We were half dead when we arrived at Chievely, [Chieveley] owing to the intense heat, and through having such a great weight on our backs. We suffered to from thirst, as we could not get any water whilst on the march, the consequence was about 250 men of the Brigade fell out and didn't get into Camp till all hours. We pitched Camp at 5p.m. [1]

13th Dec. Capt. A. C. Jeffcoat DSO

Struck camp at 1 p.m. and started to march to Chieveley in the heat of the day with coats and kit in new style. Marched in column over the veldt, heaps of men fell out and raided water cart on arrival. Hart came up and cursed and threatened to send us back to Durban. C Coy on outpost.

Circumstances, however, dictated that the Royal Inniskilling Fusiliers hadn't to wait long to be thrown into action. Within days of their arrival in South Africa they were to engage in one of the bloodiest and most memorable actions of the war, the Battle of Colenso. This battle was the first stumbling block in a series of actions deemed necessary if

Ladysmith, which had been besieged by the Boers since 27 October, was to be relieved.

Unfortunartely the battle plan adopted by General Sir Redvers Buller[1] was one which, on all accounts, was drawn up with little or no knowledge of the Boers, either strategically or tactically.

The 2nd Brigade under the command of Major-General H.J.T. Hildyard[2] was chosen to deliver the main assault by crossing the Tugela River by the Iron (Wagon) Bridge and seize the kopjes to the north. The 5th Brigade under the command of Major-General Hart was to cross the river at Bridle Drift, a point immediately west of the junction of Doornkop Spruit and the Tugela River and make progress down the left bank towards the north of Wagon Bridge.

Major-General G. Barton's[3] 6th Brigade was given the task of guarding Major-General Hildyard's right flank, whilst still further west Colonel Dundonalds[4] Mounted Brigade was ordered to make for Hlangwane to safeguard the right flank and to take up a position on Hlangwhane Hill. The reserve was assigned to Major-General N. G. Lyttelton's[5] 4th Brigade who were instructed to form up west of the railway station. There they were to hold themselves in readiness to lend support to either Hart's 5th Brigade or Hildyard's 2nd should it become necessary.

The battle began at 4.45 a.m. with the bombardment of the Boer-held Fort Wylie by naval 12-pounders and from the right by six naval 12-pounders belonging to the 14th and 66th Field Batteries under the command of Colonel C. J. Long RA.[6]

The bombardment continued relentlessly throughout the day. Shell after shell was hurled against the Boers until eventually whether out of frustration or impatience Colonel Long committed the cardinal error of allowing his guns to outstrip his infantry cover. Against express orders and the advice of his junior officers, he ordered the artillery to push forward in the hope that his 15-pounder field guns would prove more effective.

This was to prove a costly error. Advancing to within 800 yards of the Tugela River and approximately 1200 yards from Fort Wylie the Boers by their seeming inactivity sucked Colonel Long and his artillery into a deadly trap. Misjudging Boer strength and tactics, the more manoeuvrable field pieces, followed by the cumbersome naval guns, galloped forward, outstripping their infantry escort, Hildyards 2nd Brigade.

Under a murderous hail of Mauser rifle fire directed from Grobler's Kloof and Red Hill, nearly two-thirds of Long's artillery strength lay dead or wounded. Captains Goldie and Schrieber were killed and Colonel Long himself seriously wounded, shot through the lung. One man's misjudgement and failure to assess the Boer strength properly cost the British dearly.

15th Dec. 99 L. J. Bryant

The Battle of Colenso was fought on this day; this being General Sir Redvers Bullers First Attempt to Relieve Ladysmith; This is also the first occasion for our Regt. to be under fire in this Campaign.

The force struck camp at 2 a.m., we fell in at 3 a.m. and marched off the scene of operations to take up our respective positions.

My Regt. is in the 5th or Irish Brigade, along with the Dublin Fusiliers, Connaught Rangers and The Border Regt.

Our Scouts had reported all clear and we were marching along not thinking that the enemy were so near us and we were marching in Mass of Columns when all of a sudden two shells from the Boer Guns burst amongst our Brigade and our Colonel gave us the order to "extend" and so we went into Action. Our Brigade formed the left flank of the operations, under the command of Major General Fitzroy Hart, and our formation was intended to be as follows:-

Firing line, Dublin Fusiliers and Connaught Rangers; Support, Border Regt, Reserves, Inniskilling Fusiliers, but the Boers opening fire suddenly took us all by suprise that we had no time to get into our proper formation, so the consequence was all parts of the Brigade were in the Firing Line, altho' we still had our Support and Reserves.

The Boers were entrenched along a high range of Kopjes and they also had trenches dug at the bottom of the Kopjes, and we could not see any of them as they kept well under cover. Whilst they were practically safe in their trenches, we had no cover at all as we were on level ground so making a good mark for the enemy and they took good advantage of it too and made things very hot for us.

The Tugela River flows between the Boer positions and us, and they had damed the river and also put barbed wire entanglements in the river just under the surface, so that if we tried to cross we would get entangled in the wire and so be shot down or else drowned.

The fight lasted about 9 hours and altho' we advanced up to the waters edge we could not cross it, and so had to retire as the Boer position was too strong to take.

15th Dec. Capt. A. C. Jeffcoat DSO

Got up at 2 a.m. and struck camp after waiting about during the great Brigade drill started for Colenso at dawn. Order of battle was we were on the left of the line; Hildyard in the centre; Barton and the Imperial troops to the right and Littleton [Lyttelton] in reserve. GOC marched us up to within 1500 yards of the position in massed quarter column. One shell burst in front of the Brigade, the second in the centre killing 10 Dublin fusiliers and the third behind us. The whole Brigade started to deploy as hard as they could. No orders were issued. Regiments and companies went forward in whatever line they found themselves. The whole Brigade got mixed up. The rifle fire was terrible, the shells whistled over our heads and burst amongst us sending up clouds of dust. Our guns shelled their trenches for some hours but never seemed to be able to silence their guns. There were two big disappearing guns on the hill to our left that did frightful execution.

Colonel Long's actions were to cost the British dearly. Forced to retreat under heavy Boer fire, twelve guns were abandoned and in danger of falling into enemy hands, a mortal sin in any military engagement of the period.

To try to retrieve the guns Lieutenant Roberts,[7] the only son of Field-Marshal Lord Roberts, and two other officers, Captains Schofield and Congreve, ventured forward. Boer Mauser fire proved too intense, however, resulting in the death of Lieutenant Roberts and serious injury to Captain Congreve. Captain Schofield remained unscathed and was successful in bringing off two guns of the 66th Battery.

The whole spectacle had been witnessed by General Buller whose staff doctor Captain Hughes was killed outright by a shell which fell amongst the group. His aide-de-camps Lord Gerard, also had a narrow escape when his mount was shot from beneath him.

A further effort was made to retrieve the remaining ten guns by Captain Reed who having borrowed three teams of horses from the 7th Field Battery pushed forward with a squad of men into the murderous crossfire. Though successful in harnessing up an ammunition wagon they were instantly cut down, Captain Reed being severely wounded. The guns were now abandoned and a general order to retire given.

As a result of their efforts to save the guns at Colenso Lieutenant Roberts, Captain Congreve, Captain Reed and Captain Schofield were awarded Victoria Crosses. However, General Buller refused to cite Captain Schofield for the VC, stating that he did nothing extraordinary having performed his actions whilst under orders. As history can testify Buller's apparent insensitivity was overruled, and Captain Schofield became one of five recipients of VCs gained at the Battle of Colenso, the other being Corporal Nurse.

The British defeat at the Battle of Colenso was a major setback for those besieged within Ladysmith. Had the British taken the key position of Hlangwane on 15 December, the position of the Boers would almost certainly have become untenable, forcing them to fall back to Pieters. In doing so they would have exposed their rear to the Ladysmith Garrison under Sir George White[8], who would have been strong enough at the time to break out with his Cavalry and Artillery if necessary.

However, defeat at Colenso can be attributed more to an amalgam of events rather than one overall incident. Besides the failure of the British to take Hlangwane, it seems remarkable that they had learnt so little of Boer tactics following the Battle at Modder River just two weeks previously.

General Buller and his Staff had time in the intervening period to realize that it was probable, if not certain, that since the Boers used entrenchment to such good effect then, it would only seem logical similar methods would be used again under similar circumstances.

Another contributing factor was the catalogue of logistical and tactical errors made by commanders on the spot. It is easy, however, in hindsight, to attribute blame that does not take into account the heat of battle. Maps of the district, which, though Natal had been a British colony for more than two generations, proved totally inadequate and untrustworthy, and often compounded mistakes.

However, given all that had taken place, we must not forget that the greatest contribution to the British defeat was, in fact, the skill of the Boers themselves. It is easy to pillory certain aspects of British tactics and the General Staff but we should not for a moment lose sight of the determination and guile of the Boers. They had at their disposal a very able and experienced soldier in General de Villebois-Mareuil whose assistance had been sought by Dr. Leyds at the very outbreak of hostilities.

Count de Villebois-Mareuil[9], retired from active service in the French Army since 1896, was persuaded to travel to South Africa as a mercenary in order to work out a stratagem for the Boer forces in Natal. He was personally responsible for the disposition of the Boers at Colenso and elsewhere along the Tugela River, and was present and actively directed the repulse of General Buller's attack. He was killed, however, in an action near Boshof, in the Orange Free State, when his forces were surrounded and attacked by Lord Methuen[10] on 5 April 1900.

Although the British Army suffered a truly demoralizing defeat at the Battle of Colenso, all was not lost. It was a costly error in an unforgiving atmosphere. In hindsight the outcome should have been different, but, although a defeat, it was only a setback, not an insurmountable obstacle.

15th Dec. 99 L. J. Bryant
The losses on the British side were very heavy, amounting to about 1200 casualties. Our Regiment losses were 19 killed and 97 wounded, not counting prisoners, which however were very small. Our side also lost ten Guns which fell into the hands of the Enemy, altho' a plucky and daring attempt was made to recover them, but the Boers opened a terrific fire on the Gunners and they had to give up the attempt, this not before they had done as much as any mortal man could do. Shortly after the Battle was over, the Boers robbed our dead. We retired back to Chieveley again and pitched Camp for the night.

17th Dec.
We arrived at Frere about 6 a.m. and pitched our Camp at 7 a.m. The remainder of the day we had to ourselves.

17th Dec. Capt. A. C. Jeffcoat DSO
Started 1 a.m. and marched back to Frere camp. As usual we were worried by Hart. I was in advanced guard with C Coy. We have come back to our old camping ground but I have a tent to myself. A & B have no officers left. Total eclipse of the moon disorganised night march.

On 18 December 1899 Sir Redvers Buller was replaced as Commander-in-Chief of the Army in South Africa by Field-Marshal Lord Roberts, though he stayed on as commander of the army in Natal. This appointment came just days after his son was killed at the Battle of Colenso. At the same time Lord Kitchener of Khartoum was recalled from the Sudan and appointed to Lord Roberts' Staff.

18th Dec. Capt. A. C. Jeffcoat DSO
Went out to number 4 picket and relieved Coy F Dublins. My first outpost duty. Very hot all day. Rather a nice farm in front looted by the Boers with an excellent well. Spent the day in hearing the experiences of the NCOs of my coy. Very few got through without some graze.

The Battle of Colenso dealt a severe blow to the morale of the troops and taught a less than cautious Command that they were up against more than a motley collection of dirt farmers. The Boers were a toughened people, experienced horsemen and crack shots, who were well disciplined and organized, as the actions of Black Week demonstrated.

The regimental archives of the Royal Inniskilling Fusiliers record that as a result of the Battle of Colenso the Regiment lost its second in command, Major F.W. Charley, killed in action, and Captain C.F. Loftus, three sergeants and eighteen ORs died of wounds. Those wounded included nine officers, five sergeants and seventy-six ORs; a further five ORs were recorded missing in action. The temporary loss of those wounded, especially Major A. J. Hancocks, Captain E. J. Buckley (Adjutant), Lieutenant H. A. Leverson, Second Lieutenants Best, Devenish, Meldon and Whiffen, and Major Brannigan RAMC (attached) would prove an obstacle to the further participation of the Regiment until a later stage of the campaign.

Following the order by General Sir Redvers Buller to retire, the Royal Inniskilling Fusiliers fell in, struck camp at 12 midnight and marched the eight miles back to Frere with the remainder of the Fifth Brigade. Arriving at approximately 6 am on 17 December the troops spent the next few days engaged on Outpost duties.

20th Dec. L. J. Bryant

Stood to Arms at 3 a.m.

Every Regt. has to do this parade so as to be ready in case of emergencies. It is carried out as follows:-

Rise at 2-45 a.m., Fall in at 3 a.m. properly dressed and with rifles and equipment. Stretcher Bearers with their stretchers. We then march off to our respective places just beyond the Camp and Stand to Arms till sunrise. No talking or smoking is allowed whilst on parade or before parade, nor are lights of any kind to be shown either when getting up, or on parade. We had the rest of this day to ourselves.

20th Dec. Capt. A. C. Jeffcoat DSO

English mail from mother and card from Mrs. H. Busy collecting kit of wounded men. We have started a mess of 6 in my tent. Feeding like fighting cocks on bully beef and jam. Rumour of Hart going. Hope its true, Colenso bridge destroyed by our artillery.

Out of the line, time was spent resting and regrouping. Outpost duties, fatigues and picket duties continued as usual whilst awaiting reinforcements and fresh supplies. Minor skirmishes occurred in and around Colenso but on the whole the area was relatively quiet, broken only by the engagement of the naval guns, which occasionally opened up on the Boer lines to keep their heads down.

On the 20th a picket of seven men of the 13th Hussars, belonging to Dundonald's Mounted Brigade, were surprised by a group of Boers with the loss of two killed, whilst the remaining five succeeded in escaping. Natal Carbineers, however, lay in wait and repelled the Boers the following day, when as usual they attempted to rob the dead. The weeks that followed the battle were often spent in long periods of inactivity, but since it occurred over the Christmas period, the troops were happy to take advantage of the lull.

22nd Dec. Capt. A. C. Jeffcoat DSO
Auctioned kits of 7 men killed in coy. Had letter from Hancocks who is doing well but very down on his luck.

Two days before Christmas 1899, Winston Churchill finally rejoined the Natal Army, having escaped from captivity in Pretoria on 12 December. Having scaled the wall of the compound in which he was held he followed the railway line which he surmised correctly led to Delagoa Bay. Concealing himself first on board a coal train and then a train bound for Lourenco Marques he spent long days and nights hiding in the bush, avoiding Boer patrols, before eventually reached Delagoa, from where he boarded a steamer bound for Natal.

25th Dec. L. J. Bryant
Christmas Day was spent as follows:- We had Divine Service at 7 a.m. and the remainder of the day we got to ourselves. The Regt. passed away the time by playing two Football Matches. One against the Borders at 3 p.m. and the other against the Connaughts at 5 p.m. The Borders beat us by 2 goals to none, and we beat the Connaughts by 1 goal to none. We got two pints of beer, by paying for the same through our accounts, altho' one pint was supposed to be free of charge. Our fare for the day was as follows:-
Breakfast:- Bread and Jam, and Coffee, without milk.
Dinner, Boiled Meat, and a few vegetables.
Tea, What was left over from Breakfast, and tea, no milk. For Extras, we got one pineapple between every 15 men, just for the occasion.
It was raining all the morning.

25th Dec. Capt. A. C. Jeffcoat DSO

Christmas usual 3.30 parade, served at 8 communion in Border Mess, tent very hot. None of the Christmas provisions sent from England have arrived including the Queens chocolate. The Queen sent good wishes. Very quiet day but expect alarm shortly.

Chapter Three

1900
Spion Kop, Vaal Krantz

The New Year and the dawn of a new century found the "Skins"[1] still encamped at Frere, whilst the build up of troops continued. Time on their hands, the troops passed the days and weeks in the usual round of fatigues, outpost duties and general "bull". Private Bryant's diary catalogues the duties and pastimes they engaged in during this spell of inactivity. His entry for 5 January is quite humorous and tongue in cheek, whilst at the same time portraying the usual hardship and gripes synonymous with life in the ranks.

A shipment of 10,000 plum puddings donated by Messers. Lyons, having arrived from England intended as a Christmas gift for the troops, was shared out amongst them, although not as equally as Lyons might have at first intended!

1900

1st Jan. 1900 L. J. Bryant
We broke the New Year in by going for a Short Route March of 5 or 6 miles. We started on our March at 9 a.m. & returned to Camp again at 12.30 p.m. We struck our Camp at 2 p.m. to give the ground an airing, and repitched it again at 3 p.m.

The rest of the day we had to ourselves.

The following message from Her Majesty the Queen, was read out to us. Viz:- "I wish you all a Happy New Year, God Bless You." (Sgd) V. R. I.

2nd Jan. Capt. A. C. Jeffcoat DSO

English mail expected, letter from Dove, only English letter. Bathed in very cool and deep pool but very muddy. Heavy firing at Chieveley last night. Great scorpion hunt.

5th Jan. L. J. Bryant

The Regt. went out on another Short Route March of 5 or 6 miles to day.

We all got a small piece of plum pudding given to us at dinnertime. The puddings were in small cups, and were sent to the Troops at the Front, as a Xmas gift, by a Firm in London. We got one small pudding between every two men (in our Regt.) altho' the Firm intended us to have one each. The following Inscription was on the cover of the puddings,:- Lyons and Co. send you this pudding, hoping it may contribute something to a Merry Xmas. Good Luck to you. Some of our officers had as many as three puddings each, but as it was that rich, they only gave us one between 2 men, as they probably thought it would make us sick.

5th Jan. Capt. A. C. Jeffcoat DSO

Route march passed a dead bullock which we heard afterwards had been shot by the Borders because it had knocked 2 of them over but everyone tells them they mistook it for a boer!

Not on such a light note, however, the New Year brought renewed hardships for those besieged within Ladysmith. The early hours of 6 January opened with a renewed Boer artillery barrage of the beleaguered town. The troops massed at Chieveley could do little more than bide their time and listen to the thunder of the guns as they continued all morning unabated. Heliograph[2] messages were picked up from within Ladysmith, which kept Buller informed of Boer movements.

"9 a.m. Enemy attacked Caesar's Camp at 2.45 this morning in considerable force. Enemy everywhere repulsed, but fighting still continues."

"11 a.m. Attack continues, and enemy has been reinforced from south."[2]

Caught unprepared and not wishing to be drawn prematurely into a second attempt upon the Boer lines at Colenso, any thought of a full all-out attack was quickly discarded. At the same time, however, it was unthinkable that the Relief Column, under strength though it was, should stand idly by whilst Ladysmith was overrun. By 2 pm, however, it was decided that rather than remain a passive onlooker the army should commit a token force which, whilst not weakening their overall complement, might divert Boer attention from their primary target, Ladysmith.

Orders were given for General Hildyard's 2nd Brigade, General Barton's 6th Brigade accompanied by three batteries of artillery and covered by a bombardment by the naval guns to venture out and engage the Boers.

Whilst the infantry advanced in scattered order their flanks were cover by the 13th Hussars, having moved out of Springield whilst Thorneycroft's[3] Mounted Infantry deployed in the direction of Hlangwane.

6th Jan. L. J. Bryant

The Boers made a determined attack on Ladysmith today, to try to capture it, but were repulsed with heavy loss. We had to sleep with all our straps on, big coats being rolled on the belt, so that we would be able to turn out at a moments notice, in case of emergency. Nothing occurred here.

Sir George White's garrison within Ladysmith still remained under severe enemy attack.

"12.45 p.m. Have beaten enemy off at present, but they are still round me in great numbers, especially to south, and I think renewed attack very probable."[3]

"January 6, 3.15p.m. Attack renewed. Very hard pressed."[4]

In the end it was the weather that came to Sir George White's aid. Due to lack of light and severe thunderstorms, the Boers were halted. However, the day's incidents brought home to the General Staff the urgency of the situation. Ladysmith could not repulse many more attacks of this nature. If the siege was to be broken, immediate action was required.

8th Jan. Capt. A. C. Jeffcoat DSO

No news about the attack on Ladysmith except Boers repulsed. Rode to station with Bell and went to see Gibton in stationary hospital, he is worse and is going to Maritzburg tomorrow. Welsh and Gordon went to hospital with dysentery and go on to PMB. Deberry has come out to join his 1st Battalion at Chieveley.

Three days later the advance for the relief of Ladysmith commenced. Under atrocious conditions Lieutenant-General Sir Charles Warren's[4] Division marched from Estcourt to Frere. Finally, on the morning of 10 January the army prepared to advance. Intensely hot after the thunderstorms of the previous few days, it was well into the afternoon before the column began its march westward. In total it consisted of some 15,000 infantry, 2,500 cavalry and mounted infantry, and fifty-eight field guns, not including the Mountain Battery which it was deemed would be of no particular benefit in the type of engagement which lay ahead. To the rear followed an interminable motley collection of ox-wagons, carts, ambulances, cannon and all the paraphernalia of war, which such a large column on the march requires.

10th Jan. L. J. Bryant

The Brigade fell in at 6.45 a.m. and marched to Pretorius Farm (8miles). Our Regt. had to guard the Convoy, which was a very large one, extending for nearly 20 miles, in length. The first Coy. started at 7 a.m. and my Company which was last did not start until 5 p.m. We arrived at Pretorius Farm at 8 p.m. The Connaughts, being in hours before us, volunteered and pitched our camp for us.

10th Jan. Capt. A. C. Jeffcoat DSO

Got up at 3.30 a.m. and struck camp. Breakfast at 4 and then marched over to where the supply was posted, as we have been detailed as escort. 1 coy detailed to every 50 wagons to escort them 8 miles to Pretorious farm halfway to Springfield. The start off was very bad as many of the teams had been inspanned for weeks and would not pull together.

11th Jan. L. J. Bryant

We had a rest. Two prisoners were brought into Camp to day, & were taken before the General, & they turned out to be two of our own Scouts. The men in our Bge. were greatly taken in over it, as thinking they were Boers, they started to make a fool of them by asking them such questions as, How did you enjoy your Xmas? & How was Joubert getting on.

The stand to Arms parade was cancelled for our Brigade, from this day.

12th Jan.

Five prisoners were brought into Camp to day, & detained for the night.

13th Jan.

The above mentioned prisoners were sent on to Frere to day. Had the usual parade."

The passage of the column was a slow and arduous affair. Laden down by vast amounts of baggage and ancillary equipment, the column found itself clogged up and halted by flood-swollen spruits and rivulets, which had turned the normally arid veldt into a quagmire of mud. The General Staff would have been wise to recall the comments of Napoleon I almost a century previous, when he observed that no other army carries with it as much as the British. And as the strength of an army should be gauged by its numbers, multiplied by the number of miles it can cover in any given period, it therefore followed, using this criteria, that 4000 or 5000 lightly equipped and mobile Boers were a match for Buller's entire force.

Not wishing to repeat the disaster of 15 December, Buller bypassed Colenso and marched towards the Upper Tugela where he hoped the flood-swollen river would be more easily fordable and not as well defended. This, however, was to prove not to be the case and his troops would have to endure some bitter exchanges before the month was out.
The Royal Inniskilling Fusiliers arrived at Springfield on January 15th.

15th Jan. L. J. Bryant

Fell in at 1 p.m. and marched to Springfield (6 miles) arriving there at 5 p.m. We could see the Shells fired from our Naval Guns at Chieveley bursting on the Boer position in the distance. Pitched camp at 7 p.m.

16th Jan.

Fell in at 5p.m. and done a forced march to Spearmans Farm (15 miles). We left our Camp standing and 'B' Coy. were left behind to strike the Camp and pick up our kits and escort them to our Base later on. We bivouacked for the night about 3 a.m. and we were half frozen with the Cold and Rain, as we had to lay down on the ground with nothing to cover ourselves, except our thin Khaki Clothes.

We were just dozing (after our arrival) as we were very tired, when a false alarm was raised and we were quite surprised and confused, as we thought we were going to be attacked. Needless to say we didn't get much sleep after that.

On 17 January the Inniskillings crossed the Tugela by means of pontoon bridges and advanced on the Boer positions. Stretcher-bearers, who made several trips across the Tugela, brought up supplies but little progress was made, as the Inniskillings had to wait for the main force to arrive.

17th Jan. L. J. Bryant

We crossed the Tugela (over pontoon bridges) & advanced towards the Boer position. The Stretcher-bearers had to re-cross the Tugela to draw rations from the Supplies for the Troops. We had to go over the pontoon bridge again & half a dozen mules were crossing over at the same time but stopped in the middle of the bridge & 2 blocked the passage through. A couple of men were trying to make them go on but two mules fell over the side of the bridge & were drowned. Soon after that I tried to get past the mules, but one of them kicked out & I fell into the river, Stretcher & all. I had my straps on, but lucky for me I came up just near the side of the bridge. The water was very deep & a swift current was running at the time. I had to sleep this night (& many others) without a shirt on, as I threw the one I had away as it was full of holes etc. It came on to raining during the night, & I was shivering all the time with the cold, so I didn't get much sleep.

18th Jan.

We are still in the same place, as we are waiting for the Convoy to cross over.

19th Jan.

The Convoy having crossed over the Tugela safely, our Regt. was put on guard over it. We had our Great Coats given to us to keep out the cold.

The main force of the Army, three brigades with six batteries under the command of Sir Charles Warren, was concentrated at Springfield whilst the central thrust was entrusted to General Coke's[5] and General Lyttelton's Brigades at Spearman's Camp and Potgeiter's Drift.

The British right flank was covered by Bethune's Mounted Infantry whose task it was to pay particular attention to Skiet Drift, near which the Boers were thought to be gathering in force. It was intended that whilst Sir Charles Warren's main force, accompanied by the Cavalry Division under Lord Dundonald, advanced north-westwards to Trichardt's Drift and attempted to cross the Tugela, a diversionary movement would take place. A demonstration of force was to be made by General Coke's and General Lyttelton's brigades from their respective positions, fanning out in open order from Spearman's Farm and Potgeiter's Drift and advancing upon the Tugela. Although in clear view of Boer entrenchment on the surrounding hillsides nothing happened, which led many to believe that perhaps the Boers were intent upon repeating their tactics which had proven so successful both at Modder River and Colenso.

As night fell, troops were still streaming across the Tugela. By dawn General Lyttelton's Brigade had occupied a forward position on a line of kopjes known as One Tree Hill, whilst under cover of darkness General Hildyard's 2nd Brigade had retired from their advance eastward. It had been hoped to convince the Boers that the main attack would come from the east, whilst, under the cover of darkness, the 2nd Brigade wheeled about and advanced upon Trichardt's Drift, ten miles to the west, and waited anxiously, in sight of the steep slopes of Spion Kop, for the word to advance.

As day broke the weary troops waited. Whether the General Staff considered it imprudent to launch a full-scale attack with men tired and exhausted is difficult to tell. The fact that the advance was dangerously delayed enabled the Boers to fully comprehend the situation and re-enforce their position ready for a full-scale frontal attack.

Assessing the events, Warren called his staff together and informed them of the situation and advised them of a change of plan. In a communiqué despatched to General Buller dated 19 January he concluded,

> I find there are only two roads by which we could possibly get from Trichardt's Drift to Potgieter's, on the north of the Tugela, one by Acton Holmes, the other by Fair View and Rosalie; the first I reject as too long, the second is a very difficult road for a large number of wagons, unless the enemy is thoroughly cleared out. I am, therefore, going to adopt some special arrangements which will involve my stay at Venter's Laager for two or three days. I will send in for further supplies and report progress.-Warren[5]

Delayed by a combination of cumbersome supply trains and an inability by those in command to assess the situation, the attack was postponed until 20 January. The following extract from Bryant's diary is an invaluable insight into the Battle of Spion Kop as seen through the eyes of a Fusilier.

20th Jan. L. J. Bryant
The Battle of Spion Kop, was commenced today; This being Bullers Second Attempt to Relieve Ladysmith.

Our guns opened fire about 8 a.m. and shelled the Enemy's position till 7 p.m. It came on to rain again and we got drenched to the skin. We had hardly anything to eat all day.

21st Jan

Firing started early today and continued until evening. Our Brigade was not in action today.

22nd Jan. Capt. A. C. Jeffcoat DSO

We lay here in the blazing sun all day with shells bursting over, forward and bullets whizzing over our heads and doing nothing. Private Devenny from my team was killed from a shrapnel shell, one of the ones taken at Colenso. Our Howitzer and field battery fired at random all day with liddite and other shells. But we lay idle, each regiment taking it in turns to go into the firing line.

23rd Jan. L. J. Bryant

The Battle is still raging and we have driven the Boers from several of their positions. We all ran short of Tobacco and Cigarettes, and as we could not do without a smoke, we collected all the Tea leaves we could lay our hand on and after they were dried we smoked them in our pipes for Tobacco or else rolled them up in any paper we could get and so made cigarettes.

We also eat our Emergency Rations, as we had nothing else to satisfy our hunger, but we had to pay for another Ration afterwards, for eating them without permission from the General.

We have not had the chance to get a wash for 6 days now.

24th Jan.

The Lancashire Brigade charged Spion Kop (from which the battle takes its name) very early this morning and succeeded in driving the Boers off it, so that they had to take up another position. The Brigade were open to a murderous cross fire from the Boers, which did considerable damage to them, as we could see from our position, but they held their position all day.

25th Jan.

The battle is still going on, but the Lancashire Bgd. had to retire from Spion Kop during the night, as they were not able to hold the position any longer, under such a fire as was opened on them, and they received no assistance from anywhere.

26th Jan.

A, C & D Coys. rejoined the Battle again this morning, and we learnt from the men that they had been lying near some of the trenches (which the Boers had retired from) and were there for five days. They were subjected to a heavy shell fire from the Boers Big Guns, and a few of the shells bursting amongst them. We had 17 casualties in our Regt. in this fight.

27ᵗʰ Jan.

We again had to Retire. The rain came down in torrents and we had to 'Stand to' in it for 2 hours and we were drenched to the skin. About 7.30 p.m. the Boers opened a terrific rifle fire, at nothing, thinking no doubt that we would attack them during the storm. We started our Retirement about 8 p.m. and retired to Acton Holmes, (7 miles), half of us were falling asleep whilst on the march, we were that done up. Our losses in the Battle were again heavy, viz. 1700 casualties. We heard afterwards that the Boers were retiring from Spion Kop, the same time as we were, and so opened a terrific rifle fire to cover their Retirement.

By 28 January the Royal Inniskilling Fusiliers were once more back in camp at Spearman's Farm. Buller's second attempt to relieve Ladysmith had petered out once more.

The Royal Inniskilling Fusiliers, as part of General Hart's Brigade, had borne the brunt of the fight, occupying as they did the centre, whilst General Hildyard's Brigade advanced on the left and General Woodgate's[6] occupied the right. Bastion Hill and Three Tree Hill, small ridges on the much larger Spion Kop were occupied but proved impossible to hold. Devoid of cover, they resembled the centre of a vast natural amphitheatre, overlooked on all sides by Boer entrenchments, which poured a murderous fire on the advancing troops. The Inniskillings and others elements of the Irish Brigade had to endure a Boer artillery barrage, not only of pom-poms but also the British 15-pounders lost at Colenso.

The General Staff at this time seemed to be fraught with indecision and recrimination. After almost a week of stagnation General Coke was ordered to launch an all-out attack on Spion Kop, something he was loath to do without proper knowledge of what lay in store. Again Sir Charles Warren postponed a main assault.

Indecision was not confined to the Brigade commanders, it stemmed from the very top. Rather than issuing decisive clear-cut orders, General Buller convened a council of war, often viewed as the last refuge of the irresolute, at which he criticized Warren whilst avoiding any all-out responsibility.

The operations in and around Spion Kop from 20 to 27 January appear to the observer a catalogue of missed opportunities, miscalculations, tactical errors and indecisive leadership. Not for the first time could it be said that horses were lead by mules!

The engagements of the previous week had cost the British dear in both manpower and supplies but, above all, morale. Fierce though the fighting was, casualties to the Royal Inniskilling Fusiliers proved remarkably few. Captain D. Maclachlan, wounded on the 21st, died some ten days later of his wounds, whilst only two ORs were killed and nine wounded.

Morale low, General Redvers Buller addressed the troops in the hope of allaying their apprehension and instilling confidence once more. To this end he visited Spearman's Farm on 29 January and addressed the assembled troops, which included the Royal Inniskilling Fusiliers.

29th Jan. L. J. Bryant

We shifted Camp very early this morning one and a half miles, so as to be nearer the water.

All the Troops fell in at 2 p.m. and formed Square, as Gen. Buller wished to say a few words to us. Amongst other things General Buller told us that he had found the key to Ladysmith, and he said he hoped to be there in a week. He also told us not to be disheartened for all would come well in the end. He praised us for the work we had done, and for the hardships we had endured. He then called for three cheers for H. M. the Queen, which were heartily given, as were 3 more for Gen. Sir Redvers Buller himself. We then marched back to our respective parade grounds and dismissed.

Buller now believed that he had indeed found a chink in the Boer armour that encircled and cut off the approaches to Ladysmith. Improved reconnaissance had in his estimation found the key to Ladysmith i.e. Vaal Krantz. Vaal Krantz marked Sir Redvers Buller's third attempt to break the Boer stranglehold around Ladysmith. Reinforced by a draft of some 3000 fresh troops, replacing those lost at Colenso and Spion Kop, he believed he would now accomplish his task at the third attempt. In addition to this fresh influx of troops he received two siege 5-inch guns and a huge 6-inch naval gun.

Together with another Field Battery and a Horse Artillery Battery, replacing the field pieces lost at Colenso, he now believed he was as strong as at any previous time in the field. Add to this the 14th Hussars and Colonel Wynne[7] to replace General Woodgate killed at Spion Kop, Buller believed he now possessed the upper hand.

Again, in an effort to outwit the Boers, the main force remained encamped at Spearman's Farm whilst six naval 12-pounders, two field guns and the mountain battery were placed on Zwart's Kop. Together with reconnaissance patrols and the shelling of the Boer trenches at Colenso, it was hoped to divert attention away from Buller's real aim, Vaal Krantz.

Between Spion Kop to the west and Doorn Kloof to the east lay a comparatively low ridge opposite Spearman's Hill and Zwart's Kop. At the eastern-most section of this ridge lay an area called Brakfontein which commanded the stretch of land between Potgeiter's Drift and Ladysmith. It was here that Buller believed he had found the Boer leader, General Botha's [8] Achilles heel.

The period before the battle was given over to various preparations, picquet duties and the addition of reinforcements. The Inniskillings received a draft of some ninety men mainly from their 3rd and 4th Battalions as well as a number passed fit to return to duty again having been wounded at Colenso. Conditions were hot and wet, which made the troops uncomfortable having to "stand to" in full kit, whilst not afforded the luxury of sufficient water for either drinking or normal everyday ablutions.

By 4 February preparations were complete and the order to move out given.

4th Feb. L. J. Bryant

Had Divine Service as usual at 7 a.m.. We fell in about 8 a.m. and marched to Vaal Krantz (6 miles). We bivouacked for the night, and got one blanket between every two men. The rainy season being on us, we had to carry our oil sheets on our belts, instead of rolling them up in the blankets.

4th Feb. Capt. A. C. Jeffcoat DSO

We expect to move today across the Tugela at Potgeiters drift and attack a very strong position across the Ladysmith road. Thank goodness we have two 4.7 Naval guns and six 12 pounders not counting the Howitzer and Field battery, in all over 80 Guns.

Generals Hart and Hildyard moved their respective Brigades across the Tugela whilst General Lyttelton withdrew his troops from One Tree Hill to be replaced by General Wynne. At 7 am on the morning of the 5th the six batteries of field artillery in position by One Tree Hill opened a barrage upon the Boer lines. The order was given for two battalions, the Yorks. and Lancs. and the South Lancashires, to advance in extended order in the direction of the Boer lines at Brakfontein, but still the Boers held their fire. It was only when within distance and through fear of being overrun that the Boer artillery opened up upon the advancing troops.

The Boers positioned a huge 6-inch Creusot on Doorn Kloof whilst two Krupp field pieces were entrenched on the eastern slope of Spion Kop. In addition, spread at intervals along their lines were the dreaded "pom-poms" which the British troops particularly disliked, and not without cause. In response the British artillery, aided by the directional observations of the wars balloons, opened a fierce barrage upon the Boers, hurling 50-lb lyddite shells in a never-ending stream. Under such conditions it is remarkable that anyone should have remained alive, but although they sustained heavy casualties, the Boers held fast.

At this point in the battle it seemed to the Boers that indeed they had the upper hand again, as the British were seen to be retiring back across the Tugela. Artillery pieces, ammunition wagons and men were observed drawing back to a safe distance. What the Boers failed to grasp was that such manoeuvres were all part of Buller's plan to distract attention from his intended target, Vaal Krantz.

5th Feb. L. J. Bryant

The Battle of Vaal-Krantz was started today; Bullers Third Attempt to Relieve Ladysmith. Our Guns opened fire at 7a.m. We made a faint attack on the Boers left flank, and then attacked their right flank, and drove them off one of their positions. The Irish Bge were not in action this day.

6th Feb.

Firing was resumed by our Artillery and Naval Guns at 6.30a.m. The Boers had shifted their guns during the night and they opened a hot fire on our Artillery. The Boers ceased fire 3 times during the day, and we drove them off another part of their position, and took two prisoners.

Whilst the British reformed, the Royal Engineers were given the task of constructing a further pontoon bridge across the Tugela at Munger's Drift to complement those already constructed east of Potgeiter's Drift, a move all too readily detected by the Boer artillery, which wasted no time opening up upon them. Nevertheless, the bridge was completed with minor casualties.

7th Feb. L. J. Bryant

Our Regt got up at 2 a.m. and shifted to another place. My Company, E, went out as escort to the Guns and we also had to watch the pontoon bridge (which our Engineers had just put across the Tugela) and see that none of the Enemy tried to cross over it or destroy it.

The Boers opened fire on the Bridge with their Guns, but did no damage to it, altho' a couple of men who were having a swim in the River had to get out on the double. We rejoined the Battalion again at 7p.m.

With the 1st Durham Light Infantry on the left and the 3rd King's Royal Rifles on the right, the attack on Vaal Krantz began. Though under heavy fire from the vicinity of Doorn Kloof, they pressed steadily forward, until by mid afternoon the eastern slopes of Vaal Krantz were in British hands. However, as before, poor intelligence and a lack of knowledge of the countryside hampered their advance. The eastern end of Vaal Krantz proved impossible to hold as it was surrounded and overlooked by a much stronger Boer entrenchment on the western end of the ridge and from Doorn Kloof and several surrounding dongas. The British also found their artillery advance had ground to a halt as the ridges on Vaal Krantz were so steep and razor sharp that transportation of the guns under such exposed conditions would prove suicidal.

Fighting continued throughout the day until by late evening the Boers counter-attacked from the west. General Lyttelton's Brigade, reinforced by the 2nd Devons, held on and repulsed the attack, but it was now clear to all that their position was becoming increasingly more untenable, clear, that is, to all but command HQ apparently. The stalemate continued for several days as the Boers made repeated attempts to dislodge the British. General Hildyard's Brigade was drawn up to relieve General Lyttelton's men on Vaal Krantz as positions changed hands throughout the day and night.

History, it seemed, was repeating itself over a very short period of time. Doorn Kloof was fast becoming another Spion Kop! Buller's "key to Ladysmith" counted for very little. The real key to breaking the siege was in this case Doorn Kloof, not Vaal Krantz, as he had surmised. Without first securing the heights of Doorn Kloof possession of Vaal Krantz was inconsequential. Any attempt to execute a flanking movement on Brakfontein was now called off and, not for the first time, a general recall issued.

8th Feb. L. J. Bryant

We once more had to retire, altho' the Boers got as good as they gave. Our casualties were 400 in this fight. We retired back to Springfield very early in the morning; General Buller himself conducted the Retirement. Our Naval Guns covered our Retirement. The Boers started to shell our Hospital and also sent a few shells after us, but done no harm. We arrived at Springfield at 6 p.m. after marching 15 miles.

8th Feb. Capt. A. C. Jeffcoat DSO

Springfield. We struck camp at 1 p.m. on the 4th, Sunday after church and marched nearly to the river...Captain Forty joined us. At 7 a.m. we were explained the plan of the day.

From Springfield the Royal Inniskilling Fusiliers, as part of Hart's 5th Brigade moved out on 10 February and marched back the eight or so miles to Pretorius Farm.

At this point I would like to take issue with Mr Winston Churchill who commented upon the progress of the Army during the South African campaign. Indeed, as previously stated, their advance was certainly hampered by thousands of tons of ancillary equipment, but Churchill, at the time preoccupied with making a name for himself, failed to differentiate between the needs of a large, increasingly mechanized army and those of a mostly mounted mobile guerrilla force such as the Boers.

Commenting upon the fact that he had never before witnessed officers accomodated in tents whilst on active service, either in India or the Sudan, he further cited the fact that enlisted men were provided with canvas shelters and lived far too well to be best able to counteract the enemy. Such luxuries he termed "poor economy".

Indeed there was a lot of truth in the observations made by Churchill, but his comments were tainted with more than just a hint of pompous snobbery which detract much from what he had to say. Such an ambitious adventurer, for he was little more than that, could scarcely comment upon the realities of life in the ranks, its deprivations and hardships. On the other hand Bryant is far more able than I to take issue with Churchill's condemnation of his "elaborate" lifestyle. Churchill's use of the words 'poor economy' gives one a fleeting insight into just how individuals such as he valued the price of a man's very life.

The following few extracts from Private Bryant's diary speak for themselves.

10th Feb.

Struck our Camp and marched to Pretorious Farm (8miles) at 8 a.m. It was a very hot day and we only got a very small taste of coffee to drink before we started on our march. About 250 men of the Brigade fell out during the march through weakness, and owing to the excessive heat. One man died with Heat Apoplexy. Arrived at Pertorious Farm at 1 p.m.[26]

11th Feb.

Reveille went at 2.30 a.m. We fell in at 4 a.m. (after striking Camp at 3.15 a.m.) to march to Chieveley (15 miles), but we did not start on our march until 5 p.m. & we arrived at Chieveley at 3 p.m. & pitched our Camp at 3.30 p.m.

Chapter Four

Inniskilling Hill (Hart's Hill), Relief of Ladysmith

Dejected and weary the men of the Royal Inniskilling Fusiliers struck camp at 3.15 am on the morning of 11 February and prepared to fall back to Chieveley where they were to remain until the 22nd of the month. During this period they were to remain at a heightened state of readiness, bedding down on the hard earth whilst awaiting orders to join Buller, already engaged at Colenso in his fourth attempt to relieve the beleaguered Ladysmith.

As the men waited for the order to move out, snippets of information filtered through to them in Battalion Orders regarding the state of the war elsewhere. In an effort to bolster their spirits, every effort was made to try to keep them informed of the progress of the war, especially the movements of Lord Roberts who at that particular time had invaded the Orange Free State. Any news especially of an uplifting nature was welcomed by all.

16th Feb. L. J. Bryant
We pitched Camp once more, at 6.30 a.m. The following Telegram from Lord Roberts to Gen. Buller was read out to us; French forced his way through the Boer lines and relieved Kimberly [Kimberley].[1] He also captured a Boer Laager, containing food and ammunition. Kelly-Kenny [2] is chasing Cronje,[3] who is Retiring Northwards with 10,000 men.

With the close of February, so too came a change in fortune, not only for those besieged within Ladysmith but the entire war effort. General Buller's fourth and final attempt to raise the siege would herald one of the British Army's first victories in a campaign, which, up until then, had been fraught with setbacks and disasters. The events of Modder River, Magersfontein, Colenso and Stormberg[4] may indeed have been behind them but still ahead lay a formidable task.

For the Royal Inniskilling Fusiliers too, it would herald their most memorable contribution to the entire campaign, the attack on Railway Hill, later to be known as Hart's Hill and even more so, *Inniskilling Hill.*[5] During this episode the Inniskillings would not only lose their Commanding Officer, Lieutenant-Colonel Thackeray,[6] but also a huge percentage of their Officers and ORs. So much so that, following the relief of Ladysmith, the regiment was so depleted that General Buller ordered it withdrawn from Hart's Brigade and detailed to remain as part of Ladysmith's garrison until fresh drafts of Inniskillings could arrive.

However, before any of this could take place, Ladysmith had to be relieved. The closing days of the siege and the advance of the relief force is best accounted for by someone who was actually there, someone who experienced at first hand the dangers and hardships entailed. To this end I give over the next few pages to those whose own words can convey far more than I could ever hope.

17th Feb. L. J. Bryant
Half the Battalion were on Fatigue repairing the Railway line near Colenso; Buller having made the Boers retire from their position there. We received the Queens present of a Box of Chocolate, which Her Majesty intended as a New Years Gift, for the Troops at the Front, on that day.
18th Feb.
Went on Outpost duty at 6 p.m. The Boers turned their Search light on us, but 3 shells fired from our Naval Guns soon made them stop showing it anymore for this night. A Severe Storm came on.
19th Feb.
Came off Outpost and went on Inlying Picquet at 'Retreat.' A Second Thunderstorm came on.
20th Feb.
Relieved off picquet and went on Outpost again at 5 p.m. Had more rain in the night.

21ˢᵗ Feb.

Came off outpost at 6 a.m. and had to go on again at 7 p.m. We then got orders to return to Camp again about 8 p.m. The Boers again put their Search Lights on us. We struck Camp at 10 p.m., fell in at 12 M.N., and marched to Colenso, re-crossing the Tugela.

21ˢᵗ Feb. Lieut. D. G. Auchinleck

Rained all last night. Troops in front still advancing. Great amount of Boer ammunition and stores have been captured on Monte Christo and Hlangwane. Got orders in the evening to move off to Colenso at 12 midnight Dublins having occupied it this evening. Shelling went on all day.

22ⁿᵈ Feb. L. J. Bryant

We arrived at Colenso at 6 a.m. after marching about 9 miles or so. We passed by the Railway Bridge which was totally wrecked, it having been blown up by the Boers, and we rejoined Bullers Main Force once more. The Boers thinking that they would never be put out of Colenso, had brought their beds etc. down with them and had them in bomb proof shelters. We bivouacked for the day, which was a very hot one, and some of the men of the Brigade went exploring and came across boxes of explosive bullets which the Boers had been using.

22ⁿᵈ Feb. Lieut. D. G. Auchinleck

We amused ourselves all morning examining the enemy's trenches and picking up odds and ends as trophies. Found any amount of cartridges and other things the enemy had left behind in their hurry to get off. In the afternoon we moved on to the next hill and bivouacked there that night. Desultory firing went on all day till the evening when we heard a heavy musketry fire a little way to the front. Very few bullets came our way.

"Explosive bullets" were sometimes referred to as "man-stopping", "dum-dums" or "soft-nosed bullets" because when they penetrated the body they spread out or mushroomed, inflicting terrible wounds on the victim by leaving a gaping hole at the point of exit.

The dum-dum[7] bullet was so called because it was first manufactured at the arsenal of Dum-Dum in India. The dum-dum causes such terrible wounds by having the nickel coating on the top of the bullet filed away which allows the lead to expand. Such soft-nosed bullets were discovered in several Boer trenches not only at Colenso but also Paardeberg[8] and elsewhere. However, this practice was not confined solely to the Boers. Major-General Gatacre [9] whilst in the Sudan ordered both officers and other ranks under his command to spend long hours under the fierce sun filing off the tips of their bullets, as he declared such ammunition was the best way to stop the Dervish. After the Battle of the Atbara, however, he often marched his men out into the desert to fire off the remaining rounds before the Sirdar, Kitchener, joined the force for the march on Omdurman.

23rd Feb. L. J. Bryant

The Battle for the Relief of Ladysmith is still being fought. Our Brigade had to shift to another place, and we lay down near one of our Howitzer Batteries; we had a few casualties whilst shifting our position. The Imperial Light Infantry (a Colonial Corps) were attached to our Brigade, in place of the Border Regt. who were elsewhere. A few shells kept coming pretty near to us from the Boers Guns, as they were trying to find the range of our Howitzer Battery, and succeeded after we left. The Irish Bge. received orders to go into Action during the afternoon.

The Inniskillings were to form the Firing Line; the Dublins and Connaughts the Supports, and the I. L. I. [Imperial Light Infantry] were the Reserves. We had to cross over a small Railway Bridge, whilst on our march to the place of our operations, and we were open to a very murderous fire from the Boer Mausers,[10] as they had the range off to a .T. and we had to run the gauntlet, but did not have many casualties for all that.

We had to drive the Boers from three positions, the last being called Pieters or Railway Hill, from which the Battle takes its name. The Boers evacuated the first position, and our chaps charged the second position and drove the Boers from it. The last position was a very precipitous and stony hill, but the Regt. under Lieut. Col T.M.G. Thackery, made a dash for it at once, but such a murderous fire was opened on them, that they could not stand it and were repulsed with heavy loss. Col: Thackeray was one of the men who fell mortally wounded in that desperate charge. Not to be denied , the men under command of Major Saunders, with a Company of the Dublins and Connaughts, again made a rush for the position, but were again repulsed with frightful loss, being to weak to stand long under such a fire as was brought to bear on them.

Darkness having then set in, the Battalion retired back to the position they had won and held it for the night. The Boers were sniping all night long.

23rd Feb. Lieut. D. G. Auchinleck

Turned out to be the most eventful and fateful day of the war so far for the Inniskillings. Regt. started at daybreak and very soon they got into the shell fire. Reached the ridge about 8 a.m. and halted and waited there; Howitzer Battery took up a position near. At 12.30 the Regt. Marched off to attack hill which proved almost impregnable, marched 3 miles along railway in single file under a heavy musketry fire, across one bridge, afterwards christened Pom-pom Bridge on account of the fearful Pom-poms and musketry fire which swept it. During this bit we lost 20 or 30 men. Arrived at our place of formation, we at once formed for attack A & F firing line B & D Supports, E, H, G and C Reserve. We drove the attack half way up the hill without losing very much, capturing a Boer Laager. The fire then became very heavy and many men fell but no officer yet. We waited here some time pouring volleys into the Boer trenches. A few of the Connaughts and Dublins came up on our right and the I.L.I. on our extreme right. We then advanced over the railway cutting and took up position on the far bank. The fire was still very heavy, sweeping the whole ridge and was here we rallied preparatory to the charge. Then the Regt. Charged and men, and officers fell in dozens; after going some way the Regt. rallied and charged again and this time got to within 50 yards of the enemy's trenches. Here the fire was awful coming from four different directions and it is marvellous how the men faced it. With the help of supports we might have got right to the top but as it was, the regiment lay there all night and the enemy kept up a incessant fire. Now as to my own doings, shortly after the Regiment started, I got orders to move the Transport round to where they were yesterday and a very lively half hour we had the shells dropping round us all the way. However we got round with no casualties and spent the morning listening to our guns shelling. A few of the Boer shells came over our way but we were well sheltered under the hill and so they fell beyond us.

In the afternoon I got orders to take the rations up to the Regiment and started off about 5 p.m. with my wagon along the railway being told I should get a truck on which to take the rations up to the front. But when I got there, there was no truck to be found so I decided to walk up to the Regiment and find out where they were so that I might take the things up first thing in the morning, so off I started with Britton of the Dublins up the line and a very nasty walk it was; coming towards us all the time the bullets were falling round us prety thick and when we had gone about 4 miles we could not find the

Brigade anywhere so we decided to turn back and wait for daylight. The same ordeal had to be gone through on the way back and I hope I shall not have another walk like this one; we got back in the middle of the night and tried to get some sleep but it was hopeless, the bullets whistling over us all night and a continual roar of musketry fire was kept up away on our right where our poor fellows were.

23rd Feb. Capt. A. C. Jeffcoat DSO

Moved at daybreak and marched to the right in fours under a heavy shell fire and took up a position under cover but as the Howitzer battery took up a position below us we came under shell fire. At about 11 a.m. the CO came and told us that the Brigade was to attack a hill on the right, our right leading supported by the Connaughts and I.L.H. So at 12 we started off along the railway in file and came under fire almost at once. It was a great trouble getting the machine gun along especially crossing the first bridge. About a mile on we emerged from the cutting and found ourselves under a heavy fire, losing many men.

24th Feb. L. J. Bryant

The Boers came around the Railway Line and tried to Flank our Regt., but failed in the attempt, and the Devons coming up to relieve our Regt. we retired out of Action and lay down near the banks of the Tugela and had a rest which we badly needed.

We had a Muster Roll Call,[11] and we found out that our losses in yesterdays action amounted to 69 men killed and 175 or so wounded. Total 246. We lost our Colonel and Second in Command in yesterdays fight, and the Dublins also lost their Colonel. No further fighting took place to day as it was raining all day.

24rd Feb. Lieut. D. G. Auchinleck

Up early and set to work to load the truck which turned up before daybreak. Very heavy firing going on in front. Got the truck moving the rations up as far as Pom Pom bridge under a very heavy fire. Unloaded there and came back and took my Wagon back to the remainder of the wagons. Then I went back to see if I could see any of the fighting and the enemy's guns began pelting shrapnel and other shells on to the slope of the hill where I was. The 11th Bds and Howitzer Battery were there and while it lasted it was bad (2 hours). I then went back to my wagon and the firing went on all day. I took up another day's supplies in the evening without much difficulty. Got them off in charge of Morley who had come back that morning and was going up to join again and then received an order to send up another day's supplies as the transport was to move tomorrow so by the time I got back it was after 2 a.m. and I was jolly tired. All last night the Regt. lay just behind the crest behind a rough stone wall with the Boers plugging away at them with orders to hold the hill at all costs and they would be relieved at daybreak by another Brigade. Daybreak came but no Brigade and the Dublins and Connaughts having retired behind the hill about 8.30 a.m. when the remains were relieved and retired back to the river the task which they had been set, being found impracticable.

24th Feb. Capt. A. C. Jeffcoat DSO

At dawn we went on to try again on our right and heard from stragglers the news of the cutting up of the regiment. They had pushed under a heavy fire and taken the first hill, then as the supports did not come up they tried to take Harts Hill [Inniskilling Hill] a very strong position, and got up to the top but as the cross fire was so terrible the Colonel and most of the officers were hit they had to retire…leaving the dead and wounded on the hill. The Colonel, Major Sanders and young Stuart and 60 men killed, 8 officers and 200 men wounded and Best missing. They must have had a terrible time.

25th Feb. L. J. Bryant

General Buller obtained an Armistice for 12 hours so that our wounded etc. could be brought in as they were lying were they fell since the 23rd Inst. The Stretcher Bearers then went out and brought in the dead and wounded, the men could not have been brought in before, as it would have been certain death to attempt to go near the place, let alone carry a man away on a stretcher. Some of our wounded men, who had been lying quite near the Boer position, told us that they suffered fiercely from want of water, and that the Boers came down afterwards and gave them water to drink, but that the Boers robbed our dead, as usual. The Armistice being over at 7 p.m. the Boers started sniping; their bullets were flying just over our heads and settling in the Tugela, which when they struck made little lights, as they were explosive bullets which the Boers were using.

One of those to be rescued during the armistice was Major C. J. Lloyd Davidson who had lain wounded on the slopes of Inniskilling Hill. Interviewed at a later date for the regimental history he recalled:

"We lay behind this wall throughout the day, our guns firing over us and our shells sometimes throwing dust and earth over us. Rain fell heavily, which was a blessing. I remember opening my mouth to catch what I could, being very thirsty then the sun came out, burning hot. The firing never ceased throughout the long day, all going just over us, as it appeared, and the Boer rifle fire hitting the rocks all around us; if anyone moved or helmet showed, a dozen bullets came at us. About dusk some stretcher bearers came up and carried me down to a culvert under the railway embankment, where I was left all night. Next morning (Sunday 25th), during the truce for the collection of the wounded, I was carried to a dressing station near the river bank of the Tugela. I'll never forget the relief it was to be away from the sound of the whistling bullets." [12]

25th Feb. Lieut. D. G. Auchinleck

Up 5 a.m. and got the oxen inspanned. Did not move off till some hours after as the pontoon bridge was blocked with transport, a few shells came over us in the morning but nothing to speak of. At last we got off and crossed the river again and went away past Hlangwaur Hill and after great difficulty about finding where we were to go to, parked the wagons near Sir Chas. Warren's Headquarters about 1$^{1/2}$ miles in rear of the Battalion. Having seen everything settled I rode off to see the Regt. everything being quiet as an armistice to bury the dead was in force till 8 p.m. this evening. I found them on the river bank and it was here I first heard the true account. The Colonel, Maj. Sanders and poor Walter killed; Davy, Foot, Evans, Bill, Crawford, Potts, Devenish, Ridings wounded. Jones broke his arm during the retirement and poor old Best was taken prisoner, nobody knows how. A terrible job, leaving only 8 officers with the Battalion. I had a long talk with them and later took back a lot of things belonging to the killed to the wagons so that they might be safe in case the Regt. moved off. Just as I started, the Boers began firing again and when I got back to the wagons a perfect fusillade started, one bullet striking a mealie bag on which I was leaning. Jolly glad to lie down, sniping continued all night.

25th Feb. Capt. A. C. Jeffcoat DSO

We got an armistice to bring in dead and bring down the wounded, poor fellows had been out on the hill for 48 hours without food or water. I went down to the river and had a wash and saw the remnants of the regiment.

26th Feb. L. J. Bryant

Our Artillery were shelling the Enemy's positions all day to-day, and our Engineers put up another pontoon bridge across the Tugela, just near where we are lying. The Boers again opened fire at 7 p.m., and kept it up all night.

26th Feb. Lieut. D. G. Auchinleck

Nothing much in way of fighting went on today, our guns shelling the Boer position in a half-hearted way, preparing for the big battle to-morrow. In the morning I went over to the Hospital to see our fellows but they had all gone down to Maritzburg and Mooi River so I came back and had lunch withd the Dublin Transport. In the afternoon Morley turned up with a party for the rations so we started off with them and I took them in a wagon as far as I could when his party took them on. I went down with him to see the others and stayed with them a short time. Rode back with Brooker our Bdr. Supply Officer and got to bed as early as possible.

26th Feb. Capt. A. C. Jeffcoat DSO

We were sniped all day and kept up a fire on their trenches as also did the artillery; the day being spent in moving the artillery more to the right and building a pontoon Bridge below us and bringing up more troops. Heard of Cronje's capture.

27th Feb. L. J. Bryant

Our Regt. went into Action again to-day, as a Reserve Force. Captain Gibton took over the Command on the Battalion as we only have 4 Officers left and he is the Senior. General Buller having shifted his Guns to another position turned the lot on the Boers position, which they effectively shelled with Lyddite[13] and Shrapnell[14] all the morning and afternoon, so that the Boers dare not lift up their heads, knowing that they would get a warm reception. We had about 94 Guns playing on the Boer trenches and they were firing Salvoes (volleys) and the noise they made would make your head split.

About 3 p.m. our troops charged the Boer positions in overwhelming numbers and the Boers ran for their lives out of their trenches, a lot of them showing the white flag and holding up their hands, but the chaps were that mad they took no notice of them at the start and down they went. The Boers must have lost pretty heavy to-day; our losses being 1500. We had 4 casualties in our Regt. to-day.

27th Feb. Lieut. D. G. Auchinleck

MAJUBA DAY. The greatest day of the war. Rode over to the hospital in the morning to see Steward and on the way over heard the official telegram from Roberts about Cronje. As far as I remember it ran like this - "Cronje and all his forces surrendered unconditionally this morning at daybreak and is now a prisoner in my camp. Strength of force will be communicated later.

I hope Her Majesty will consider this event satisfactory, occurring as it does, on the Anniversary of Majuba." This was great news to start on and then I heard we were to make a big attack in 3 parts. Stewart had gone away so I returned and watch the fight for some time from the Naval guns and 5 inch guns. Our guns 80 or 90 in number, began shelling the Boer position about 8 a.m. and kept up a terrific fire all morning at a range of from 3,700 to 5,000 yds.

At about 11 we saw the right attack start and gradually it developed, every inch of the ground being contested stubbornly by the enemy. When this had thoroughly developed, the centre attack commenced and shortly after the left.

The Boers stuck to their trenches magnificently under the most awful shell fire and maxim fire in addition to the rifles but in the end they were simply compelled to go and at about 5.30 or 6 o'clock the whole Boer position was ours... The concentration of the artillery fire with the shells bursting on the 3 hills was an extraordinary sight, such a fire never having been seen before, I suppose. Got to bed early after the most eventful day of my life. We took about 250 prisoners.

27th Feb. Capt. A. C. Jeffcoat DSO

At about 2 p.m. the infantry started to advance, we could not see what Barton's brigade was doing but they took Pieters Hill, the Scotch fusiliers losing heavily.

The infantry in front then started in skirmish order sweeping round from the right, the S. Lancashires driving the Boers out at the point of the bayonet. The Light Infantry then advanced and took Harts Hill without much trouble so the whole Boer right was turned and all the Boers cleared out to Umbulwana during the night. We fired altogether 11,500 rounds in shells. We at last had a quiet night's rest.

Chapter Five

Ladysmith

For those besieged within Ladysmith the morning of 28 February 1900 began as it had for some time previous, a continuous round of caring for the sick and wounded whilst remaining in readiness should there be a renewed Boer attack. However, the events of the previous few days were finally coming to their conclusion, the long-held hopes and aspirations of the besieged were about to be fulfilled. Around noon the British 4.7 Naval guns began bombarding the Boer entrenchment at Umbulwana, approximately four miles from Ladysmith and on which "Long Tom,"[1] the huge Boer gun which had been the scourge of the inhabitants, was mounted. Out of necessity the range and accuracy of the Naval guns was essential, owing to the fact that immediately below the slopes of Umbulwana was situated the neutral camp of Intombi. It was to this camp that the sick and wounded, along with those residents of Ladysmith who wished to escape the terror of the siege, had been evacuated some time earlier. According to an inhabitant of Ladysmith;

> Something very unusual was taking place, as our Naval guns had not fired for six weeks previous to this. One of the shells from our guns carried away the derrick which had been erected to remove the guns on Umbulwana. The firing continued from about twelve noon till 4.15, when suddenly a tremendous shout was heard, and looking in the direction of Caesar's Camp, the vanguard of the relieving force was seen coming along. Young and old, those too feeble from the long-standing sickness and lack of the common necessaries of life, all

bounded in the direction in which the relieving force was coming. Shouts from every side were heard. Bells rang, guns fired and as the vanguard of the Imperial Light Horse and the Natal Carbineers came in, the sight can be more easily imagined than described.[2]

The news that the siege had finally been broken and Ladysmith relieved was greeted with jubilation throughout the Empire, but nowhere more especially than in South Africa and the United Kingdom. The first real breakthrough had been achieved in a campaign whose progress had hitherto been less than encouraging.

According to missionaries belonging to the South Africa General Mission, a group caring for the troops by providing Soldiers' Homes, the relief was greeted with a mixture of jubilation and joy, tinged with sadness within Ladysmith itself. However, any celebrations were marred by the stark realities of war. The ravages of the siege and the sacrifices of both defenders and relief column alike were all too evident.

"The siege was over now. As we passed through the battlefields, the awfulness of war was apparent on all sides. Intombi was reached with its tent hospitals, with 1,500 sick, suffering and convalescents. The silent graveyard adjoining with its six hundred graves, told of 'Pestilence that walketh in darkness,' the majority having died of fever and dysentery. The walking skeletons spoke of famine, while the look of strain on many a face revealed to us something of those long hours of anxiety."[3]

The sight which greeted the relief column was similarly grim. Now that the battle was over the troops had time to survey the Boer trenches, a chance to see exactly what and who they had been pitted against. The destruction and loss of life on both sides was glaringly apparent.

28th Feb. L. J. Bryant

There being no more fighting to do at present, a lot of the troops went round and had a look at some of the Boer Trenches; the Trenches where between 4ft. 6 & 4 foot 10 inches deep and were covered with cartridges etc, some of them were full of dead boers, which had been thrown in anyhow & covered with a little dirt, so eager were the Boers to get away when our Troops charged their position, that they didn't have time to carry their dead & wounded with them as they usually do, but just through them in the trenches & put a little dirt over them, the consequence was here & there a foot or part of an arm was sticking up out of the dirt.

We also had a look at some of their wounded, some of whom were turned quite yellow from the effects of Lyddite. One or two of the Boers told us that it was not their faults that they were fighting against us, for, they said that they would be shot by their own men, if they refused to fight against us, when asked twice by their Commandant, never mind whether they were sick or not.

With the Relief of Ladysmith accomplished, Hart's Fifth Irish Brigade was left to count the cost, especially the Royal Inniskilling Fusiliers, who not only lost their Commanding Officer Lieutenant-Colonel T. M. G. Thackeray in the first attack on Inniskilling Hill (Pieters or Hart's Hill) but also their Second in Command, Major F. A. Sanders, amongst the second wave to brave the hill. In all the Royal Inniskilling Fusiliers lost 72% of its officer strength and 37% of its enlisted men killed or wounded in this single engagement.

$$5^{th} \text{ Irish Brigade}$$
$$\text{Casualties}[4]$$

Officers

	Killed	Wounded	Missing
Brigade Staff			
R. Innis. F.	3	9	1
Conn. Rangers		7	
R. Dublin F.	2	4	
Imp. Light Inf.		1	
Bearer Company			
Total Casualties	5	21	1

Other Ranks

	Killed	Wounded	Missing
Brigade Staff		3	
R. Innis. F.	56	159	23
Conn. Rangers	19	105	8
R. Dublin F.	9	53	28
Imp. Light Inf.	2	19	
Bearer Company		1	
Total Casualties	86	340	59

Having sustained such heavy casualties in the run-up and eventual relief of Ladysmith, it is ironic that on 1 March 1900, when the Relief Column marched triumphantly into Ladysmith, to the cheers and adulation of the townsfolk, the Royal Inniskilling Fusiliers, the Border Regiment and the Connaught Rangers should be omitted. Placed on fatigues to guard the convoy, they were given the task of pulling the guns across the pontoon bridge that spanned the Tugela. It wasn't until 4 March that they were allowed to enter Ladysmith, and only then to pass through on a route march.

1st Mar. Capt. A. C. Jeffcoat DSO

All the other troops have pushed on but the Irish brigade is left behind to get the baggage across the river. Were on fatigue all day regulating traffic and keeping road in order. Rode with Hessey over to the Boer position. Harts Hill was very stiffly held, our fellows must have got enfiladed all the way up. Beyond there is a plain for 4/5 miles to Umbulwana.

1st Mar. Lieut. D. G. Auchinleck

Spent the morning completing the list of wounded which took us from 5-9 a.m. I then went back and spent the day with the battalion. Hessey, Jeffcoat and I rode all over the Boer trenches, a wonderful sight. A great many of their dead buried in the trenches, just as they were. Women found in the trenches also. Regiment on fatigue most of day.

2nd Mar.

Walked down and saw our graves and took a general look around. Fatigue at pontoon bridge still going on but Transport started off at 3 p.m. but had to outspan on top of the hill as there was such a block at the bridge, very quiet day.

During the days and weeks following the Relief of Ladysmith letters and telegrams of congratulations and condolence arrived almost daily. Sometimes addressed to the troops as a whole, at other times specific to the Inniskillings, nevertheless Private Bryant faithfully entered the details in his diary, thus providing us with a brief insight into attitudes both at home and abroad.

3rd Mar. L. J. Bryant

The following Message from H. M. the Queen to Gen: Buller, was read to us this morning viz:

Thank God for the news you have told me. I congratulate you, & all under you, with all my heart.

Sgd. V. R. I.

Our Brigade fell in at 4 p.m. and marched to Pieters Station ($2^1/_2$ mls.) & bivouacked for the night.

General Bullers Speech to the Troops
on the Relief of Ladysmith.

The Following letter from Gen; Buller to all the Troops appeared in our Bn. Orders today. Viz;

Soldiers of Natal

The Relief of Ladysmith unites two Forces, both of whom, during the last few months, have striven with conspicuous gallantry, & splendid determination to maintain the Honour of our Queen and Country.

The Garrison of Ladysmith, have, during the last four months, held their position against every attack, with complete Success, & endured privations with Admirable Fortitude.

The Relieving Force, had to force its way through an unknown Country, across an unaffordable River, & over almost inaccessible heights, in face of a fully prepared & tenacious enemy.

By the Exhibition of the True Courage that burns steadily, as well as flashes brilliantly, it has accomplished its Object, & added a Glorious page to the history of the British Empire.

Ladysmith has been held, & is now Relieved. Soldiers & Sailors, Colonials & Homebred, have done this by one desire.

The General Commanding, Congratulates both Forces upon the Martial qualities they have shown. He thanks them for their determined efforts, & he desires to offer his Sincerest Sympathy to the Relatives & Friends of those Good Soldiers & Gallant Comrades who have fallen in the fight.

Signed Redvers Buller, General.

The Relief of Ladysmith, coming close on the heels of Kitchener's success at Paardeberg on 17 February, in which he defeated and captured General Piet Cronje, coupled with General French's[5] successful relief of the besieged Kimberley on the 15th, gave the public a reason to celebrate, which up until then had been muted. Congratulations on the troops' success poured in from all areas, from Heads of State, to societies and towns. It appeared at this stage that previous disasters were now firmly behind them and the campaign had taken on a new impetus.

4th Mar. L. J. Bryant

We fell in at 5 a.m. and marched into Ladysmith; passing through the town on our march. We marched 15 miles, and it was very hot all day. We bivouacked for the night, about 2 miles from the town.

4th Mar. Lieut. D. G. Auchinleck

Fell in at daybreak and marched to Ladysmith. Great delay on the way on account of deep drift across the Klip River. Regt. arrived about 2.30 p.m. I did not get in till 5 and then could not find the Regt. Had an awful job galloping all over the shop, and gave it up in despair about 10 p.m. Even the orderly which Gen. Howard gave us could not guide us right.

5th Mar. L. J. Bryant

Under canvas once more. We had a rest today. The following appeared in our Orders today:- the G.O.C. has to communicate to the Troops, the following Telegram he has received from the C. in Chief, viz;- Please to convey to all Ranks under your command, my Appreciation, as a Soldier of the Splendid work at Ladysmith. They fought nobly, & deserved the Success. The achieved also Congratulates Gen. White & those under his command, for the Gallant manner in which they have maintained the old fighting tradition of our Army, under very trying circumstances.

(Sgd.) Wolsley, Commander in Chief.[6]

The G.O.C. has also to inform the Troops, both of the Relief & Defence Forces, that he has recd. Congratulations from all parts of Cape Colony, & Natal, from most of the Great Towns & Societies of the United Kingdom; from Lord Minto, in the Name of Canada; from Lord Ranfurley in the Name of New Zealand; from Lord Curzon in the Name of India, & from the Governor of the Australian Colonies in the Name of their people.

Sgd. H. S. Mills, Colonel, Chief of Staff.

5th Mar. Capt. A. C. Jeffcoat DSO

Wagons arrived after breakfast so we pitched camp, I have taken over H Coy. And we have started a regimental mess and fixed up Boer tent as a mess tent.

7th Mar. L. J. Bryant

Nothing unusual occurred. The following appeared in Bn. Order:- The Major General has recd the following Telegram; from the Cardiff Exchange, "Congratulations on the Magnificent Conduct of the Irish Troops."

7th Mar. Lieut. D. G. Auchinleck

Up at 5.30 a.m. Had to go round the country trying to find decent water for drinking purposes. This took a long time. In the afternoon rode down with Boston to tea with Beves and bought a shell. Went to the ordnance to see about getting a water cart with no result, Bed early.

8th Mar.

Started off at 2.30 a.m. and walked into the station at Ladysmith with Scotch Cart full of wounded officers kits. Had to take them down to Colenso and bring back pony for Bell. Met Beves who was going down on leave and we started at 5.15 a.m. on a workman's train. Got as far as Pieters where they had to stop to mend a culvert. Beves and I started off and I showed him where we had done all the fighting and also our graves. Then we waited for the train to pick us up again. Arrived about 12.30 and we went on to Colenso; first train through from Ladysmith to Colenso. Beves was astonished how we ever got through such a network. Arrived at Colenso 10 o'clock and was busy all afternoon getting the kits off and trying to find Bell's pony which I at last succeeded in doing late at night. Could not get back that night so got Sergt. Cummings to give me a shake down. Very comfortable night.

9th Mar. Lieut. D. G. Auchinleck

Started to ride back to camp 22 miles about 10 o'clock. Very interesting ride seeing the back of the Boer position. On the way met the Proprietor of the Railway Hotel (Leonard) Ladysmith and rode in with him. Stopped at a farmer's who had remained on his farm all the time and had an interesting talk with him. Got into camp after doing business in Ladysmith about 5. Found the Somerset L. I. had marched in to relieve us and we were to go on the lines of communications till we had got some new officers etc.

For the Inniskillings, however, life, now the battle was over, was about to take a new twist. Such was the extent of the casualties suffered by them during the Relief of Ladysmith that it was decided the Regiment should be withdrawn from the strength of Hart's 5th Brigade and detailed to assist the Ladysmith garrison until numbers could be brought up to strength once more. As a result they were to remain in and around the vicinity of Ladysmith until early August 1900, by which time those wounded would have been discharged from hospital fit for duty. Furthermore, any shortfall in regimental numbers would be catered for by fresh drafts of both officers and other ranks.

The following is a breakdown of the numbers of Inniskillings served in South Africa with the battalion

	Officers	NCOs & ORs
Strength of Battalion before mobilization.	24	766
Reservists who joined at mobilization	7	449
Total	31	1215
Left behind with "Details" at Mullingar	2	244
Embarked with Battalion	29	971
First Draft		115
Second Draft		260
Third Draft		100
Fourth Draft		170
Fifth Draft		122
Sixth Draft		23
Seventh Draft		258
Eighth Draft		54
Ninth Draft		42
Tenth Draft		100
Eleventh Draft		102
Joined the Battalion at various times		44

11th Mar. L. J. Bryant

Our Regt. struck Camp at 11 a.m. and marched to Devon's Post (about 4 miles off). 'C' & 'F' Coys. Marched to Intombi Hospital (about 8 miles) to do duty there. Our Regt. being in such a weak state, (owing to our heavy losses during the Relief) are now put on the Lines of Communications to recruit our Strength. The Somersets take our place in the 5th Brigade. We were loudly cheered by the Dublins and Connaughts as we marched away.

11th Mar. Lieut. D. G. Auchinleck

Church Parade 6.40 a.m. Afterwards got orders to move, 150 men and I officer (Morley) to go to Intombi Hospital on Detachment. The remainder to go to Devonshire Post to supply picket line etc. All very sick about it. Started off 1 p.m. and arrived 3. One of my wagons broke down but I managed to get it fixed up alright. Went into Ladysmith to see about water cart again and I think have managed it this time. Atkinson joined us just as the Battalion marched off. Rather a surprise as we did not expect him so soon. Got camp pitched and squared up. Had meal and then to bed.

12th Mar.

Had a lovely sleep last night Morley goes off at 3 30 a.m. to
Maritzburg to get men's kits etc. a 2 day job. He is covered with
errands for us. Rode down with him to the station and went round
Ladysmith to get some odds and ends. Wilcox of the Gloucester
Regt. came to dinner. Bed 9.30 p.m. The following telegram was
received from G.O.C. – "Fighting was proceeding at Mafeking on 8th
inst. The Boer force in battle on Modder River was estimated at
14,000. Kruger arrived in time to see his men in full flight and tried
in vain to rally them. We occupy Norvals Pont the Boers having
completely retired to their own territory. Two of the centre spans of
the Bridge are destroyed. Brabant has occupied Jamestown without
opposition. The Boers are retiring on Bethulie and Aliwal. The
Advanced Guard of the Carnarvon Field Force has entered Carnarvon
and was well received." Sir R. Buller has received the following
telegram   from President Hiberinans, Warick, Queensland
"Hiberinans, Warick, Queensland send congratulations Irish
Regiments, Brilliant victories."

As the Inniskillings settled down to a welcome period of rest after the
hardships and deprivations of the previous few months, word reached
Ladysmith on the 15th that Lord Roberts had entered Bloemfontein.
Amid celebrations marking the event, telegrams arrived almost daily
from home and abroad bearing condolences and congratulations on the
Regiment's recent endeavours.

16th Mar. L. J. Bryant

The following telegrams were sent to our Regt. :- From Gen. Stokes.
"Deepest Sympathy; Brave Regt."
From members of the Northern Counties Club, Derry:-
"Congratulation all ranks, bravery in the field.......
Deepest Sympathy on Heavy Loss."
From Durban Light Infantry :- "We drink success to you, as the
Future Irish Guards. God Save Ireland."

To commemorate the actions of the Irish Brigade during the lead up to
and eventual relief of Ladysmith, Queen Victoria decreed that a fourth
Brigade of Guards be raised, which would be known as the Irish Guards.
As a result on 1 April 1900 in accordance with Army Order no. 77:

"Her Majesty the Queen, having deemed it desirable to commemorate the bravery shown by the Irish regiments in the recent operations in South Africa, has been graciously pleased to command that an Irish regiment of Foot Guards be formed. This regiment will be designated the Irish Guards."

In order to form the nucleus of the new regiment elements were drawn from the existing Foot Guard regiments, i.e. 200 Irishmen were drawn from the 1st Grenadiers. Their Colonel-in-Chief was the Queen, their Colonel was Earl Roberts and Major R. J. Cooper who had already seen action with the Grenadiers in South Africa was promoted Lieutenant Colonel and became their first Commanding Officer. Other officers appointed to the new regiment were the Earl of Kerry, Lord Oxmantown, Lord Settrington, Lord Herbert Scott and the Earl of Kingston.

To differentiate the Irish Guards from the existing Guards regiments their uniform was as follows: of scarlet and blue facings, its distinctive features were a silver embroidered shamrock at each end of the collar, the star of the Order of St. Patrick on the shoulder-strap, a plume of St. Patrick's blue on the side of the bearskin, a field-cap with soft projecting brim piped with green with a green band, and the buttons on the tunic would be arranged in groups of four, four and two.

16th Mar. Lieut. D. G. Auchinleck

Rode into Ladysmith in morning to get 4 wagons wheels mended. Saw the official telegram about Bloemfontein; It ran as follows – Following received from Intelligence, Cape Town 14th "Lord Roberts occupied Bloemfontein yesterday; Union Jack flies over the Presidency vacated by Mr. Steyn. The Mayor, State Secretary, and other officials met Lord Roberts two miles outside the town and presented him with the keys of the public offices; the enemy has withdrawn from the neighbourhood; the inhabitants gave the troops a cordial welcome."

This was pretty good news and we all hope it will settle matters to a great extent. Did nothing much in the afternoon. Major Mackenzie arrived this morning and takes over command of the Regt. Saw Turner, son of Mr Turner of Winchester, this morning who was at Twyford and was called E.V. Wrote to mother very short and uninteresting letter, expect English mail to-night. English mail didn't arrive even to-day. Our mail seems to have got all mixed up now that we have left 5th Bde.

Spent a fairly busy morning and in the afternoon got orders to take wagons to Colenso and bring back beer for the men tomorrow (St. Patrick's Day) and men's kits brought by Manley as far as there. Manley got back here this afternoon. I started off at 5 p.m. with two wagons, one mule and one ox-wagon. I went on with the mule wagon so as to hurry the beer back. Got an awful attack of neuralgia and spent a miserable night. Arrived 10 p.m. and started the beer back at 12 midnight. Was too seedy to ride back with it so I sent pony back and decided to go back by train in the morning.

17th Mar. L. J. Bryant

St. Patrick's Day. The following telegrams were sent to our Regt.:-

From Secty. Irish Association,:- Durban Irishmen send heartiest Greetings on this glorious day. Ireland mourns with you the loss of the Gallant Sons who have died the death of Heroes.

From P. M. Burg:- Maritzburg Irishmen send Fraternal Greetings for St. Patrick's Day, & heartfelt Congratulations on your Gallant work in Natal.

We thoroughly enjoyed ourselves today considering the circumstances.

The morning opened with very wet weather as it was raining, but happily the rain ceased about 9 a.m. & we had fine weather afterwards for the rest of the day. Every man of the Bn. was served out with a green piece of ribbon made into a Boa, to wear in his Cap or Helmet.

We played a football match against the Gloucester's but it was a very poor game although there was some excuse as they were still weak not having properly got over the effects of the Siege. Our side should have won, as it was the game ended in a draw, nothing being scored.

We got 2 pints of beer today by paying for the same; & in the evening we had a Bonfire and an open air concert, to which the Glosters were invited, & we passed a very enjoyable time together.

The Programme for the night was as follows:-

1. Song. The Anchors Weighed.
Encore. Song. The Minstrel Boy.
2. Recitation. Barbara Fritz.
3. Song. For Old Times Sake.
Encore. Song. More work for the Undertaker.
4. Song. The Song that will live for Ever.
Encore. Song. Good Bye Mick.
5. Song. Only a Leap.
Encore. Step Dance.

6. Song. I looked for her in the Market
Encore. Song. Won't she be surprised.
7. Song. The Sandy Coloured Loom.
Encore. Song. Up I came with my little lot.
8. Song. Not Now.
Encore. Song. Come to me.
9. Song. The Old Brigade.
Encore. Song. Soldiers of the Queen.
10. Song. Jack's fond of his Beer.
11. Dance. Irish Step.
Encore. Song. Norah.
12. Song. Whilst the dance goes on.
13. Recitation. The Fireman's Death.
14. Song. Around the Old Camp Fire.
Auel Lang Syne.
God save the Queen.
We got an Issue of Rum each after the concert was over & after exchanging cheers with the Glosters we retired to Bed, about 10 p.m..

17th Mar. Lieut. D. G. Auchinleck

St. Patrick's Day. Started off for Colenso 9 a.m. Got to camp about 10.30. Beer arrived 11 a.m. Very glad to get back. Absolutely tired out and a very painful jaw and throat. Received two parcels, one from cousin Sidney with shamrock which I am sorry to say was all decayed, curious it arrived on exactly the right day. The other parcel was my camera, such a nice one, sent by A. J. am anxious to get some photos taken. All sorts of congratulatory telegrams from everyone all over the country. Played a football match against the Gloucester Regt. in the afternoon which resulted in a pointless draw. In the evening after an enormous dinner, soup, curry with rice, potatoes and French beans, Roly Poly pudding followed by pineapples, oranges cakes and marsala we had a sing-song. Bed pretty late.

18th Mar.

Got up very early and rode with Major Mackenzie, and Morley to see the VC presented to Capt. Reed R A and Sergeant Nurse R A who got it at Colenso Dec. 15th. A most disappointing performance, Buller seemed so casual about it. Got back in time to have breakfast and be on Church Parade at 9 a.m. Hessey went of to Mooi River and Maritzburg to see Davy, Foot etc. Heard that Gibton was in a dangerous condition and had been given up last night but had rallied slightly this morning. Hope he will pull round alright. English mail came in the afternoon. Letters from mother, Bess, Norrie, Iris,

Amanda, 2 from Hancocks and several illustrated and daily papers from mother. Wrote to Hancocks and Jim.

During the period the Inniskillings were assigned as part of the garrison at Ladysmith they were employed on a variety of duties in and around the town to a radius of approximately twenty miles. Picquet duties, fatigues and minor detachments continued on a daily basis whilst the Regiment awaited fresh drafts of men to supplement its depleted ranks. It was at this time that Lieutenant-Colonel R. Lloyd Payne[7] DSO assumed command of the Inniskillings on promotion from the Somerset Light Infantry on 22 April 1900 following the death of Captain W. L. P. Gibton from dysentery on the 19th of the month. Captain Gibton had commanded the Battalion from 24 February until 12 March 1900.

19th Mar. Lieut. D. G. Auchinleck

Up very early. Rode down to Intombi Hospital (by road about 4 or 5 miles) with Maj. Mackenzie. We were on Court of Inquiry on Dundee prisoners. A very long job got through 91 prisoners between 9 a.m. and 2 p.m. Had lunch with R.A.M.C. there; then went over and saw Morley and had a long chat with him while the groom vainly endeavoured to catch the ponies. At last he got one of them and the Major started off home. In the middle of our talk we got a Heliograph message giving us the sudden shock of hearing poor Gibton died at 12.00 this morning. It is awfully sad, another one gone. Went over and took a photo of the cemetery at Intombi where there are 630 buried since the commencement of the siege; also Intombi camp with Umbulwana in background and Det. Camp. Dinner very late. Bed 10.30. Got very nice letter from Davy.

19th Mar. Capt. A. C. Jeffcoat DSO

Gibton died and buried.

21st Mar. L. J. Bryant

Had kit inspection to day by our C.O. and he informed half of us were deficient of them. No. 4943 Lance Corporal J. Gallagher (Band) died of wounds received in Action on the 23rd of Feb. last. He died at Moi River. A small draft arrived from P.M. Burg for our Bn. to day. The Glosters held an open air concert etc. this evening to which we were all invited, & we spent another enjoyable evening together. The Glosters got up a small band for the occasion, numbering 12 performers.

23rd Mar. Lieut. D. G. Auchinleck

Rode into Ladysmith in afternoon to try to get my photos printed; went into a shop and to my surprise a man said "Are you Mr. Auchinleck?" When he said that I at once recognised him as a son of Mr. Adams who had been out here for nearly four years and had been thro' the siege. Very curious meeting here. He kindly promised to do my photos for me which was a great relief. English mail went out to-day. Letters to Betty, Cha, Madi, Miss Mandi, Arthur, Stuart, Sydney and Sergeant Cummings Burton and Lemon Duton. Atkinson did the funerals to-day.

24th Mar.

Up 6 a.m. and had to go off at once and arrange about a funeral which came off at 9 a.m. A very long job. Bought 2 chickens for the mess. A lovely cool day. Atkinson sprained his thumb last night rather badly and his arm in a sling. Maj. Deeble R.A.M.C. who was our doctor at Enniskillen came up from Intombi and had tea with us in the afternoon. He had been thro' the siege. Had to settle about another funeral in evening.

25th Mar. L. J. Bryant

Divine Service was held as usual. I with five other Band chaps went to a rest Camp to do duty there, under Band. Sergt. Lee of our Regt.

25th Mar. Lieut. D. G. Auchinleck

Rest Camp Notes

Orderly Officer to-day so having had breakfast at which Stewart turned up again. I marched the Roman Catholics to service at the convent. Did not go in myself but had a long talk with some of Buller's Staff who are quartered there. Got back to camp about 12 o'clock. We had a luncheon party to-day. Mr. & Mrs. Hamilton and Capt. Kennedy (Staff). Mrs. Hamilton is a sister of Maj. Mackenzie's he is Postmaster General of Natal. They stayed all afternoon and I took a photo of the group and then they went all round the Sangers. Rode into Ladysmith to see about my photos but they were not finished.

26th Mar. L. J. Bryant

We took over the Rest Camp from the Glosters today; Our duties being as follows:-

To clean up the camp every day & keep it clean

To do Police duty on the Railway Bridge & let no person belonging to the camp loiter on the Bridge or cross over it to go into the town.

To stop any Soldier from crossing the Bridge to go into the Town, unless he has a pass authorising him to go into the Town.

This Camp is for men coming out of Hospital, & for Drafts going to join their respective units, so that they can rest here for a day or so, & also draw their Rations here.

26th Mar. Lieut. D. G. Auchinleck

Very cold night last night and an icy morning. Major Mackenzie told me I might go on a weeks leave next Saturday so I am looking forward to it greatly. Had to go to the funeral of 3 more men this morning at 9.30 a.m. Morley and Hutton are both on the sick list. The former with fever so Manley has go down to Intombi to take over detachment. Huttons with pain and a high temperature. Rode into Ladysmith with Hessey to arrange the funeral of another man at 6 p.m. This has been one of the hottest days we have had. No news in the papers for a long time.

27th Mar.

Nothing in the morning as usual. Rode into Ladysmith and Bought a tea-pot and a dozen tea cups. We will soon have quite a civilised mess. Got back about 4.30 p.m. and found Capt. Ford R.A.M.C. who came down to Finners with us for the first year we went there. Went round with Atkinson and took photos of the sangers. The R.C. Priest came to see us in the evening. Had a letter from Norrie to-day dated 1st March in which she says she has seen the account of our fight. Also one from H.M.R. of Algiers. Very tired, bed early, fearfully hot day.

29th Mar.

Came off picket at daybreak arriving in camp at 7 a.m. Jeffcoat came back from leave this morning and walked up with us from the station. He has brought all sorts of luxuries back with him from Durban which place he found very expensive. Forgot to say that I received a letter from mother yesterday dated March 1st. They had heard the news of the Relief of Ladysmith. She enclosed letters for Clandr. and A.S. Auchinleck and a most amusing cutting from the former. Rode all over Ladysmith in the morning on different jobs. Archdeacon Barker came to lunch, went round the Sangers and stayed till tea time. The weather is almost unbearable. Had to ride over to the town (about 3 miles) for Maj. Mackenzie to see about some parcels in the evening. Four more men buried this evening (Atkinson's job). After dinner Atkinson and I developed some of his photos. They were a failure as the film was bad. Stewart on picket. Heard to-day Johnny and Morley are both dangerously ill. The former from wounds the latter from enteric.

30th Mar.

First thing to-day was the funeral of 2 more men. Then came the news that Manley was pretty bad and was going to No. 18 B.F. Hospital. Rode into Ladysmith after having written a few letters to see about getting a ham cooked. Met Deeble and spent half an hour with him in the Royal with Inkson also. Got my photos which have been developed and are very successful. On the way back, I stopped at the station and saw Manley who had just arrived by train from Intombi. Looks fairly bad and is rather depressed about himself. Then had funeral of 2 more men at the cemetery and then back to camp for dinner. Jeffcoat on picket and Stewart feeling rather seedy.

31st Mar.

Steward was sent off to the No. 18 B.F. Hospital this morning and Atkinson went to Intombi to take Manley's place yesterday evening. Steward has got dysentery. This leaves only Jeffcoat and me on duty. Spent this morning after parade printing the photos which are pretty good and writing letters. Rode into Ladysmith in afternoon.

1st Apr.

Atkinson brought in detachment from Intombi early this morning. Very glad they are out of that awful hole at last. Hessey, Jeffcoat and I were on a board of prisoners of war this morning. Deeble came to lunch and stayed all afternoon. Rode with him and Hessey as far as cemetery to see about graves for 4 men, buried this evening. Atkinson and I sat up till 12 developing photos with rather poor success. Glade to get to bed.

3rd Apr.

Took a party of 60 men over to Tin Town to act as Hospital orderlies till further orders as they are so very short and over 800 sick are there. In the afternoon rode into Ladysmith and found all my photos. Part of mail arrived this afternoon. Letters from mother and Austin. Don't know where the remainder have gone.

5th Apr. L. J. Bryant

The people of Enniskillen, Ireland very kindly sent Tobacco, Cigarettes & other presents to our Regt. which we recd. today

6th Apr. Lieut. D. G. Auchinleck

Poor Sergt. Windrum died to-day so we had a big funeral in the evening. All the officers and most of the sergeants attended. The drums played us back. This is the first time we have had them playing since we came to Natal.

7ᵗʰ Apr.

Rode into Ladysmith this morning. A draft arrived early and brought with it a lot of things for the men. Kay of the 1ˢᵗ K.R.R. came to tea and also some newspaper correspondents, 'Spher' etc. Orderly Officer to-day; took a lot of photos and developed them in the evening.

The events of Inniskilling Hill may have caused fate to take a different turn from that which the Inniskilling Fusiliers had first envisaged. However, out of the line Bryant and Auckinleck still remained faithful to their diary accounts, recording even the more mundane events, from the numerous hail and sand storms that plagued the troops to giving a detailed account of how the Inniskillings entered a local football tournament and eventually, much to the dismay of the Ladysmith home support, won it.

Their first-hand accounts of the exploits of the Royal Inniskilling Fusiliers emphatically convey more of what it entailed to be Fusilier during the South African campaign than any historian could hope.

8ᵗʰ Apr. L. J. Bryant

Had Divine Service as usual & we got another lot of presents given to us.

Letter from Major General Fitzroy Harte to our Regiment.

The following letter was sent to us from Gen. Harte. Viz:-

O. C. 1ˢᵗ Bn. R. Inniskilling Fusiliers.

In leaving the Natal Command with my Brigade; I desire to express to your Battalion my great regret, that the Royal Inniskilling Fusiliers are temporarily, taken from the Irish Brigade.

The Battalion has fought valiantly, it has suffered much, & it has well earned the repose necessary to repair its losses in the Battle and Campaign.

The Gracious notice of our Queen & the Abundant public Testimonies are treasures in which the Royal Inniskilling Fusiliers have gained a large share.

I honour the Memory of your Dead & I grieve with the bereaved parents.

To the Survivors, I say, I hope I may be soon allowed to welcome you all back again to the Irish Brigade.

Sgd. A. Fitzroy Harte, Maj. Gen. Comdg. Irish Brigade.

10th Apr.

We struck the Rest Camp today, & repitched a new one, Using Indian Tents , in place of the Bell Tents, which we formerly had. We heard firing in the direction of Elandlsgate [Elandslaagte] rumoured to be the Boers making an attack on our Troops stationed there. Our Regt. had to stand to and wait further orders. We heard afterwards that the above report was true, & that the Boers were repulsed. The Dublins and Connaughts (belonging to our old Brigade) passed through here today on their way down country. We turned out & gave them a parting cheer.

10th Apr. Lieut. D. G. Auchinleck

Heard heavy firing in the direction of Elandlsgate [Elandslaagte] while we were having breakfast… At 12 o'clock we got the order to be ready to turn out at a moment's notice. The hills to our front being lined by the Fusilier Bde. Nothing however happened. I had to go on picket on the Helpmakaar and Colenso roads much to my annoyance but it was a lovely night though very cold, so I did not mind. Nothing startling occurred.

11th Apr.

Orders about waiting to turn out were cancelled this morning so we presume everything had settle down again. Came off picket about 7 a.m. Heard that the Boers had shelled the camp at Elandslaagk putting several shells into it. Our men were doing physical drill at the time. Maj. Brannigan and Devenish returned this morning. Devenish quite recovered from his second wound. I forgot to put in that Inkson went away last night to the great regret of every officer and man in the Regiment. He got a tremendous sent off and we are all dreadfully sorry to loose him. Rode into Ladysmith in the afternoon. Atkinson rather seedy; Jeffcoat went on picket and had a very wet night. Heavy thunderstorms lashed about 5.30, very brilliant flashes of lightening. Tried to get a photo of the lightening but was unsuccessful. Heard of poor Morley's death this afternoon from Enteric.

12th Apr.

Kit inspection at 6.30. One of the mules died last night and another one is very ill. Hope it is not a form of 'horse' sickness. Vet. Surgeon came to see the mule and said it was horse sickness. He turned out to be one of the Cochranes of Strabane. I recognised him as one of them directly I saw him although I had never met him before. Heard that Hutton was in a very critical condition.

15th Apr.

Church Parade at 8.30 a.m. Major Hessey and Jeffcoat went down to the church in Ladysmith. Got a wire at 10 o'clock saying 2nd Lt. Hutton sinking low, no hope, so I galloped off at once to see if I could do anything but arrived too late. We are all dreadfully sorry about him. Major Hessey spent the afternoon arranging about a coffin and gun carriage.

15th Apr. Capt. A. C. Jeffcoat DSO

Hutton died of enteric in Ladysmith.

At this point Capt. A. C. Jeffcoat's diary comes to a sudden and abrupt close. No reason is given why the diary was terminated nor does he take up the narrative again at a later date.

16th Apr. Lieut. D. G. Auchinleck

I was in command of funeral party for poor Hutton's burial. Started to march to Tin Town Hospital at 6.45 a.m. and got back to the cemetery at 9.30. Very impressive service (1st person we have buried in a coffin), was awfully seedy all day with a cold and headache (Influenza). Steward went down country by early train to-day.

18th Apr.

On a Board of Indemnification in the morning and then continued my letter to Norah. In the afternoon I rode over to Tin Town with Jeffcoat to see Atkinson and Devenish. Had a game of cricket there with the doctors and made a 0. Then developed some photos in a real dark room they have got there; very successful. Got back at about 8 o'clock; had dinner and played croquet with Crawford. Bed 9.30.

21st Apr. L. J. Bryant

Our new Commanding Officer (Lloyd Payne) took over the command of our Bn Today. He formerly belonged to the Somersetshire Regt. & has the DSO.

21st Apr. Lieut. D. G. Auchinleck

A lot of work to do in the morning as we wanted to get off to the Cricket Match early. Started to ride over to Tin Town about 11.30 and had lunch at 12.00 with the R.A.M.C. The match began at 1.45. Inniskillings 1st innings. We made 91 Crawford and I putting on 33 for first wicket. Crawford made 13; I got 33. R.A.M.C. made 68 so we won. Had tea and a lovely bathe in a deep pool. Rode back to find Col. Payne had arrived and he had mail for us from Peggy and Mado who had seen him off which seemed to bring home a lot closer to here.

22ⁿᵈ Apr. L. J. Bryant

Had Divine Service as usual. The C of E Religion fell in under the command of Col. Lloyd Payne & headed by the drums marched to the church in the Town & held a Memorial Service for the Dead.

22ⁿᵈ Apr. Lieut. D. G. Auchinleck

Church Parade at 8.30. Marched into All Saints Church and had a Memorial Service in memory of those of the Regiment who had fallen. Very impressive service and lovely sermon by Archdeacon Barker. Capt. Secombe of A.S.C. came to lunch and stayed all afternoon. Very hot day so we were all lazy in the afternoon.

23ʳᵈ Apr. L. J. Bryant

Colonel Payne fell in the Bn. on parade this morning to give them a lecture on taking over command of the Battn. Amongst other things he said that he hoped before long, that he would have the pleasure of leading the Bn. into action again once more etc.

23ʳᵈ Apr. Lieut. D. G. Auchinleck

Parade 7.15 a.m. feeling very seedy all day and had a bit of fever in the evening (102.6). Was told I was to go down to Durban next day for change of air etc. Brannigan thought I had enteric fever.

24ᵗʰ Apr.

Got up feeling not much worse but the temperature had gone; started off with Capt. Clelland for Durban by the mail at 9.10 a.m. had a most fearfully tiring journey and was dead beat at the end of it. Arrived in Durban at about 9 p.m. and drove straight to the Marine Hotel.

25ᵗʰ Apr.

Up pretty early and saw a civilian doctor called Chefuree who advised us strongly to report myself on the "------" in case anything serious was wrong with me so off we went and I saw Dr. Pullen. He examined me thoroughly and said I was completely run down, and my liver was in a very bad state; gave me medicine and said there was no necessity for me to remain on board unless I liked to, so I went back to the Marine Hotel.

16ᵗʰ Apr. - 8ᵗʰ May.

Stayed at Durban and enjoyed myself very much indeed. Joined the Club which was a very nice one and amused myself, driving, sailing and going for walks, buying photos of the war etc. Bought some Indian embroidery work and several things of that sort to send home. On the 5ᵗʰ May the Sporting Club races came off and they were tremendous. Six races mostly for ponies.

9th May.

Spent the day with Burgess R. N. He saw me off at 6 p.m. this evening. Travelled up with Joel and Britton in a reserved carriage which was very comfortable. Bitterly cold night.

10th May.

Got to camp about 6.30 and found everybody fast asleep. Jeffcoat was in Maritzburg on duty. Great news from the Free State. Received any amount of letters.

13th May.

Church Parade 9.20. Crawford came in in the morning and I rode out with him to lunch, for the first time saw Lombard's Kop at close quarters. It is exactly like the side of a house. Brannigan and Gordon arrived later and I rode back with them.

14th May.

Orderly Officer again to-day. Rode in Ladysmith and bought a warm coat, British which are ripping things. Had to spend the afternoon in camp. Played 'Bridge' in the evening and then had to go round the Town guards which is no joke. Got back about 12o'clock.

17th May. L. J. Bryant

Mafeking [8] Relieved

The following telegram was posted up outside the post office today:-
The Federal Forces abandoned the Siege of Mafeking on the arrival of the Relieving Force.

Our Regiment struck camp at 6.45 a.m. & marched to Observation Hill about 3 miles distant, & camped there.

17th May. Lieut. D. G. Auchinleck

Started changing camp at 8 a.m. and it took the whole day as there was such a tremendous lot of things to be taken. Each wagon had 2 loads and then it was not all taken. Finished work about 6.30 p.m. We have now got a Marquee as an Officers Mess which is much more comfortable and a great deal warmer in the evening. Great 'Bridge' is played every evening.

19th May.

Pickets have been put on again. I went out at 4. 30 p.m. to Cove Hill which is nearly 2 miles to the rear of our camp and accordingly rather useless. Fearful cold and miserable night tho' I slept most of the time. False alarm by sentry who took a visiting patrol for the enemy, forsooth! Because they would not answer the challenge. Got back to camp 8.30 a.m. Rumour of Relief of Mafeking.

20th May.

Rumours of another move to-day. Lt. Col. Currin came to see Col. and it was at last decided we might stay where we are. Pickets changed. Now we have to throw out 3 pickets night and day to our front which is a little bit more sensible but still it is apparently unnecessary as the enemy is a small matter of 50 miles away. I was Orderly Officer to-day which is not much fun, what with the rest camp 3 miles away and guards at night.

21st May.

Relief of Mafeking in the paper this morning and we are all heartily glad. Also several other bits of good news. Hoopstad, Lindley and Christiana occupied and everything seems to be going as well as possible. Went to funeral in the afternoon after playing croquet with Crawford.

22nd May. L. J. Bryant

The Townspeople of Ladysmith celebrated the Relief of Mafeking today. They had sports during the Morning & Afternoon & in the Evening they ignited a huge Bonfire & let off fireworks. The Band of the Glosters played a programme of Music from 7 to 9 p.m. & were also at the sports.

22nd May. Lieut. D. G. Auchinleck

Up early. News this morning contains occupation of Klerksdorp, there is a rumour that Bobs [Lord Roberts] is at Johannesburg which is unlikely. Also that Boers have blown up Laing's Nek tunnel and retired.

26th May. L. J. Bryant

A chronic Sandstorm came on, lasting for 6 hours, smothering everything in dirt.

31st May.

The Regt. Struck Camp at 7 a.m. Fell in at 9 a.m. & marched to Besters Farm, (18 miles) arriving there around 5.30 p.m. They then had to lie down on the ground all night (which was a very cold one) & they had nothing to wrap around them, as the Transport broke down on the road & did not arrive that night.

1st June. Lieut. D. G. Auchinleck

Up early getting everything squared up for the march. Too much baggage for the wagons and they were all overloaded. When we had gone about 2 miles I was sent back by the C. O. to see about a lot of wagons and stores being returned to the ordinance and Transport Park. This took some time and I did not get off from Inniskilling Hill until 4. 45 and did not exactly know my way. Mr. Blackbeard was with me. We got about 9 miles out and then could not find the way, as it was pitch black. Maj. Hessey's servant said the Transport was stuck so we all put up at Bester's Farm and had a fair night's rest.

2nd June.

First thing at daybreak I sent Blackbeard back to try and find wagons and hurry them up and I went on and found the regiment alright. Had some breakfast (coffee and biscuits) and started off again to find Transport. Spent about 5 hours but failed to find it so rode back to camp just in time to see two of the wagons arriving with Ricardo and rear-guard, and one more arrived shortly after. The other two were badly stuck, one with a wheel smashed, the other with the pole broken. Took out 2 wagons with us (Ricardo and self) and got one wagon load in, the other we got started and told Blackbeard to bring it in that night if possible. Ricardo and I got back to camp about 8. 30 p.m. Glad to get dinner and bed.

5th June. L. J. Bryant

The news arrived here that Lord Roberts had entered Pretoria. We first heard the news at 9.30 p.m. There was Great Rejoicing in the Town; A large crowd marched through the Town cheering and singing Patriotic Songs, whilst kids were running about kicking up an Infernal row, by beating tins, so that we couldn't go to sleep for hours. Then the Bells were rung & fog Signals let off.

5th June. Lieut. D. G. Auchinleck

Cavalry patrol got into rather a tight corner. Boers let them get to within 150 yds. near Colworth Station and then fired; wounded 3 men, one dangerously and killing 3 horses and wounding one out of a total of thirteen. Enemy supposed to be about 200 strong. Pickets strengthened in consequence of this.

6th June.

Struck camp and pitched it a little further forward under the hill which forms our line of resistance. Got leave to go in by the train and see Edie and Gervans and spent one of the best days of my life. Called on Archdeacon Barker and dined at Crown Hotel. Talked the whole of the spare time. Hired a pony as I had orders to be back that night. Got back to Besters about 11.30 p.m.

12th June.

Parade 9 a.m. Outpost scheme; paraded for picket 4.30. Great excitement at about 5, detached post reported men walking about on hill in front who looked as if they were building a sangar. Have sent out a strong patrol and am writing this while waiting for them to return and report. Went in to dinner. Traile relieved us for an hour.

15th June.

Adjutant's parade this morning. Very interesting parade. Jeffcoat and I went into Ladysmith by train. Shopping all the afternoon; put up at the Crown Hotel. Very Comfortable. Only one bed between 2 of us.

16th June.

First person I saw when I left my bedroom was Tom Murphy much to my surprise. Looks very seedy and is rather deaf. Started off for Colenso at 10 and walked from there all over to Old ground as far as Pieters arriving there about 4 p.m. I took a lot of photos on the way. At Pieters Station we met Col. Hadder who I had met on the 'Simla' and his daughter and travelled up with them to Ladysmith showing them all the points of interest on the way. Got back to the Crown Hotel in time for dinner and arranged to have two beds as Jeffcoat said I kicked him too much. Went round to the Royal Hotel after dinner and called on Col. & Miss Hadder. Spent a very jolly evening, dancing on the veranda etc. Bed about 10 p.m.

17th June. L. J. Bryant

A draft of 240 men arrived here for our Regt. & joined the Bn. this evening.

19th June. Lieut. D. G. Auchinleck

Parade 9.30. All marched down to the Klip River about 3 miles to our right with rifles and magazines charged and had a thorough wash up of both bodies and clothes. Got back about 12.30. Did nothing in the afternoon. Rather a hot day. Mail.

20th June.

Company Officer's parade to-day. Had to have 3 of my natives licked to-day for getting drunk. Otherwise all went well.

23rd June.

No parade to-day. The Sports began at 10 a.m. and were the greatest fun and success especially the Mule Race which caused many falls and roars of laughter. Continued after lunch and ended about 3.30 p.m. Then we had an officer's pony race. Lady Grey won easily. Colonel 2nd, Jeffcoat 3rd, Kenny 4th. I ran with the others. I wrote an account of the sports for "The Impartial Reporter" which was very amusing. Played Bridge after dinner.

28th June. L. J. Bryant

The Regt. Struck camp & trained it down to Free State Junction, which is about 2 miles from here, & camped there.

30th June.

The Regt. Played another Football Match against the Town Eleven. The game ended in a draw of one goal each, the Town equalising in the last minute of the game.

A detachment of our Regt. Stationed at Tin Town, got up a Scratch Team and played a Cricket Match against the Leicester Volunteers. This is the second match played between the two teams; our team winning the first match by 4 wickets; we also won this match by 60 runs. Scores Innis. Fus. 148 runs, Leicesters 88 runs.

4th July.

We got served out with another lot of presents today; amongst the articles being a Cardigan Jacket, which we greatly appreciated, as the Nights are very cold now.

6th July. Lieut. D. G. Auchinleck

Moved to Tuitwa [Tintwanyoni] and Jonono's Kop. 4 Coys. to former, 3 to latter, and 1 Coy. left at Tin Town with E.W.A. Everything went off well. Very sickening being split up like this.

12th July. L. J. Bryant

The people of Ladysmith got up a Football tournament; the Winner to receive a Gold Medal each. Our Regt. entered for it & played against the 5th Lancers today, in the First Round. The game ended in a win for our team by 1 goal to nothing.

The Regt. marched from Tinwangoui [Tintwanyoni] to the O. R. Colony Junction again (8 miles). 'E' Coy marched from Jonona's Kop (15 miles). The Bn. then trained it up to Besters Farm & camped there once more.

14th July.

Our Regtl. Football Team travelled down from Besters to play the Royal Garrison Artillery in the Second Round of the Ladysmith Football Tournament.

The Match was played in a Sandstorm and ended in a draw, nothing being scored. The Sandstorm having passed over the Ladysmith Town Eleven played the 13th Hussars for the same competition. The match was fast & furious although the teams crossing over with one goal each to their score. The Hussars scored again after ten minutes & altho' the Town Eleven had the best of the play afterwards they could not add to their score & so lost by 1 goal. The result came as a great surprise to the townspeople who had assembled in very large numbers, & also the Town Eleven themselves, as they were confident of winning the tournament, in fact they said that our team was the only team they were afraid of out of the whole lot. The Hussars by winning this Match now enter for the Final Round.

17th July.

Our Regtl. Eleven played off their tie with the Artillery today in boisterous weather. & beat them by 4 goals to nil. Our Team now play the Hussars in the Final.

21st July.

Our Regimental Football Team travelled down from Besters today to play the 13th Hussars in the Ladysmith Football Tournament.

A large crowd assembled to witness the game, soldiers being very prominent. The Hussars were made strong favourites; all the townspeople being anxious that that they should beat us. The game commenced at 2 p.m. & was stubbornly contested. Our Side scored first after 25 minutes play but the goal was disallowed owing to a player being ruled offside, & the game proceeded as brisk as ever. The Interval arrived with a blank score. The second half was also well contested both goals having narrow escapes. Our team scored a goal after about 20 minutes play, which somewhat damped the ardour of the Hussars Supporters. The play after this slackened down a little, but towards the end the Hussars tried hard to equalise, but our defence was too good for them to pierce & had to retire beaten by 1 goal to nil, after a very hard fought game. A lot of money changed hand after the game was over, which was well worth going to see. Our team therefore became the winners of the Tournament & possessors of the Gold Medals.

The Games Played in the Tournament & their results are as follows:-

First Round

1   Ladysmith V Lancaster Volunteers

The Lancasters scratched.

2   13th Hussars V 60th Kings Royal Rifles

The K. R. R. scratched

3   Inniskillings V 5th Lancers

Inniskillings won by 1 goal to 0

Second Round

1   Inniskillings V Royal Garrison Artillery

A draw, nothing scored.

2   Ladysmith V 13th Hussars

Hussars won by 2 goals to One

Replayed Tie

Inniskillings V Royal Garrison Artillery

Inniskillings won by 4 goals to none

Final Round

13th Hussars V 27th Inniskillings

27th Inniskillings won by 1 goal to none.

Four Coys of the Regt. marched down to the O. R. Colony Junction and camped there as a detatchment. The Battn. Is now split up as follows:-

Head Quarters. Besters Farm. A & D Coys Detachments. Walker's Hoek. C & G Coys   O. R. C. Junction B E F & H Coys.

Chapter Six

"Our Doings in the Transvaal"

By the beginning of August 1900 the Royal Inniskilling Fusiliers' period out of the line at Ladysmith was drawing to a close. Fresh drafts of troops having arrived to supplement those wounded and sick who had already rejoined the Battalion, it was now decided the Inniskillings should rejoin the Natal Army.

Having struck camp and bidden farewell to Ladysmith the Inniskillings marched the eleven miles to Elandslaagte Railway Station where they bivouacked for the night prior to loading their kit and entraining for Ingagane. Once the whole Battalion had assembled they travelled to join the Natal Army under General Sir R. Buller at Paardekop, a railway station on the line between Volksrust and Elandsfontein.

On their arrival the Inniskillings were assigned to the 4th Division 8th Brigade under the command of Major-General F. Howard.[1] They now constituted the 8th Brigade along with the 1st Leicestershire Regiment, 2nd Liverpool Regiment and the 1st King's Royal Rifles. From August 1900 until the end of the year the Regiment was to take part in a variety of engagements throughout the Transvaal.

In mid-August they marched through Amersfoort and Twyfelaar taking part in the action at Geluk on the 25th and 26th before joining Major-General W. Kitchener's 7th Brigade to take part in the assault and capture of the farm at Bergendal along with the 2nd Rifle Brigade.

. British troops arrive at Cape Town docks for service in South Africa.

. Troops disembark with their kit at Cape Town docks.

3. Indian troops and Indian servants for British officers pictured at the docks on their arrival at Cape Town.

4. British troops board the ill-fated armoured train at Chieveley.

5. A Creusot 15-cm (6-inch) gun. Such guns were used to good effect at Ladysmith and Mafeking.

6. A 4.7″ Naval gun mounted on a limber and operated by sailors of the Royal Navy.

7. Sick and wounded troops at Wynberg being discharged from hospital.

8. 'Soldiers' Home Tent', No. 2 Base Hospital, Wynberg.

9. The Relief Column crosses the Tugela River on its way to relieve Ladysmith.

10. An artist's impression of troops of the Relief Column as they wade across the Tugela River.

11. A 6-inch Howitzer Battery with the guns shown in their usual firing position of thirty-five degrees.

12. British troops line a makeshift perimeter defence. Their bivouacs can be seen beneath the level of the firing step.

13. Field Marshal Lord Roberts arrives at Cape Town.

14. Lieutenant the Hon F.H.S. Roberts, King's Royal Rifle Corps, son of the Field Marshal, was killed in action at the Battle of Colenso, 15 December 1899, while trying to save the guns. He was awarded the Victoria Cross.

15. A street scene in Durban following the Relief of Ladysmith.

To the Glory of God and in Memory of the following Officers, Non Commissioned Officers & Men

FIRST BATTALION THE ROYAL INNISKILLING FUSILIERS.

ROLL OF OFFICERS, NON COMMISSIONED OFFICERS, AND MEN, WHO WERE KILLED IN ACTION OR DIED OF WOUNDS RECEIVED IN ACTION AT BATTLE OF COLENSO. 15TH DECR 1899.

MAJOR J.F.W. CHARLEY, 2ND IN COMMD. CAPTAIN F.C. LOFTUS

SGT J. IRELAND	PTE W. HILL	PTE J. McQUILLAN
,, J. McGHEE	,, D. KINCAID	,, R. RORISON
,, R. WYLIE	,, M. KENNEDY	,, J. ROWE
LCPL T.L. BOURKE	,, H. LEITH	,, J. SMITH
,, S. DOBBIN	,, R. McCAULEY	,, J. WALLACE
,, T. KELLY	,, J. McCARRY	,, F. WILLIAMS
PTE J. HENDERSON	,, A. McGINTY	,, W. WRIGHT
,, J. HICKEY	,, J. McMULLAN	

ROLL OF OFFICERS, NON COMMISSIONED OFFICERS, AND MEN, WHO WERE KILLED IN ACTION OR DIED FROM WOUNDS RECEIVED IN ACTION AT VARIOUS PLACES DURING THE SOUTH AFRICAN CAMPAIGN.

CAPTAIN D. MACLACHLAN,	SPION KOP, NATAL
LIEUT G. J.R. WALKER	NEAR LICHTENBURG, W. TRANSVAAL
,, R. A. CHALONER	ROOIWAL,
PTE W. BARRETT	KAFFIR KOP, O.R.C.
,, W. COTTER	BERGENDAL, E. TRANSVAAL
,, W. DEVENNEY	SPION KOP, NATAL
,, P. DEVENNEY	WITPOORT, N.E. TRANSVAAL
,, W. DONEGAN	KRUGERSDORP, ,,
,, J. KEEGAN	STERKFONTEIN, ,,
,, R. ROWE	KLIP RIVER, ,,
,, O. SOMERS	ROOIWAL, W. TRANSVAAL
,, E. THORNTON	THORNDALE, N. ,,

ROLL OF OFFICERS, NON COMMISSIONED OFFICERS, AND MEN, WHO DIED FROM DISEASE DURING THE SOUTH AFRICAN CAMPAIGN 1899-1902.

CAPTAIN W.L.P. GIBTON	QR MR SGT J.S. BROWN	SGT P. MOONEY
LIEUT C.W. MORLEY	SGT W. BINFIELD	,, A.J. WINDRUM
,, J.T. LOWRY	,, W. BROWN	,, T. WRIGHT
2ND LIEUT A.R. MILLER	,, T.A. CLARKE	CPL R. CLARKE
,, ,, S.H. HUTTON	,, J. CLELAND	LCPL H. FITZSIMMONS

DRMR J. DILLON	PTE T. GOODMAN	PTE C. McAVINNEY	PTE B. O'LOAN
PTE W. BARNETT	,, G. HAMPSEY	,, J. McBRIDE	,, S. PRIOR
,, J. BAXTER	,, W. HUGHES	,, J. McCREADY	,, J. QUINN
,, W. BRENNAN	,, J. HYNDMAN	,, W. McGARRY	,, T. QUINN
,, J. CAMPBELL	,, M. KAVANACH	,, J. McGIFFEN	,, P. TALMAGE
,, H. CAULFIELD	,, M. KAVANACH	,, J. McGUIRE	,, T. TIERNEY
,, J. CLARKE	,, D. LEAHY	,, L. McMANUS	,, J. TINNEY
,, COLLINS	,, C. LAUGHLIN	,, R. McSHANE	,, W.H. WALKER
		,, L. NASH	,, G. WEIR
		,, W. NIXON	,, J. WHITEHOUSE
		,, J. NOBLE	,, J. WRIGHT
			LCPL M.E. WHITE
			BOY R.H. ARTHUR

16. A memorial to the officers and men of 1ST Battalion, The Royal Inniskilling Fusiliers who were killed in action or died of wounds at the Battle of Colenso, 15 December 1899.

17. A group of Inniskilling Fusiliers pictured outside the blockhouse they manned.

18. A group of sergeants of the Royal Inniskilling Fusiliers take time out to pose for the camera.

19. An artist's impression of the battle to take Hart's Hill (Inniskilling Hill).

20. This sketch was drawn in the Transvaal by De la Rey as a design for a Christmas card for the Royal Inniskilling Fusiliers.

21. One of the chocolate boxes sent to the troops for Christmas 1900 which arrived several months late.

Special Army Order.

SOUTH AFRICAN FIELD FORCE.

ARMY HEADQUARTERS,
PRETORIA.
24th January, 1901.

DEATH OF HER MAJESTY QUEEN VICTORIA—

The following telegram has been received from the Adjutant-General, War Office, dated London, 23rd January, 1901:—

> "Commander-in-Chief deeply regrets to inform you of the death of Her Majesty Victoria, Queen of the United Kingdom of Great Britain and Ireland and of the Colonies and Dependencies thereof, Empress of India, who departed this life at 6-30 p.m., 22nd January, at Osborne House, Isle of Wight."

The following from Lord Kitchener has been sent in reply :—

> "The news of the Queen's death has been received with the greatest grief by the Army in South Africa. In their name I beg to express our sincere condolences with the Royal Family on the great loss sustained by them and the Nation."

By Order.

W. F. KELLY, Major-General,
Adjutant-General.

22. A facsimile of a Special Army Order announcing to the troops in South Africa the death of Her Majesty Queen Victoria on 22 January 1901 and the reply sent on their behalf by Lord Kitchener.

23. The painting depicts the first attempt by the Royal Inniskilling Fusiliers to storm and take Hart's Hill (Inniskilling Hill) prior to the relief of Ladysmith. During this attempt they lost their Commanding Officer. At the second attempt their second-in-command, Major Charley, was also killed. Such were the casualties sustained that the Regiment was taken out of the Irish Brigade until their numbers could be brought up to strength once more.

24. Troops of the Royal Inniskilling Fusiliers are engulfed by members of the public upon their triumphant return to Londonderry in 1903.

Marching into Machadodorp as part of the 8th Brigade the Inniskillings camped for a period at Helvetia before dividing into two halves, the left remaining at Schoeman's Kloof whilst the right half-battalion headed up the Badfontein Valley to Witklip. By 9 October the Battalion had reunited once more in a force under the command of Lieutenant-General N. G. Lyttelton CB making for the Middelburg area. Most of October, November and a significant portion of December was spent in and around the vicinity of Middelburg engaged in various actions such as that at Witloof before the Battalion was unexpectedly ordered to entrain for Pretoria. The purpose of their sudden departure from Middelburg was made evident on their arrival at Pretoria, as the Inniskillings immediately marched for Commando Nek to reinforce Major-General R.A.P. Clements'[2], beleaguered force after their disastrous run in with the Boers at Nooitgedacht in the Magaliesburg Valley. By late December the Battalion was again involved with Clements' column as it moved west against De La Rey at Thorndale.

2nd Aug. & 3rd Aug. Lieut. D. G. Auchinleck

Received orders 4.45 p.m. to go to Ingagane and Dannhavser by rail, Transport to go by road so the Regt. got off about 8 p.m. and started with Transport about the same time and picked up the wagons at Walker's Hock. Had a very bad march into Ladysmith as the wagons got stuck twice arriving at the Junction 5 a.m., fearfully cold. Rode down to the station to see the Regiment off. They started about 8 a.m. in a great fuss and hurry. I got off at 9 with Transport and made the first outspan at 12 at Modder Spruit going on again at 3 o'clock and arriving 2 miles beyond Elandslaaght [Elandslaagte] just at dark. Just after starting on this track from Modder Spruit I had a running shot at a buck but missed. Sent wire to G.O.C. telling of arrival and then got to bed after a meal.

4th Aug.

Left Elandslaaght rather late 9 a.m. as I met Blackbeard with the other six wagons empty so we had to distribute the loads. The next track was a very long one, 12 miles as we could not water before but it was very dull. We outspanned at Busi Spruit just beyond Meran. I had a splendid bathe here and we started off for Glencoe at 4.30 p.m. arriving there at 9 p.m. Had an excellent dinner at the refreshment Room in the station then drew a days' fodder for the oxen, and then I was told I was wanted at the telephone. Kenny sent out the following instructions which were a very pleasant surprise. Regt. goes by rail to Sandspruit (which is in the Transvaal) to-morrow night. Send all stores by rail at once and come on with Transport to Ingagane and report to S.S.O. I then went up to the wagons and about 10 minutes after getting there received a wire from G.O.C. L. of C. Newcastle as follows:-

The ox-transport Inniskilling Fusiliers to march back to Ladysmith. The officer in charge should hand it over to H.S.C. there and proceed by rail to Sandspruit as soon as possible. This was rather a surprise so I gave orders to inspan.

6th Aug. L. J. Bryant

Our Doings in the Transvaal

We started on our journey at 1.15 a.m. & arrived at Paarde Kop, Transvaal at 3 p.m. A blinding sandstorm came on during the morning, & lasted all day; we were blinded by the sand and covered in dirt. We got our dinner & tea together at 4 p.m., it consisted of Bully beef, Biscuits, & Tea, & the whole lot was covered in sand. We are now in the 8th Brigade, & 4th Division. We fell in at 5 p.m. to join our new Bge. at Meerzicht about 10.30 p.m. after marching 10 miles, & bivouacked for the night, which was very cold.

Got blankets at 11 p.m.

6th Aug. Lieut. D. G. Auchinleck

Started for the last march into Ladysmith 5.45 a.m. and outspanned Modder Spruit 8 a.m. Had a shot at a vulture but missed again. Having had breakfast and a wash, I started off for Ladysmith leaving the wagons to follow later. Got into Ladysmith at 12.30. Saw Maloney L. Transport Officer and arranged about handing over wagons etc. also arranged with S.S.O. and railway authorities to start off 5.45 tomorrow. Wagons got in 4 p.m. and everything went well. Settled bill at Adams & Co. got receipt for wagons etc. Sent wires to G.O.C. L of C and Adjutant telling them my movements, Slept Railway Hotel.

7th Aug. L. J. Bryant

We had to escort the Convoy in today's trek; the convoy is a very large one, numbering about 800 wagons & it extended for about 15 miles in length. There was a very high wind blowing all day, & the grass caught alight in several places, & the wind soon made it into a big fire. We started on our trek about 2 or 3 p.m. & marched 8 miles. We got no breakfast before we started, as altho' the water was boiling for the coffee our C. O. made the cooks throw it out as he thought we were going to start at 8 a.m. or so, but he never told the cooks to make more coffee. As we did not get our blankets till about 12 M. N.

we made ourselves warm by following up the grass fires, as it was a bitterly cold night.

7ᵗʰ Aug. Lieut. D. G. Auchinleck

Started from Ladysmith by the 5.45 a.m. train (the Kaffir Mail). When we got to Glencoe we had to change and as there was no room in the mail train for the men we had to go up in the next goods train. We spent a fearful day of it arriving at Charlestown about 8.30 p.m. The Reversing Stations and Laings Nek were really wonderful, the curves of the railway extraordinary. I went and called on the Stationary Hospital and the 1ˢᵗ Dublins and then to bed. Fearfully cold ice everywhere in the morning.

8ᵗʰ Aug. L. J. Bryant

We marched about 7 miles today, & arrived at Amersfoort safely with the Convoy about 4 p.m.

8ᵗʰ Aug. Lieut. D. G. Auchinleck

Started 6.30 a.m. and got to Sandspruit about 7.30 no sign of the Regt. there so I went on to Paardekop and there found out that they had gone with Buller (8ᵗʰ Bds.) and no one was allowed to go on as it was not safe. I gave up all hope when all of a sudden they wanted an escort for the mails so I was sent by the merest bit of good luck. Started at 1 p.m. and got to Amersfort where the whole army was bivouacking at 6.30 and handed over the mails. I was delighted to at last get back to the Regt. Had something to eat and then to bed. The coldest night I have ever spent in my life.

9ᵗʰ Aug.

On the move; we all stood to arms 5.30 a.m. had breakfasts, then inspanned at 8.30 but we are still here, as I am writing, at 11 o'clock and the Transport is so enormous. I see no chance of getting off for an hour or two yet. There are over 600 wagons here. From what I have seen of the Transvaal so far, the chief differences from Natal are:- the ground is not so mountainous....there are not so many stones and stony kopies. We got off at last at 10 o'clock and had a fairly easy march about 9 miles and outspanned about a mile beyond Reitspruit. 4 Coys A.B.F. & D on outposts. Had something to eat and then had to take blankets and get coats round to A & B Coys which was rather a poor job in the dark. Got back about 11 o'clock having been to give the orders to O.C. Leicesters. Very glad to get to bed after a pretty long day. Took 3 prisoners.

10ᵗʰ Aug.

Up 5.30 standing to arms, not quite so cold but cold enough. Had breakfast 7 a.m., started off 9 a.m., everything went off much better to-day. Regt. rear guard to baggage for the 3rd time in succession. Had 2 drifts to cross and then the Vaal River. Camped about 1/2 a mile N. of river getting there pretty early 4.30 p.m. Regt. did not get in till 7 p.m. Shortly after the Transport got in our guns and pom poms fired a few shots but I have not heard at what. A horrible night blowing a hurricane, could not get any sleep. Took 4 or 5 prisoners. We crossed the Vaal by a bridge called Uitspan Bridge (eight spans) which was quite a fine stonework bridge. The river was almost dry but must be a fine big river in summer with high steep banks.

11th Aug.

Up 5.30 a.m. Regt. are to-day in advance of baggage. They started at 8 a.m. There was fearfully cold wind this morning. Strathcona's Horse passed out thro' our camp about 7.30 a.m. They are a very fine lot of men. I started at 10 a.m. with baggage and had not gone 1/2 mile when we got to a spruit. Thank goodness it was not bad so we got over it without much trouble. Good road but it was the worst day I have ever spent, a blinding dust storm went on the whole day and you could not open your eyes. Then to cap everything when we got into camp at Klipfontein, grass fires got up in every direction. We had to put the first one out which took over an hour. Then another sprung up. Thank goodness to the leeward side of us, burnt the K.K.Rs. things, blankets, haversacks, everything and the ammunition was going off all over the place. It really was terribly dangerous and everybody was moved on to the burnt parts and were not allowed to light fires except on burnt ground which was quite dangerous enough. Everybody very tired, Lt. Dundonald got into Ermelo unopposed.

12th Aug.

Wish I was in Dunaree. ['Oh to be in Dunaree....'] Up 5.30 a.m. Fearfully cold wind and frost. Baggage started 10.30. Regt. at 12 as flank guard to baggage. Had a most successful march without a single black sighted. Ermelo is a very pretty little town with a Post Office, Court House and a large goal. When I got in I discovered 150 had surrendered and handed in their arms. The enemy is said to have gone off to the East and Dundonald's cavalry have followed them. The Regt. got in early and then I went to the N.N.F. canteen and got a lot of things. Had to walk 2 journeys and on the way saw the rifles, which had been handed in being smashed up. I wish I had my camera. Bought a couple of chickens and we had an excellent dinner of curried chicken and beef and tinned tomatoes. Not very tired tonight so sat up and talked.

13th Aug.

Up 5.30 a.m. Eggs for breakfast which the Col. bought. Regt. went off as advanced flank guard at 8.30. Baggage started 9.30 a terribly long and tedious march all up hill. It must have been 15 or 16 miles. Halted at Klipfontein Farm. Rather a nice little camp. Very near water. Everybody very tired. Managed to get a wash for a change. Have caught a cold which is a beastly nuisance. One of the mules is sick and a pony has been lost. We seem to be going on the direct road to Belfast and leaving Carolina on our right. We are getting anxious to know what is going to happen when we get to Belfast, as there does not seem to be going to be much opposition on this march.

14th Aug.

Regt. started at 9. Transport at 10. A very bad road with 2 or 3 steep hills. Passed a lovely farm and commandeered 6 wagon loads of hay and 2 tons of mealie. The farm has 12,000 acres and the people appear to be very well off. Very few outhouses. The march was a short one about 8 miles. I got 2 chickens and the Regt. got one and 3 sheep so we are well off for grub. We encamped at Kranspan in sight of Carolina. Strathcona's Horse got tied up in the afternoon and we saw another squadron going out to extricate them but I have not heard the result yet. Had an excellent evening meal *with* Stewart, Hickman, Ricardo and Hessey.

15th Aug.

Regiment right Advanced flank guard; started at 8.30 a.m. Transport started at 9.25. Nothing very startling happened on the march and we were in sight of camp, about a mile off, at 3 but by no means there. There was a fearful spruit to cross and a 4.7 stuck for over 1/2 an hour and I thought I should never get my wagons across. At last they started another drift which was worse than the first and I got my 10 wagons across with two sticks and got into camp about 7 p.m. We got several wins thro' to-day from French's Column. We are to rest in this camp which is called Twyfelaar and is on the Komati River for seven days while all the mule wagons go off the day after to-morrow to Wonderfontein to get supplies and I hear we are to concentrate here and go on somewhere else. I do wish I could get some clean clothes. I have nothing but what I stand in; everything else I left behind in Paardekop.

20th Aug.

Rumours of a move to-morrow, getting rather sick of this place and wish we were on the move again.

21st Aug. L. J. Bryant

We resumed our Advance across the Transvaal & marched 8 miles; camping at Van Wyks Wlei.

21st Aug. Lieut. D. G. Auchinleck

Orders came to move last night so we started this morning. Transport at 9 a.m. Regt. was extreme rear guard and did not get off till 1.30 in spite of orders to be ready to move at 10.30. Got to camp about 2 with Transport and was then ordered to go back as Regt. was to camp S. side of spruit. When I got there fresh orders came to go and encamp near Supply Park so we did not get settled till 7 o'clock. The mules were inspanned for 11 hours which was a cruel shame; everything very badly managed. Camp called Van Wyks Vlei.

22nd Aug. L. J. Bryant

Advanced 8 miles today, & came in touch with the enemy.

22nd Aug. Lieut. D. G. Auchinleck

Halting here to-day for some reason. I believe to let Gen. French get round with his cavalry. There were several casualties yesterday. Mostly 18th Hussars, Lt. Field amongst them, altogether about 18. Supplies (mess) are running very short; no porridge for breakfast this morning. We have heard big guns going on all day about 5 or 6 miles in front. Gen. Howard came over to see us in the afternoon. Played Bridge and then supper and bed.

23rd Aug. L. J. Bryant

We done no marching today. The Boers hold a very strong position near here, & our Artillery were shelling it all day.

23rd Aug. Lieut. D. G. Auchinleck

Started off this morning. Regt. at 7.45 a.m. as left Advd. Flank guard. Transport at nine a.m. We had only 5 miles to go and when we got on the last ridge before the camp we saw pom-poms, shrapnel and Long Toms going at us so we knew there was a bit of a fight in front. Crossed the drift and then I went on a little bit to try and find out where the camp was to be when 4 Long Tom shells fell quite close to me which was rather a surprise. Got to camping ground alright and then I went out to see Regt, found them in support of the Liverpools, the latter had a few casualties, one man killed that I know of. Gunners 1 killed and 2 wounded. The enemy seem to be going to make a stand. To-morrow may show. Regt. got into camp about 7 p.m.

24th Aug. L. J. Bryant

We advanced to Geluks Farm (8 miles) but had to move very cautiously. Immediately after arriving at Geluks Farm my company had to go and escort the Guns, which were shelling the Boer position all day. The Liverpools advanced too near the Enemy position & lost very heavily when they found out their mistake & started to retire for the Boers opened a hot fire on them. Went on Outpost.

24th Aug. Lieut. D. G. Auchinleck

Up 5.30 a.m. Stand to arms. Remained here all to-day. This camp is called Geluk Farm, continual sniping went on all day at the outpost. Boers pretty close perhaps 1,000 yards. Our guns fired occasional shots and the Boers fired a few shells into camp without doing any harm. Shrapnel burst too high; the casualties to the Liverpools turned out to be very much more serious than at first supposed, 100 killed and wounded. Capt. Plomer missing, Pte Kennedy of ours very slightly grazed yesterday and to-day Henderson of G Coy was hit with a spent bullet which went thro' some papers and lodged in his purse.

25th Aug. L. J. Bryant

Our Artillery opened fire very early this morning; Our Engineers were making a sangar for our 5 inch Gun when the Boers sighted them, & sent a couple of Pom-Pom shells amongst them, which made them stop working but otherwise done no harm. Got relieved off Outpost by another Coy. of our Regt. A shell from the Boers Long Tom burst in our camp today, but did not explode.

25th Aug. Lieut. D. G. Auchinleck

Up at 5.30 standing to arms; fearfully cold night and morning. After breakfast we heard there was a canteen in, so I went over and got what I could so we are now a bit better off. Pretty heavy firing went on all morning but ceased about 12. Could hear fighting a long way to our left and we believe it is Pole Carew's [3] Division. Two of the 6th Dragoons came over to see us in the morning and I went to the canteen again in the afternoon to see if I could get a few things for them which I managed to do. Johnston, son of Col. Johnston of Snowhill Enniskillen came to see us in the afternoon. He is a sergeant in Strathcona's horse. Continual sniping all day at our pickets and in the evening one shell fell lee the camp about 50 yds. from us which was most unpleasant. Orders to move came about 11.30 p.m.

26th Aug. L. J. Bryant

We shifted our position today, & worked round till we got on the Boers left flank. Our Regt. received orders to reinforce the 7th Brigade, which we did. 'E' Coy went on Outpost & we had to dig trenches to lay down in, & were up half the night doing them, & we got into them about 2 a.m. & tried to get a little sleep. It was a very cold night, & we were half frozen with the cold, as we only had our great coats with us.

26th Aug. Lieut. D. G. Auchinleck

Started off Regt. 8.45 Transport 9.30 Regt. Right Rear flank guard. A very heavy fight all day. Devon and Manchester Regiments in front; could not make headway enough to take the position so it was rather a disappointing day. The Boers fired a good way many shells at our ridge, most shrapnel, which burst too high. The consequence of the day was that I had to go the whole way back to the Regt. and did not get into camp till about 11 o'clock, then I was sent off to find water cart etc. and got to bed 1.30 a.m. Camp called Vogelsruispoort

27th Aug. L. J. Bryant

We went into Action again today, & took part in the fight at Bergendal Farm, so our C. O. had his wish fulfilled. The Boers started snipping very early this morning, & my Company had to Retire out of the trenches about 7 a.m. to rejoin the Battn. again. The Boers didn't fire a single shot at us, whilst we were retiring, altho' they were snipping pretty heavily before our retirement.

We rejoined the Bn., & then marched off to reinforce the 7th Bge.; about 1 p.m. after marching about 6 or 7 miles, we then supported the Rifle Brigade in an attack on the Boer position. A party of the Boers with a pom-pom were entrenched in a farm house; most of the Boers were in the Johannesburg police, & they turned the pom-pom on us & gave us a warm reception. Our Artillery were shelling the Enemy, & their Llyddite & Shrapnel Shells were bursting right over the Boers & must have created fearful havoc amongst them.

We started our Advance about 2 p.m. & had to advance over a plain which gradually sloped towards the Farmhouse, & we were open to a hot fire for a time. The Boers up to this had made a good stand, & caused a lot of trouble amongst us, with their pom-pom. About 3 p.m. our Regt. with the Rifle Brigade charged the position & the Boers took to their heels when they saw the fixed bayonets.

The men in the Farmhouse were all either killed or captured, & there was a race between the two Regts. as to who should capture the pom-pom, but our Regt. got there first. We also captured a lot of ammunition & a lot of prisoners. The Rifles lost heavily but we only had 17 casualties, all wounded.

27th Aug. Lieut. D. G. Auchinleck

Up 5.30 a.m. Started 7 a.m. and we got orders that we were attached to the 7th Bde. to-day so I joined them with my baggage. A great fight to-day, our Artillery making grand shooting at a stony Kopje and farm house to our left front. About 3 p.m. the position which the Boers were going to hold for ever was taken by the R. B., ourselves, the Inniskillings being the first up by around 50 yds. Davy, Ricardo, Sergt. Craig, McCormac were the first up of all and Davy collared the Boer Pom-pom. 'B' and 'A' took 19 prisoners and altogether it was a great victory and a great surprise for us to be in the first line when we started rear guard. Gen. Lyttleton and Col. McGreggar congratulated the Regt. on being to the front again; we then advanced to the next ridge and kept firing at the beggars till dark. I think they have cleared back to Machadodorp. Got into camp early. Camp is called Bergendal.

28th Aug. L. J. Bryant

We rejoined our Bge. after yesterdays fight, & we were fell in ready to continue our Advance, when Gen. Kitchener (who commanded the 7th Bge.) rode up to our Colonel & said he wished to say a few words to us on our conduct yesterday.

He told us he was very pleased at the Gallant Conduct shown by the Regt. yesterday, and he said if we had been a minute later in reinforcing the Rifles the Attack would surely have failed. He said that not only was Gen. Buller watching us, but that Lord Roberts also had an eye on us, & that both appreciated the magnificent conduct shown by the Regt. in yesterdays fight. General Kitchener also said that he would write to Gen. Harte about our splendid conduct yesterday & tell him how pleased he was with the Regiment. He then rejoined his Bge. again. Our C. O. told us afterwards that he was very glad that he had the pleasure of leading us into action, & hoped he would soon have the pleasure again. He also said that he took no praise himself for our Conduct yesterday as it was the N.C.O.s & men themselves who deserve all the praise.

We advanced 18 miles today, & arrived at Machadodorp. The Boers intended to make another stand here, but we arrived on the scene too quick for them, so they took to their heels again.

28th Aug. Lieut. D. G. Auchinleck

Up 5.30 Standing to arms; all quiet, started off 8.30 a.m. and had a very long march 15 or 16 miles but got into Machadodorp with practically no opposition about 5.30 p.m. Just at the end snipers had a few shots at us but we soon cleared them away and Long Tom fired two shells without doing any harm. This place is only a few tin houses and filthy dirty and we were rather disappointed. Had to find 4 pickets. Very close night.

29th Aug. L. J. Bryant

We advanced 9 miles today & bivouacked at Helvetia. Gen. Pole-Carew's Bge. & French's Column are camped not far from us. Had a little rain during the day.

29th Aug. Lieut. D. G. Auchinleck

Up 5.30 a.m. Regt. moved off about 8.30 a.m. The first train into M. arrived at 9 loaded with supplies. There has been no firing up to now (10 a.m.). Baggage awaiting orders. About 12 o'clock the good news came in that the Boers had succeeded the ridge in front and at 2.30 the baggage moved off on a fearful road, hills like the side of a house and one hill over a mile long which was fearful hard on the mules. Got into camp about 7 o'clock. Two coys. did not get in till 10.30 and 12m.n. This camp is called Helvetia. The country here is as bad as Natal, precipitous holes and deep chasms. No fighting except artillery.

31th Aug.

No standaing to arms so had a good long sleep till 7 a.m. Had a fearful attack of colic last night. The worse pain I have ever felt. Congratulatory telegram from Gen. Cooper Light brigade. Wrote a lot of letters as mail went out 10 a.m. this morning. Gen. French failed to capture Reupr yesterday at Watervalonder…. But released prisoners who marched into our camp in the afternoon. 1,800 of them

1st Sept. L. J. Bryant

Our Regt. & the Leicesters moved off this morning & advanced 6 miles. The Left Half Bn. our our Regt (E, F, G & H Coys.) then went on detachment on Schoeman's Kloof, whilst the remainder of the Column advanced another 6 miles & camped at the Crocodile River. The other half Bn. of our Regt. stopped there for a few days & then marched to Witklip (9 miles) & went on Det. there.

1st Sept. Lieut. D. G. Auchinleck

Started off again towards Lydenburg 1/2 Bn. at 6.40 a.m. the other 1/2 rear guard. Baggage started 8 a.m. Long march and halted to camp at the Little Crocodile River having left the left 1/2 Battalion at a place called Schoeman's Kloof as a sort of post to guard the road. No opposition to-day. When we left Schoeman's Kloof we went down into a big Valley surrounded by very steep precipitous hills and when we arrived in camp about a dozen grass fires sprang up some way to our front and made a lovely sight. The 1/2 Bn. got in about 8.30 p.m. Officers here were Col., Davy, Ricardo, Hessey, Johnston, Traile, Ray and myself with Father O'Donnell attached and Maj. Woods R.A.M.C.

2nd Sept.

A late start. Regt. at 9.45 baggage at 10. Crossed the Crocodile river and passed Badfontein Hotel. Read Telegram from Queen to Buller on parade and his answer. Soon after starting 2 Long Toms opened on our Advd. Troops and the Transport parked just beyond Badfontein Hotel and remained there all day. The Long Toms fired about 120 rounds and wounded 5 or 6 men, nothing much happened. The Boer position looked a very strong one 3 companies out of 4 on picket. Bed early.

3rd Sept. L. J. Bryant

The Boers sent in a Kaffir with a white flag, to tell us that they had a wounded man of ours in a Farmhouse. The Stretcher Bearers had to go out & bring him to our Camp. As he was about 4 miles from our Camp, we took a Scotch Cart with us. The man belonged to the 5th Lancers & he told us he was very kindly treated by the Boer woman who was looking after him. 'E' Coy were on making Fortifications today. We got 3/4 rations today.

4th Sept.

A party of Boers fired into our Camp today, to try & ascertain our strength but retired when they found we took no notice of them. They also fired on our Scouts (18th Hussars) & wounded one man & took 2 prisoners. 'G' Coy returned with our Transport & provisions today. Went on Outpost again.

4th Sept. Lieut. D. G. Auchinleck

Still here. We are told we are waiting for Ian Hamilton who has started from Belfast to turn the Boer position and will probably not move till the day after to-morrow. We heard yesterday evening that Bobs had issued a proclamation and that the Transvaal had been annexed which is, I suppose, good news but does not mean that the war is over. Devenish came over to see us and seems to have had a pretty warm time on 2nd. Another very lazy day.

5th Sept.

A very unpleasant morning, just as we were sitting down to breakfast Long Tom started shelling the camp, 2 shells particularly coming much too close to us, the gun had changed its position much more to the right and closer. Two or three regiments in consequence had to go and take our end of the hill and then Long Tom ceased firing. Snipers only opposed this movement.

6th Sept.

Our orders were to be in readiness to move at 9 a.m. The cavalry moved off shortly after 9 but we did not inspan till 3 p.m. to our great surprise we saw our wagons etc. going up the hill about 5 miles to our front at 1.30 so as I write (3 p.m.) it looks as if the Boers had evacuated the position, Ian Hamilton must have got round behind them. Anyhow at last we are moving forward again. Actually did not get off till 5 p.m. and had a dreadful slow dragging march. Got into camp, which was at the foot of the hills where the Boers had their Long Tom, at 10.30 p.m. Regt. got in slightly after 12, had something to eat and got to bed at 1.30 a.m. It was a lovely moonlight night so that made things a bit more pleasant.

7th Sept.

Up 5.30 a.m. Standing to arms and an early breakfast. Regt. moved off 8.30 as advanced guard to Baggage; first time we have been advanced guard for days. Baggage moved off about 9 a.m. only went to the top of the hill when the right 1/2 Bn. were left as they were bound to be. It was indeed a fearful hill for Transport. I rode on into Lydenburg, about 8 miles, in afternoon to try and get some stores and am now writing in the Standard Hotel Lydenburg 8.30 p.m. I went to see Col. Murray A.A.G. Ian Hamilton's Force. He looked very fit and was full of going on etc. The Boers started shelling us in the afternoon and kept it up for an hour at a range of 11,000 yds. I then went to the Convent with Father O'Donnell and Collins and saw Father Brown and had an excellent dinner of fried eggs etc. Have got some stores but can't start back till tomorrow with convoy.

8th Sept.

Long Toms started off again after breakfast, one shrapnel killing 2 and wounding 14 of the Gordons (Volunteer Coy). Spent the whole morning trying to get some provisions and was partially successful particularly in liquor. Our troops drove the Boers off the hills to the east in the afternoon and Long Toms once more went off. Got back to our camp which is called Witklip 8.30 p.m.

9th Sept. L. J. Bryant

Eighteen Boer prisoners were brought into Camp today. We heard big Guns firing in the direction of Lydenburg.

9th Sept. Lieut. D. G. Auchinleck

Ian Hamilton's force passed thro' our post at 1 p.m. en route to Helvetia. Ricardo and I spent the whole day in the valley foraging. Got 8 pigs, 8 hens, a turkey, a goose and any amount of vegetables. Great sport with the pigs!

10th Sept. L. J. Bryant

Gen. Ian Hamilton 's Bge. arrived here today & camped about 1 mile from us.

11ᵗʰ Sept.

The Boer prisoners were handed over to the Royal Scots, belonging to Ian Hamilton's Bge.

12ᵗʰ Sept.

A small party of Engineers were proceeding to Badfontein, 6 miles from here to repair the Telegraph wire which had been cut when they were attacked by a force of Boers. The Boers wounded a few men & captured the remainder, also captured 3 wagons that had Telegraph implements in them. They burnt the wagons but kept the teams of mules.

12ᵗʰ Sept. Lieut. D. G. Auchinleck

Convoy of 4 wagons of the Engineer Telegraph Division attacked by about 40 Boers at the bridge over the Little Crocodile. Lt. Meyrick R.E., 10 sappers and 11 18ᵗʰ Hussars being escort. Mailo luckily turned back in time. Convoy of empty wagons arrived from Lydenburg.

13ᵗʰ Sept. L. J. Bryant

The Engineers who were taken prisoner yesterday, were sent into camp today. Four Coys. of the Manchesters arrived here today.

13ᵗʰ Sept. Lieut. D. G. Auchinleck

Convoy passed thro' Crocodile Valley safely. Farms being burnt as a punishment for attack on Telegraph Division. 8 of our mules were driven off by 6 Boers when being watered 2 miles from camp along the road to Lydenburg.

14ᵗʰ Sept.

Full convoy arrived from Schoeman's Kloof. Heard Kruger was at L. Marques and Bolton resigned. Home mail arrived.

16ᵗʰ Sept. L. J. Bryant

The Det. of our Regt. stationed here fell in at 9.30 a.m. & marched to Badfontein (6miles) & camped there as a det. Men with very bad boots *are doing duty on Aileen Kopje, with a Maxim.*

17ᵗʰ Sept. Lieut. D. G. Auchinleck

Quiet day. Had long telegraph giving us all the news as follows:-
"Kruger is going to Europe on 6 months leave leaving Schalk Burger as President. Botha has handed over command to V. Given owing to indisposition. French is in Barbeston and has captured 43 locomotives, much rolling stock and any amount of supplies. P. Carew is at Godwan. Boers admit 40 casualties N. of Megarieo where they were driven by Clements. Hart occupied Potchefstroom 11ᵗʰ after forced march, cavalry 45 35 miles and surprised Boers.

Some killed, a few escaped and remainder arrested only casualty Lt. Maddocks killed."

Nothing startling but very satisfactory news.

18th Sept.

My natal [birthday] day. What a place to spend it in. Nothing of note happened except convoy returned from Schoeman's Kloof. 4 of the 5th Lancers and Maude came to dinner. Champagne and Brandy particularly appreciated.

20th Sept. L. J. Bryant

'F' Coy. escorted one of the wagons to Schoeman's Kloof for more provisions. The other 3 Coys. were on fatigues making fortifications. A part of Boers surprised a small party of our Scouts today who were on observation duty. The Boers killed one man, wounded 2 & took the remainder prisoners, but let them go after taking their arms, etc. off them. The Boers came within 2000 yards of our Camp, but hastily retired after we opened fire on them with the maxim. A flock of Locusts passed overhead today.

20th Sept. Lieut. D. G. Auchinleck

Spent the whole morning shopping but did not get much. Started back 2 p.m. and got into camp at 6 p.m. An old Boss (Cross) came into camp to-day. Cavalry patrol of 4 men fired on at Badfontein, 1 man killed, one dangerously wounded and 2 horses killed and 2 missing.

22nd Sept.

Davy went down to take command at Badfontein. Heard some distant guns about 8 a.m. We were all just sitting down to wash and shave about 9.30 when we heard rifle shots from the direction of the watering place.

We were up on the ridge in a quarter of an hour. It turned out that about 50 Boers had attempted to ambuscade the watering party but had significantly failed. We got 10 or 12 shells at them as they were retiring and 3 of them fell off their horses.

We had one gunman badly wounded in the thigh. Spent the rest of the morning knocking down the wall, cutting down trees and burning a farm house near the watering place to which some of the Boers opened fire.

24th Sept. L. J. Bryant

On Making Fortifications. We have to build a stone wall about 6 foot high all round our Camp, & make loopholes in it to fire out of. We also have to dig trenches all around the place.

27th Sept. Lieut. D. G. Auchinleck

Quiet morning. Long wire received from Hd. Qrs. Pretoria. Paget ⁴ has captured a large number of cattle, sheep and horses. Eland's River garrison beat off an attack without aid. Komate Poost Bridge reported to be blown up. Mercenaries have gone to Lourenco [Laurenzo] Marques.

29th Sept.

Nothing of note. Building forts. Killed a black mamba snake just beside the mess shelter. Large swarm of locusts came over the camp in the afternoon.

1st Oct.

Two Boers surrendered yesterday to the post at Badfontein. Another small convoy arrived from Schoeman's.

2nd Oct.

Convoy went out 5.30 a.m. and I went with it as far as Schoeman's Farm to collect tin (corrugated iron) for shelters to provide against the rain which is expected shortly. Got back with 2 wagon loads about 11 o'clock.

3rd Oct.

It started raining last night at 11 p.m. and rain and hail has continued ever since 11 a.m. Everything wet thro'. Wrote letters all morning, terrible hail, thunder and lightning.

4th Oct.

Rain continued the whole day with very little fine, convoy came from Lydenburg in the afternoon and lost a good many animals owing to the very heavy state of the ground. 36 died in the last 6 miles.

6th Oct. L. J. Bryant

Still working on the fortifications. A & C Coys took the Convoy to Witklip this morning. Our Orderly Sgts. came around this evening to take down the names of any men who wished to stop in the country after the war is over, also the men's trades.

6th Oct. Lieut. D. G. Auchinleck

Buller came thro' with S.A.L.H. [South African Light Horse] and S.H. [Strathcona's Horse] on his way to Machadodorp and probably home. The force is to be disbanded. In the evening the Boers sniped the covering party to our watering party. Soon made them retreat with the aid of shells.

8th Oct.

Moved camp across to the other hill and just as we had settled down into the grand tin houses which Ricardo had built an order came that we were to move to-morrow. Very glad to move but not to leave the house. E and K Coys. with Davy, Kenny, Leo, Jeffcoat and Martineau arrived about 7.30 p.m. from Badfontein.

9th Oct. L. J. Bryant

The Bn. fell in at 12.30 p.m. to rejoin our Bge. again, who were marching down country from Lydenburg. 'H' Coy. rejoined the Bn. again, marching from Lydenburg (12 miles). Before the Bn. started on the March our C.O. told us that Gen. Buller when he passed through Witklip, told him, that he was very pleased with the work done by the Regiment in the Campaign.

He also told him, that he might not have taken particular notice of the work done by the Irish Bge. & especially of the Inniskillings at Pieters Hill [Inniskilling Hill] yet he said he would be sure he would mention us in his written dispatches.

He also said he was very pleased at he work the Regt. has done at Bergendal (Belfast) & and he said that the men fought just as bravely as they did at Pieters Hill. We then marched off & rejoined our Bge. again, marching about 4 or 5 miles only.

9th Oct. Lieut. D. G. Auchinleck

Up early, great packing up for move. (now waiting orders 9 a.m.) Wrote a letter to Norrie and Managers of L. & C. B. Co. Ltd. Of Ireland yesterday. Wrote to Mado in morning. Fell in at 1 p.m. and marched off to Zwaggers Hock. Joined the column about 3 miles out consisting of Leicesters, K. R. R. [King's Royal Rifles] and Gordons, 18th Hussars 21st R. F. A. [Royal Field Artillery] one 5" gun R. E. [Royal Engineers] and 2 supply columns. Camped there for night just under Spitzkop called Zwaggers Hock. Anniversary of mobilization.

10th Oct. L. J. Bryant

We resumed our trek down country & advanced 10 miles, camping at Elands Spruit. The Boers indulged in a little snipping at us, during the march.

10th Oct. Lieut. D. G. Auchinleck

Up 4.30 a.m. Breakfast 5.00 a.m. Advance Troops moved off 6.15 a.m. Went thro' very hilly close country particularly the first part which was a regular defiler. A little sniping in front, one of the 10th Hussars hit in four toes. Terrible road for Transport about 9 miles. Camp Elandspruit.

11th Oct. L. J. Bryant

Marched to Dullstroom (12 miles). We got one biscuit & a half for our daily ration.

11th Oct. Lieut. D. G. Auchinleck

Up 5 a.m. Breakfast 5.45 a.m. Marched over a terrible bit of country, all up and down and covered with rocky kopjes to Dullstroom. Nice little place of about a dozen houses. Continuos sniping all day. Marched 8 or 9 miles. Got in 1.30 p.m. Plenty of time to do things comfortably.

12 Oct. L. J. Bryant

Marched 12 miles & arrived at Witklip. A party of Boers, with a Pom-Pom, had taken up a position in the surrounding hills & we were near walking into a trap, which they had laid for us, owing to bad scouting on our Cavalry's part, but the Boers opened fire too soon & we found out our mistake just in time, or else we would have had a hot time of it. We scoured the hills & the Boers made off. We had two casualties in our Regt. 1 man killed and 1 wounded. Went on Outpost duty about 5 p.m. & the Boers sniped at us, until it got too dark, but they did no harm. A severe Thunder Storm came on during the night, & we got swamped.

12th Oct. Lieut. D. G. Auchinleck

Up 4.15 a.m. Fighting commenced at once and continuing fight was kept up all day, the Boers fighting a rear guard action in order to get wagons away. Botha turned up with very large convoy and we had to take several kopjes in order that our camp might not be sniped. We lost Deveney of A coy. killed and my old servant Fitzgibbon wounded in thigh. A rather hard day. Boers opened a pom-pom on us but soon withdrew with it. Camp near Witpoort on plain surrounded by rocky hills. Very wet night with lightning etc.

13th Oct. L. J. Bryant

Marched to Blinkwater. 17 miles.

13th Oct. Lieut. D. G. Auchinleck

Expected a little resistance so the wagons did not get off till 7 a.m. Shelling continued off and on. When we had gone about 10 miles we saw the whole Boer convoy double spanning their wagons over the mountain to N. E. A most trying thing not to be able to go after them owing to lack of provisions. Hundreds of wagons got off. A very long march, about 15 miles. Camp called Blinkwater. Heavy thunder and lightning.

14th Oct. L. J. Bryant

Marched to Hock Spruit. 12 miles.

14th Oct. Lieut. D. G. Auchinleck

Regiment advanced guard, started off at 5.50 a.m. on 2/3 of ¾ rations i. e. ½ rations. Camp at Hockspruit. Camp sniped at, 12 shots.

15th Oct.

A few prisoners, 6 or 7 taken yesterday. Marched on thro' Elandslaagte, a long march over a splendid road and camped Bankfontein.

17th Oct.

Middelburg is a very nice town with good houses and gardens, quite the best town we have seen. They have got quite a nice little officer's club with a billiard room. Went to a concert with Ricardo. Very good.

19th Oct.

Went with Leo to Rochdale Farm to complete a fort up there. Started at 8.30 a.m. and got back, wet through, at 5.30 p.m. Changed camp to Guards Hill.

22nd Oct. L. J. Bryant

Our tents having arrived from Paarde Kop the Regt. were on fatigues unloading the wagons & sorting out the Kits & Tents of the different companies. We pitched our Camp once more at 11 a.m. after being without tents for 3 months but a Thunder storm came on during the Evening & we got flooded out of them, & had to lay down on the muddy ground all night.

23rd Oct.

Had Bathing Parade. The Stretcher Bearers took over their old job of filtering water for the Bn. to drink. The K. R. R. & Gordons left here today for Pretoria to take part in a Review, which is to be held there. 'B' Coy. went on det. to Guards Hill.

At this point in the campaign Lieutenant D. G. Auchinleck's Diary breaks off. However unlike that of Captain A. C. Jeffcoat, he does resume his account, albeit after a period of six months, on 30 April 1901. Why this break should happen is unclear, whether he simply lost interest in his diary during this period or whether the distractions of Middelburg, with its polo playing, dancing and concerts proved too strong, he does not say. However, we will pick up on his diary entries once more on 30 April 1901.

24th Oct. L. J. Bryant

General Bullers Farewell Speech to the Natal Field Force.

The following appeared in the Bn. Orders being the Farewell Speech of Gen. Buller to the Natal Field Force.

Extract, Army Orders. Dated P. M. Burg. 19th Oct. 1900.

"The Natal Field force ceases to exist as a separate Command from this Date.

In making this announcement Gen Sir Redvers Buffer desires to express his Grateful Thanks to all Officers, Non Commissioned Officers and Men, of that Force for their unvarying Support, and constant co operation.

The task set before the Natal Field Force, was no small one, & it has been successfully accomplished (tho' with the loss of so many dear friends & Gallant Comrades) through the Valour, Endurance & Splendid Discipline of the Troops & the Admirable Organization of the Lines of Communications.

To command such a Force has been the greatest possible pleasure, & Sir Redvers Buller regrets deeply, that he has not been to tell each, & all of them how much he has gloried in the Honour of being their Commander.

Sgd. Kitchener of Khartoum.
Chief of Staff.

29th Oct.

Two officers & 40 men, taken from G & H Coys. formed the Escort to the Guns of the 85th battery R. H. A. & escorted them to Pretoria by rail. 'C' Coy went on det. to Rockdale Farm & the K. R. R. returned to Middelburg again today. Another Thunder Storm came on.

1st Nov.

The Column which was postponed from yesterday formed up today. The force consisted of 2 Squadrons Cavalry, 1 Bn. of Infantry, & a battery of Artillery, Royal Horse. Reveille went at 3 a.m. We fell in at 5 a.m. & started on our trek, marching 18 miles. A party of Boers kept on sniping but retired when we put the Guns on them. It was raining all night & we got swamped, as we were bivouacking. 'D' & 'H' Coys were left behind to look after the camp, also the men who had bad boots.

2nd Nov.

Raining all day. We fell in at 11 a.m. & returned to camp again by a shorter route, (12miles) as it was too wet to proceed any further. Men who wished could wear their great coats on the march. We got orders to push on as fast as possible & we arrived at Middelburg with scarcely a halt. We sent our Convoy on in advance. The Boers kept on sniping at our Cavalry who were guarding the Rear of the column. The Boers were dressed in Khaki & they followed up our Cavalry, escaping notice for a time, & they killed one man and wounded another of our Cavalry. Our Guns opened fire on them whenever a chance occurred, & we heard afterwards that the Boers losses were 4 killed & 14 wounded. We arrived at Middelburg again at 4 p.m.

3rd Nov.

Raining all the morning. We got served out with new clothing, which was badly needed.

5th Nov.

Today is the Anniversary of our Embarkation for this Country. We got served out with new boots, which we greatly needed, as half of the men were wearing boots with no soles to them.

18th Nov.

All quiet here at Rochdale. A party of Boers having attacked the Buffs at Balmoral, 4 Coys. of the King's Royal Rifles were sent to the Buffs assistance.

23rd Nov.

'D' Coy relieved off det., rejoined the Bn. again today, & 40 men of each Coy at Head Quarters were sent out to complete the Fortifications around Middelburg. C & E Coys proceeded to Groot Oliphants River Station to do duty there.

Detachment Notes. 'C' & 'E' Companies.

We arrived at Groot Oliphants about 4 p.m. & relieved the Berks. off duty. 'C' Coy proceeded to Observation Hill & went on Outpost. Half of 'E' Coy were on guard at the Station, & the other half of 'E' Coy marched back to the Railway Bridge & were then split up into 3 parties. One party guarded the Bridge, another party were stationed on a stony Kopje, whilst the third party were doing duty on a detached post. The machine gun belonging to the Berks got stuck in the mud about 9 p.m., so our party stationed on the Kopje, had to go out & pull it out of the mud & bring it back to our camp for the night.

24th Nov.

Had 'Stand To' parade ar 3 a.m. We got orders at 5.30 a.m. to get ready to return to Middelburg again, but the order was cancelled at the last minute & we had to go to Observation Hill to do duty there. We marched off at 6 p.m. & done about 3 miles & we then bivouacked for the night. The Berks. Resumed their duties at the Bridge, etc.

26th Nov.

We again got orders to get ready to return to Middelburg. We were relieved off duty by a Company of the Duke of Cornwall's Light Infantry at 3.30 p.m. & we then marched back to the Railway Station & bivouacked for the night.

27th Nov.

We returned to Middelburg again for the night

Regimental News.

We learnt that 'H' Coy had gone on det. to Aasvogels Krantz & also the 25 men of our Coy whom we left behind when we went on detachment. 'B' Coy also went on det. to Gun Hill, both Coys going on det. the day before yesterday.

One N. C. O. and a few men of our Regt. were escorting a wagon with rations for H Coy on det. & they mistook the road & would have been captured by a party of Boers, who were lying in wait for them, but the Boers were sighted by our Outpost & a wire was sent in to our C. O. & he sent an officer out on Horseback to make the men retire, before it was too late. When the Boers saw the party retire they opened fire on them but did no harm. 'H' Coy rejoined the Bn. today from off det.

28th Nov.

'C' 'E' & 'G' Companies took part in a Column today. We fell in at 5 a.m. & marched 10 miles from Camp. The Boers sniped as usual but did no harm. Another Column left Middelburg today at 12 noon to co-operate with Gen. Pagets Column from Pretoria.

On 29 November 1900 Kitchener replaced Lord Roberts as Commander-in-Chief of the Army in South Africa whilst Roberts succeeded Lord Wolseley as Commander-in -Chief back in Britain.

29th Nov. L. J. Bryant

Had the usual Stand To parade at 3.15 a.m. We went on a reconnaissance today at 9 a.m. The force consisted of 1 Squadron of Cavalry, 2 Guns & 4 Coys. of Infantry........The remainder of the Column were left in charge of the Camp. A party of Boers were scattered amongst some low stone Kopjes, from which they kept on sniping at us. They also fired at us from some farm houses which we accordingly burnt. Two Boers surrendered to us & we captured some fine cattle off them. The force was too weak to attack the Boers, but the Guns shelled the Kopjes pretty freely. We had 4 casualties in the Force, all being wounded.

30th Nov.

We fell in at 4.30 a.m. & flanked the Boers who were still amongst the Kopjes & they hastily retired. We then marched about 10 miles & bivouacked for the night. We burnt a few more farm houses during the evening because the Boers opened fire on us from them altho' they had a white flag flying from the roof, & we captured 2 wagons, & some cattle & forage off the Boers. E Coy went on Outpost.

1st Dec.

We returned to Middelburg again today marching 12 miles. The Boers as usual followed up the Rear of the Column, but a few shells from our 5 inch Gun soon made them keep a respectable distance & we arrived in Camp without any further trouble.

3rd Dec.

A party of Boers were seen by our Outpost trying to commandeer some cattle from some kaffir kraals, so our Outpost opened fire on them & they retired minus the cattle. G & H Coys had to march half way to Pan early, this morning to escort an Empty Convoy back to Middelburg. They marched about 18 miles altogether. 25 men of E Coy went on det. to Aasvogels Krantz & relieved the 25 men of the Coy. who had been doing duty there with H Coy. D Coy relieved B Coy off det. at Gun Hill.

7th Dec.

'A' & 'B' Coys took part in a Column today at 12 noon. The men of the Band & Drums who were not for the Column had to go down to the Cemetery & dig a grave for a chap of the Cornwalls, who had died. Fifty men of the Battalion proceeded to Pretoria today, to go through a course of Riding for the Mounted Infantry.

12th Dec.

'A' & 'B' Coys returned to camp today off the Column. The first day the Column marched 12 miles & 25 the second day. The next 3 days were given up to reconnaissance. They were actions in conjunction with Paget's Column & the Columns captured a Boer laager on the 2nd day, after marching 25 miles. On the 6th day the Column marched 12 miles & then trained it to Middelburg. We had two casualties in our Regt. on this trek.

13th Dec.

We received orders to get ready to proceed to Pretoria, as soon as possible. We struck Camp at 6 p.m. & marched to the station & put our baggage on the two trains that were to take us to Pretoria.

14th Dec.

We started on our journey at 1 a.m. this morning & arrived at Pretoria at 9.30 a.m. We then received orders to reinforce Gen. Clement's Column. We started on our march at 1.15p.m. & marched to Black Water Spruit, (16 miles) arriving there about 9 p.m. We had our tents with us, & also one blanket, one oilsheet & a big coat.

15ᵗʰ Dec.

Marched to beyond Rietfontein, (10 miles) & joined Clement's Force. We heard that the Northumberland Fus. who were in his Column had had a severe cutting up & that about 300 me or so, had been taken prisoners by the Boers, a few days ago, as the Boers crept up on the Camp at night & attacked it, with the above result. The Boers then retired & now hold a strong position up in the valley, & we have to drive them out of it. Went on Outpost with E Coy.

16ᵗʰ Dec.

Fell in at 13.30 p.m. & marched to Stockpoort, 8 miles. It was very hot all day.

17ᵗʰ Dec.

Marched to Haarteheestefontein, (8 miles)

18ᵗʰ Dec.

We only advanced two & a half miles today as the Boers hold a strong position amongst some Kopjes a short distance away. Went on Outpost again.

19ᵗʰ Dec.

Got up at 2.15 a.m. Fell in at 3.30 a.m. & advanced to attack the Boers position at the West end of the Valley, at Thorndale. Our Regt. formed the firing Line, & Supports, the Borders were the Reserves, & the Worcesters guarded the Convoy.

The Boers had 4 or 5 big guns & at once opened fire on us & the Mounted Infantry directly we started to advance, but we drove them out of their position & followed them up for about 15 miles. It came on to rain about 10 a.m. & we had to lay on the muddy ground all night & we got swamped, as we had to lay in pools of water all night. We only had 3 casualties in our Regt. today. We pitched our camp at Brishfontein.

20ᵗʰ Dec.

'D' & 'E' Coys formed the Support to the Worcesters on an attack on a position which the Boers were supposed to be holding. We left Camp at 5 a.m. & flanked the position but found no one there when we got to the place, as the Boers had retired during the night. We marched about 5 miles to get to the place & then returned to Camp by another road two & a half miles. The Column had in the meanwhile advanced 3 or 4 miles & we camped for the day at Boschfontein. It was raining all day & we got another soaking. Gen. French's Column arrived during the day & camped near us. The Dublin Fus. were in his Force.

21ˢᵗ Dec.

We advanced 10 miles today & found that the Boers had taken up another position not far off. Our Artillery were shelling them all day. Gen. French's Column having moved off in another direction got round on the other side of the Enemy & started shelling them. Two more Columns are acting in conjunction with us & we have the Boers under De La Ray nearly hemmed in & are only waiting another Column to hold the Nek when we will have the circle complete. We camped for the night at Water Kloof.

22ⁿᵈ Dec.

We heard that Gen. French attacked the Boers last night & gave them a good hammering but the Boers got away through a Nek, as the Column that were supposed to be holding it didn't turn up. We marched 12 miles & passed through Oliphants Nek. It was very hot all day. Went on Outpost at 6 p.m. About 300 men of the Northumberlands (who were taken prisoner by the Boers, when they attacked Clement's Force, just before we joined him) arrived at our camp today.

23ʳᵈ Dec.

Marched to Buffels Poort, 14 miles.

24ᵗʰ Dec.

Marched to Wolhuters Kop, 11 miles.

25ᵗʰ Dec.

Xmas Day. We marched to Commando Nek, 9 miles. Our fare for this day was as follows:-

Breakfast, Biscuits, Jam & Coffee.

Dinner, Boiled meat, no vegetables.

Tea, Same as Breakfast.

Extras, half a pound of Bread, & tea. We also got a pint of beer, like warm water, & an issue of rum.

26ᵗʰ Dec.

Had a Rest.

27ᵗʰ Dec.

Rested. A large convoy arrived here from Rietfontein, with provisions for Rustenburg to last the Garrison 4 months. One man of our Regt. was wounded about 7 p.m. whilst cooking some supper, through a cartridge falling into the fire & exploding. A severe Thunder came on.

28ᵗʰ Dec.

The Convoy which arrived here yesterday was split up into 3 portions. The Borders & the Worcesters escorted the first two parts to Wolhuters Kop today, & we escort the 3rd portion to the same place tomorrow. We struck Camp at 7 p.m. & bivouacked for the night, as we move off at 2 a.m. tomorrow morning.

29th Dec.

A force of Boers having been reported to be holding a strong position on the road to Rustenburg with the intention of trying to capture the Convoy if they could, the orders concerning the Convoy were cancelled, & it was sent back to Rietfontein again, until the road to Rustenburg was clear. We pitched our Camp at 9 a.m. & awaited further orders. We struck our Camp again at 6 p.m., fell in at 9 p.m. & marched to Wolhuters Kop, 9 miles to rejoin the Column again.

30th Dec.

We arrived at Wolhuters Kop at 3 a.m. & rejoined our Column. Pitched Camp at 7 a.m.

31st Dec.

Had a rest today.

Chapter Seven

1901

In early January 1901 the 1st Batalion the Royal Inniskilling Fusiliers received orders to return to Pretoria from their camp at Middelburg, where they had been on detachment for most of the previous four months. However, hardly had they unpacked their kit on arrival in Pretoria than further orders were issued returning them once more to Middelburg.

The Battalion remained in and around the vicinity of Middelburg until 30 April, engaged in a variety of detachments and escort duties, by which time they received fresh orders to break camp and march once more to link up with Colonel E. H. H. Allenby's[1] Column of the 2nd Dragoons and 6th Dragoon Guards. The Column was kept continuously on the march, first north of the Pretoria - Delagoa railway line, then south, until early June when the Column was ordered to proceed south-west of Pretoria into the Rustenburg and Magaliesburg district.

Throughout the long, hot, dry South African summer Colonel Allenby's Column was kept constantly on the move, covering a distance in excess of 940 miles between 10 June and 11 September. When finally recalled to Pretoria, the final total distance covered on marches was well in excess of the 940 miles, as this did not take into account periods spent on Convoy or detachment.

Whilst at Pretoria the Royal Inniskilling Fusiliers took part in the usual run of the mill detachments, convoy escorts and marches to which they had grown so accustomed since their arrival in South Africa. However, from 11 November until the end of the year a force of 100

NCOs and ORs under the command of Captain G. W. Kenny left the battalion, assigned to act as bodyguard to Lord Kitchener.

By the end of 1901, however, the Battalion had ceased its more mobile role, having been ordered on 13 December to proceed to Kroonstad in the Orange River Colony, from where it was despatched to built and man a line of Blockhouses[2] stretching from Kroonstad to Lindley on to Bethlehem.

The introduction of a system of blockhouses spanning the countryside by Lord Kitchener was intended as a means of restricting the movements of the Boer commandos. Specifically located near railway junctions and other vital chains of communications and supply, in all some 18,000 blockhouses were built. Constantly manned by small detachments of troops, these small fortifications made it increasingly difficult for the Boers to operate freely in their role as fast mobile guerrillas, striking when and where they pleased, living off the land.

1901

1st Jan. L. J. Bryant

Two Coys. of the Lincolns joined our Column today. We got this day to ourselves.

3rd Jan.

Got up at 12.30 a.m., Fell in at 2 a.m. & advanced on Kopjes where the Boers were reported to be entrenched, we met with no opposition, so our Regt. & the Lincolns retired back again about 6 miles an we camped at Elands Kraal about 4 p.m. after marching 18 miles. Our Camp was already pitched for us. A severe Storm came on during the morning & we got a good soaking. The remainder of Clement's force held the Kopjes for the night.

4th Jan.

Our Regt. & the Lincolns fell in at 7 a.m. & and we marched to Commando Nek (15 miles). The Lincolns stopped at Wolhuters Kop. It was very hard marching, owing to the muddy state of the road. It was raining all day, & we got another drenching.

6th Jan.

We marched to Pretoria & camped on Proclamation Hill (9 miles), we cut off 4 miles of the march by going over the Kopjes by East fort. Pitched our Camp at 11 a.m.

7th Jan.

Our part in the Column now being over, we got this day to ourselves. We had new cloths served out to us, which we needed.

10th Jan.

Struck Camp at 4.30 a.m., Fell in at 5 a.m. & marched to Rly. Station to proceed to Middelburg again. We left Pretoria at 7 a.m. & arrived at Middelburg at 5 p.m.

15th Jan.

One man of our Regt. was killed & 5 men of the Lancers were wounded today, at Belfast through the Gordon Highlanders firing on them, & mistaking them for Boers.

19th Jan.

A H & part of D Coy proceeded to Dalmanutha today. The other half of D Coy. went to Machadodorp.

23rd Jan.

We first learnt the sad News of Her Majesty's Death this evening.

24th Feb.

On fatigue digging trenches etc. from 9.45 a.m. to 11.45 a.m. All hands then fell in on parade at 12 noon & we presented arms, whilst the Artillery fired a Royal salute of 21 Guns, on the occasion of the Prince of Wales ascending the Throne as, King of England. We then gave three cheers for King Edward VII & were dismissed. The Union Jack was hoisted full mast high at the Railway Station.

25th Jan.

On fatigue the same as yesterday. We again paraded at 12 noon, whilst our Artillery fired a Salute of 81 minute Guns in Honour of the Late Queen. We should have stood to Attention for 81 minutes but were dismissed off parade after about ten minutes. All flags were flying at half-mast high to day.

28th Jan.

The Company returned to Middelburg again this morning. The 3 Companies left at Head Quarters were out on a reconnaissance to Uithigh [Uitkyk] Station since 3 a.m. & returned to Camp again at 2 p.m. This has been their duty fort the last fortnight.

29th Jan.

Head Quarter Notes

The Coys. stationed here, except 'B' Coy. went out on another reconnaissance to Uithigh [Uitkyk] Station to day. We paraded at 7.30 a.m. (after getting our Breakfast as best we could) & returned to Camp again at 2 p.m. having marched 10 miles. 'B' Coy. relieved G Coy off Detachment at Klein Oilphants Bridge, A D & H Coys. returned from off Detachment to day & rejoined the Battalion again.

30th Jan.

The Leicesters went on reconnaissance to Uithigh [Uitkyk] to day, in our place, & we got a rest to day.

31st Jan.

'C' 'E' 'F' & 'H' Coys. went on Detachment again to day, at 8 a.m. as follows:-

'C' Coy: to Carcase Hill.

'E' Coy: to Guards Hill.

'F' Coy: to Rockdale Farm,

& 'H' Coy: to the Ermelo Road.

Detachment Notes, 'E' Coy.

1st Feb.

On fatigue making fortifications.

2nd Feb.

Ditto. The following letter from Gen. Harte to our Regt. was published in our Battn. Orders to day. Viz.

Farewell Letter from Major General Harte to Our Battalion.

Head Qts Krugersdorp Transvaal

-25th January 1901-

:- In leaving to take over another Command, I wish you my brother soldiers of my Force, "Farewell."

It is an article of my faith, that you would go anywhere, & do anything, required in Battle. I leave you with deep regret, & of course I must feel this particularly for the last of my Old Irish Brigade, with which I began the war. In departing, I give you this Scrap of Advice:- Be individually, whenever opportunity, offers personally, not only kind but generous to the inhabitants of this Country, which we have taken from them, & among whom so many of our Country men & Country women, will have to dwell. It will not diminish your Soldiery Strength, & it will hasten a welcome for the present Government of Peace.

(Sgd.) A. Fitzroy Harte. Major General.

Commanding Harte's 'Force.'

25th Feb.

The Company were on fatigue every day from 10 a.m. to 12 noon, (except Sundays) making Fortifications. On Sunday there was Divine Service for the church party under Major Davidson. The men of the Coy. were doing duty as follows:- Twenty four men went on Outpost at 6 p.m. & another 24 men were on Inlying picquet, leaving about 12 men or so, to have the night in bed. When it was raining, the men on piquet had to sleep in the trenches, & not in the tents. We have had rain for the last 10 days.

26th Feb.

General Kitchener visited Guards Hill this morning at 6.30 a.m. to inspect the fortifications. He was very pleased with the work done, but half of the work had to be pulled down again as the Fort was too big for the Force that had to guard it. Major Davidson left us to day to proceed to Beaufort West, Cape Colony, to take over the command of a Draft of ours, which is stationed there, since Decr. last.

28th Feb.

On the usual fatigues. Gen. Botha arrived in Middelburg at 10 a.m. to have an Interview with Lord Kitchener. He left again at 6 p.m. this evening.

17th Mar.

St. Patrick's Day. We got an extra dram of rum given to us at 12 noon to day, by order of Gen. Lord Kitchener.

20th Mar.

All hands had to man the trenches at 7 p.m. as we were told to keep a sharp look out. We heard firing at 8 p.m. in the direction of Klein Oliphant, where "A" Company are stationed.

21st Mar.

The following item appeared in our Battn. Orders to day. Viz:- The London Gazette, dated 8th February, containing the South African Despatches, including those of Gen. Sir Redvers Buller, V.C. G.C.B. from January 1900 to 13th Sept. 1900, have been received. It will be seen from these despatches that the Gallant services of the Regiment, including all ranks, has received the well merited recognition it so thoroughly deserved, more especially for the part it took in the operations for the Relief of Ladysmith etc.

22nd Mar.

One man of our Regt., belonging to "A" Coy. whilst returning from Town to rejoin his Coy. at Klein Oliphants, during the evening, was fired upon & dangerously wounded by a man of the 18th Hussars who was doing duty on the Bridge.

The following appeared in todays Battalion Orders viz:-

Colonel Paynes Speech to the Regt. On his departure for England.

The Commanding Officer very much regrets, that in consequence of the unfortunate opening of an old gunshot injury in his leg, which will necessitate a lengthy surgical operation, he is obliged, under Medical Advice , to take sick leave and it may be a few months before he is fit to return to duty. It is now very nearly a year since he assumed

Command at Ladysmith, soon after the conclusion of the operations for its Relief in which the Regt. took so distinguished a part, and gained so much credit for its Gallantry. As he remarked to the Battalion on Parade, on taking over Command from Major Mackenzie, it was a proud moment when he was appointed to Command such a Regiment and it would be the proudest moment of his life to have the honour to lead it into action. It was therefore his desire to use every effort to recruit the ranks and obtain a fair complement of seasoned officers, so that the Regt. might be in a position to rejoin a Mobile Brigade, instead of being employed on the lines of Communication. Early in August the Regt. joined the 8th Brigade Commanded by Maj. Gen. Howard C.B. forming part of the 4th Division under Gen. Llyttleton C.B. and took part in all the operations during Gen. Bullers Advance on Lydenburg, including the engagement at Bergendal on the 27th August 1900, when in conjunction with the Rifle Bge. it assulted and carried the enemys strongly entrenched position and as shown by the despatches and his personal observations when commanding, worthily sustained their reputation for Gallantry and steadiness under heavy fire, several officers, N.C.O.s and men received mention. In all subsequent operations to date the Regt. has thoroughly upheald its prestige. As Commanding Officer he has received considerable commendation from Gen. Buller for the thorough manner in which they have supported and seconded in every way his efforts to uphold the good name of a Regiment whose Record is Second to None. Without for one moment wishing any comparison he must mention the able assistance he has received from Captain and Adjt. Hessey, Captain, and 2nd Lieut. Kenny and Sgt. Major Martin who in the thorough performance of their duties connected with respective appointments have been most indefatigable and rendered most efficient services. During 25 years service he has had some experience of many Regt. English, Irish and Scotch both on and off service but he unhesitatingly says that he has never seen men face difficulties or discomforts as he has in this Regt. he has had the honour to Command. In conclusion he feels assured that the cordial support he has received will be continued and that on his return he will find that if occasions arise further Laurels will have been gained and the Regts. prestige, if possible, increased.

Let every man remember from the moment he joins the Regt. whether on Service or off that by his individual conduct he can raise or lower its Credit. Every man should consider that the Honour and Repututation of his Regt. should be his first care.

23rd Mar.

All hands had to turn out at 1 a.m. to man the trenches, owing to heavy firing being heard at Klein Oliphants.

3rd Apr.

We heard a loud explosion about 2 miles up the Line caused by the Boers blowing up a train. The Cavalry stationed here were immediately sent out to guard the train if necessary & rifle shots having been heard afterwards, we also had to go out. We had gone about half way when we had to return again, as it got too dark. A construction train went up the Line with some Kaffirs to repair the Line.

5th Apr.

"Good Friday." Twenty men of this Coy. & a party from Head Qtr. proceeded to where the line was damaged the other day & we had to guard the line until a train conveying Gen. Kitchener to Middelburg had passed safely by.

9th Apr.

Two Boers came in & surrendered to us to day about 4 p.m. A, C, & D Coys. proceeded by train to Witbank for duty there.

25th Apr.

We have been on fatigue every day. B & H Coys. were relieved off det. by the Leicesters and they had to escort a convoy to General Beatson's Column.

At this point we can resume Lieutenant D. G. Auchinleck's diary account of the campaign. He begins again by giving us a "General Account" of all that happened during the last six months. Why he chose not to record an account of the Regiments involvement during this period, especially their actions at Thorndale, we shall never know.

Lieut. D. G. Auchinleck

General Account.
From 24th October 1900 to
29th April 1901.

Stayed at Middelburg till 30th April 1901, with several small treks into the country round and one 3 week trek with Gen. Clements in the Magaliesberg Valley west of Pretoria in which we had a fight at Thorndale and a wretched spell of bad weather. At least 4 Coys. on permanent picket all the time. A very gay little place, plenty of polo, concerts etc. and an occasional dance. Posts were called "Klein Olifants," Guards Hill, Rockdale, Ermelo Rock, Carcase Hill, Uitkyk, Western Kopies, Aasvogel Kranz and Green Hill.

30th Apr. L. J. Bryant

Regimental News

The Regt. now forms part of a Mobile Column under Colonel Allenby. We fell in at 10 a.m. & marched to Groot Oliphants, 13 miles.

30th Apr. Lieut. D. G. Auchinleck

Diary of Trek with Col. Allenby's Column.

Left Middelburg, "D" "E" "F" & "G" Coys. with the whole of our Transport started 9.45 a.m. and marched to Groot Olifant's River Station arriving at 3.30 p.m. The 18th Hussars fired on our Advd. Guard at Ceitkyk[Uitkyk]. Managed to get 3 chickens and 5 eggs.

1st May.

Started at 8.30 a.m. arriving at Witbank 11 a.m. Spent rest of the day fixing up Transport things. Found camped here Scots Greys, Carbineers, "O" Battery R. H. A. [Royal Horse Artillery] (4), Elswick Battery (4 guns) and 5" gun.

2nd May.

Remained at Witbank, wrote to Mother, the worst letter I ever wrote, everybody hard at it equipping.

3rd May.

Peter K. R. R. [King's Royal Rifles] told us this morning that we start to-morrow and probably go north. Mine blown up last night about 3 or 4 miles from here (Landor Mine).

4th May. L. J. Bryant

We started out on a reconnaissance to day & marched to Leeuwpoort, (9 miles). We are acting in conjunction with Plumer & Beaston's Columns.

4th May. Lieut. D. G. Auchinleck

Started off 6.30 a.m. Had a fearful time with the Transport, was four miles behind rear guard with one wagon all day. Our Transport is absolutely useless. Did not get into our camp with the last wagon till 6 p.m. Camp called Leeuwpoort.

5th May. L. J. Bryant

Marched to Blackwoods Camp, Kranspoort (15 miles)

5th May. Lieut. D. G. Auchinleck

Started 6 a.m. Very long march across the veldt, no road and thank goodness only one drift, arrived at place where we halted for 2 hours and Best rode over from Beatson to see us. We then marched on four miles and camped at Kranspoort the same place we camped when we went out with Campbell in December 1900.

6th May.

Started 6.30 a.m. and marched four miles and camped in a very nice camp called Zaaihoek. Bad drift just near camp. Cavalry out all day scouring kloofs capturing 30 wagons, 200 cattle and 60 men, women and children. Corp. in Scots Greys killed. Had a tremendous lot of stuff handed over to us from Beaston.

8th May.

Halted to-day. Traill abd Smythe drove into Groot Oliphants in cape cast to go to Pretoria and M. Burg respectively for stores etc. Went over to Boer laager with Smythe. Got 3 chickens, 3 ducks and 2 buckets of potatoes.

9th May.

Started 6.30 a.m. and marched into Groot Olifants River Station about 10 miles but an easy march. Draft 194 strong and eight officers arrived from Witbank after lunch. Davy, Ernest, Lexy Stewart, Dunbar, Young Harris and Manders.

16th May.

Started 6.30 a.m. and marched to Kromdraai halting from 11 to 1 p.m., 20 miles splendid going for Transport but a very trying march for the men as we did not get into camp till 5.30 p.m. Plumer's camp in sight 3 miles to the west. A little scrapping on the flanks and rear. B. supposed to have trekked to Bethel with his commandos.

18th May. L. J. Bryant

Marched to Nooitgedacht, (20 miles). We came in contact with a party of Boers & gave chase to them, but they got away. Our casualties were 2 men wounded both belonging to our Cavalry.

18th May. Lieut. D. G. Auchinleck

Started 6.30 a.m. After having marched 7 miles a squadron of Carbineers on our left flank signalled in and said Boers were in sight, so we turned sharp to our left. The guns gave them a very hot time for a bit and the scrap lasted about 2 hours. We had a sergt. And 1 man wounded (Carbineers). We picked up a dead Boer and 5 more were accounted for. Marched on – camped at Nooitgedacht. The march was about 15 miles. Some companies must have done 20.

19th May. L. J. Bryant

Marched to Bloumdal, (18 miles). Our CO told us that Col. Allenby was very pleased with our marching yesterday & he hoped we would always march as well. A young officer of ours (he came up with the last draft) strayed away beyond the Outpost last night & was taken prisoner by the Boers. They let him go this morning, after taking his watch & whistle off him, he had left his straps etc. behind him or they would have had them too.

19th May. Lieut. D. G. Auchinleck
Started 6.30 a.m., a little sniping early in the day. Marched 12 miles and camped at Bloumdal.

20th May. L. J. Bryant
Marched 10 miles & arrived at Springs. We brought in a great quantity of live stock, which we had captured during the last 6 days, & we also brought in 7 Boer prisoners & a lot of Boer families with us as well.

21st May. Lieut. D. G. Auchinleck
Went off to Johannesburg at 10.30 a.m. with Stewart, Martineau and Smythe arriving there about 1.25 p.m. Had an excellent lunch at Heath's Hotel. Had a look around the town all afternoon. Went to the Rand Club and had tea, and a game of billiards with Martineau. Ordered a special dinner at the Café Royal and it turned out most excellent. 4 kinds of Hors d'oeuvres, soup, mayonnaise of salmon, Fillets of Beef and fried potatoes, roast chicken, savoury omelette. After dinner went to the skating rink and then to bed.

22nd May.
Shopped all morning. Started back 12.50 from Johannesburg arriving at Springs in time for tea. Quite a warm night comparatively, papers and parcels in. New camera arrived from Bremton and 3 mufflers from A.M.R.

24th May. L. J. Bryant
Marched to Witklip, 20 miles.

24th May. Lieut. D. G. Auchinleck
Started 6.30 a.m. and did a long tiring march (in perfect chaos) of 19 miles to Witklip. All very tired. Col. Hippsley in command.

25th May. L. J. Bryant
Marched to Leeuwfontein 17 miles. The following were captured by the Carabini on Strehla, 8 prisoners, 1 Colt Gun & Carriage, complete with 1000 rds. of ammunition, 4 ox wagons, 4 mule wagons, 40 mules, 600 cattle, 500 sheep, 16 rifles & dynamite etc.

25th May. Lieut. D. G. Auchinleck
Started 6.30 a.m. Marched 15 miles to Leeuwfontein with a halt of an hour and a half. Big grass fire as we got into camp but luckily the wind changed in a marvellous way just as the fire got to camp. Good day for Transport except just at the end when we broke 2 wagon

poles. Carabineers captured 700 beautiful trek oxen, 600 sheep, 8 wagons 8 Drivers, a Kaffir and a colt gun complete.

26ᵗʰ May. L. J. Bryant

Marched to Hartebeestefontein, 16 miles. "H" Coy. found 240 rds. of s. arm ammunition buried in the ground, whilst they were on Outpost.

26ᵗʰ May. Lieut. D. G. Auchinleck

Started 6.30 a.m. Marched 16 miles to Hartebeestefontein. Bad day with F Coy. wagon, nearly had to abandon it. Halted for 1½ hours at Blestokfontein. A little sniping in rear.

28ᵗʰ May. L. J. Bryant

Marched 12 miles & camped to the north end of Vriefontein. One of the Scots Greys was badly injured by his horse rolling on him.

29ᵗʰ May.

A party of Boers fired into our Camp at 3.30 a.m. whilst we were asleep, but did no harm. We marched to Weltevreden, (10 miles). 3 Kaffirs were brought into Camp by our Outposts.

29ᵗʰ May. Lieut. D. G. Auchinleck

Started 7 a.m. Marched 10 miles to Weltevreden, got into camp at 12 noon. Boers fired a few shots into camp last night.

30ᵗʰ May. L. J. Bryant

Marched to Straffontein, 9 miles. We captured another lot of live stock, also 3 prisoners.

31ˢᵗ May.

Marched 7 miles & camped at Van Dyks Put. Another prisoner was brought into Camp to day.

4ᵗʰ June.

The Battalion marched to Bronkhorst Spruit Station, 8 miles & camped there. "E" Coy. then proceeded by rail to Pretoria, H Coy. following later on. D Coy. and the others of E Coy. who were on det. at Howard's Mine rejoined us to day at Pretoria. The remainder of the Column proceeds to Pretoria by road.

4ᵗʰ June. Lieut. D. G. Auchinleck

Column marched off again S.W. We (The Regiment) marched 8 miles to Bronkhorstspruit Station with orders to entrain there for Pretoria. "E and "F" Coys. went off in afternoon and Crawford, Jeffcoat, Meldon and De la C. Ray passed thro' with "D" Coy. from Wetbank. Total Bag for trek from Springs May 24ᵗʰ to Wilgerivier June 3ʳᵈ – Prisoners 12, Rifles 20, Sheep 19,850, Mealies 18.56 lbs. Surrenders 4, S.A.A. 2.500 Wagons taken. 21 Men, Women 15,000 and children 312, Horses 4, destroyed 11, wheat 3 sacks. Colt

Machine gun with mules, 38 carts taken, 4 donkeys 17 c. complete. Cattle 1038, destroyed 2.

5th June. L. J. Bryant

The remainder of the Bn. joined us here at Starlight Camp, at Pretoria to day.

5th June. Lieut. D. G. Auchinleck

Spent the whole day entertaining the Transport. Johnston and I got to Pretoria after 9 p.m. Had supper at the Grand Hotel. Camp at Arcadia, found my kit had not been brought up so had to walk back and sleep at Grand Hotel.

11th June.

Started 7.30 a.m. Marched about 12 miles to Scheerpoort. A large number of Boers reported to be in front of us. Shelled Damhoek farm and Kloof, a bridge and 2 drifts to cross. Got into connection with Ghazi Hamilton.

12th June. L. J. Bryant

Marched to Hekpoort, 15 miles. We had free gymnastics on the march, jumping over Spruits etc. Half of the Convoy got stuck in a Spruit & did not come in until all hours.

12th June. Lieut. D. G. Auchinleck

Started 9 a.m. Marched about 12 miles to Hekpoort, a terrible day for Transport, did not get into camp till 9 p.m., 6 drifts, 2 bridges and several spruits to cross.

14th June. L. J. Bryant

C, D & F Coys. proceeded with a force to Breedts Nek at 6 a.m., as a force of Boers were reported to be entrenched there. G Coy. also went with the above force later on. Our Artillery shelled the position for about an hour & then our Artillery advanced a little to draw the enemy's fire & afterwards climbed the hill & the Boers retired. The force returned to Camp again about 5.30 p.m. There were no casualties on our side.

14th June. Lieut. D. G. Auchinleck

All the cavalry and guns and 3 Coys. of ours went off at 6 a.m. to try to get Maj. Garrett and 200 of the Carbineers thro' Breedts Nek which is supposed to be held by Boers. D Coy. went off to help Hamilton in Doornkop Valley. The other 4 Coys. were left to guard the camp. The force cleared Breedts Nek alright but having done so, found that Maj. Garrett etc. could not be spared for the convoy going to Rustenburg, so the shelling was useless. No casualty on our side. D Coy amused themselves by lining the ridge while Hamilton's cavalry cleared the Doornkop Valley. They got back to camp about 4.30, 14 miles to march.

15th June.

Started 7 a.m. Rather chaos at the beginning as no one knew the right road. Marched about 6 miles to Zandfontein. Very bad grass fires in camp. Very nearly burnt out at one time.

20th June. L. J. Bryant

A & H Coys. returned to Camp to day, & D & E Coys went out clearing farms & returned to Camp at 5 p.m. We were on half rations today.

21st June.

The Carabiniers & half of the Scots Greys, with Guns, went out at 2 a.m. to surprise a Boer Laager. The result of the operations were:- 2 Boers wounded, 3 taken prisoner, captured 400 cattle, 1000 sheep & goats 20 donkeys and mules, 4 horses & 16 wagons destroyed or captured. The remainder of the Column marched to Groenfontein, (6 miles) & the above forces joined us here, during the evening.

21st June. Lieut. D. G. Auchinleck

Cavalry went off on their own at 2 a.m. We marched at 6 a.m., 7 miles to a place called Groenfontein where the cavalry joined us in the evening having been very successful, wounding 2 Boers, taking 3 prisoners, destroying 16 wagons and capturing 400 cattle, 1000 sheep and goats. 2 Scots Greys wounded on picket.

22nd June.

Started 7 a.m. Delayed till 8.30 a.m. as Maj. Russell had not come in with the wounded, the Scots Greys. 3 Boers surrendered to E Coy. at daybreak. Marched 13 miles, saw any amount of game on the left flank. Camp is called Klipkrans.

25th June. L. J. Bryant

Marched to Brakspruit, 10 miles. A Kaffir Scout belonging to another Column was coming in to Col. Allenby with dispatches early this morning, when our Outposts opened fire on him & killed him, by accident.

27th June.

The Camp Stood. A, B. C. & H Coys. proceeded to Klerksdorp early this morning for supplies. G. Coy. went half way there & escorted one days provisions back here. A party of Boers estimated at 500 strong were reported to be in a Laager amongst some Kopjes, a short distance away. It was decided to attack them at daybreak. Our C.O. told us that Hamilton's Column were to attack them on the left, Allenby's on the right, & another Column were to attack them in the

Rear. The idea was that the Cavalry were to close in & drive them from their position, so to escape being captured they would have to cross over three drifts which would be held by our Regt. This was supposed to be their only way of escape open to them & as we have to go out to take possession of the drifts it is thought that we will make a good capture. We moved out from Camp at 9 p.m. (D. E. & F. Coys.) & took possession of the drifts, 6 miles off, about 11.30 p.m. without opposition. A. B. C. & H Coys. moved out from Klerksdorp during the night & took possession of the drift there. Our Cavalry took possession of the 3rd drift. G. Coy. were left behind on Outpost to look after the Camp.

27th June. Lieut. D. G. Auchinleck

Column halted, H, A, B, & C went into Klerksdorp with supply wagons, G Coy. went over to Ghazi. Hamilton's column to get one day's supply. A great scheme is on foot but we know not what it is.

28th June. L. J. Bryant

The attack on the Boer Laager took place early this morning, but did not turn out as we expected as the greater part of the Boers got away in another direction. We captured 13 Boers, including a Commandant & also 2000 head of cattle. We returned to Camp again during the afternoon. Our Cavalry captured 4 more Boers this morning.

A. B. C. & H. Coys returned to Keerksdorp again.

28th June. Lieut. D. G. Auchinleck

Have found out last night at 9 p.m. D, E & F Coys. were paraded and we marched to hold Good Drift. We were all on picket all night and the sweep of the cavalry began in the morning. Allenby, Hamilton & Weston^{3} [Columns], results not very good. Captured 13 Boers including one Comdt. and some cattle and sheep. Marched back to camp in the afternoon and went on picket.

2nd July. L. J. Bryant

Marched to Keipplats [Klipplaats] drift, 12 miles. We got up at 6 a.m. but did not move off till 11.15 a.m. Our Cavalry went out after a force of Boers at 1 a.m. this morning & were out all day.

2nd July. Lieut. D. G. Auchinleck

Started 11.15 a.m. Marched 13 miles to Klippat [Klipplaats] Drift. Carbineers went out last night, have not yet returned.

3rd July. L. J. Bryant

The Column arrived at Ventersdorp to day, 9 miles. In the operations yesterday our Cavalry killed 2 Boers, wounded several & captured 11 Boers, 1200 head of cattle & several head of sheep.

4th July.

Marched to Modderfontein, 8 miles. A party of Boers were reported to be in a laager amongst some kopjes about 12 miles away & it was decided to make a night attack on them & surprise them. E. H. & G. coys were detailed for this duty & our orders were to charge the position at the point of the bayonet, & not to fire a shot. Our Cavalry went out early to hold a drift & we fell in a 8 p.m. & moved off. We arrived at the place at 4 a.m. in the morning but the Boers had got wind of the affair coming off & had shifted their laager during the night. We saw a few of their fires which were still smouldering.

5th July.

We marched to Varkens Kraal at 8 a.m. & arrived there at 11 a.m. marching 8 miles. The remainder of the Column arrived at 1 p.m., marching 12 miles.

5th July. Lieut. D. G. Auchinleck

E, F & G Coys. went out last night at 8 p.m. to try to capture some Boers. Unsuccessful, as Boers left at 7 p.m. They found fires alight etc. Column marched at 6 a.m., 14 miles to Varkenskraal where companies rejoined us. Camp is on a beautiful river (Mooi River).

6th July. L. J. Bryant

Marched to Holfontein, 18 miles.

7th July.

Marched to Vlakplaats, 16 miles.

7th July. Lieut. D. G. Auchinleck

Started 7 a.m. Marched 12 miles to Vlakplaats arriving about noon. Got 3 weeks sick leave and rode on to Krugerdorp about 9 miles with Jeffcoat and Bowen and just caught the train to Johannesburg arriving there about 6.30 p.m. with Bowen who is going to Pretoria. Hot bath and bed early.

8th July. L. J. Bryant

The Camp Stood. H. Coy. proceeded to Krugersdorp early this morning for some provisions. They also escorted 17 prisoners & some Boer families to Krugersdorp. They rode on wagons to K'dorp.

9th July.

The Camp Stood. H. Coy. returned from Krugersdorp with provisions to day. 200 of our Cavalry, with Guns, went out on Special Service at 12 m.n.

10th July.

The remainder of the Column got up at 2.30 a.m. & moved off at 4.a.m. We joined the force that left last night at 10.30 a.m. after marching 12 miles. Our Cavalry captured 9 Boers, in their operations, & C. Coy found 4 more hiding amongst some bushes. A few horses, cattle & sheep were also captured by the Column. We camped at Zeekoehock.

12th July.

The Camp Stood. B & H Coys, with a mixed force, went out on a reconnaissance at 7 a.m. and returned to Camp again at 1 p.m. The above force came across a party of Boers estimated about 250 strong, with wagons, they were strongly entrenched amongst some Kopjes not far from our Camp. Our Artillery were shelling the position all morning & a loud explosion was heard & it was afterwards rumoured that a party of 40 Boers were trying to get a wagon full of ammunition out of danger when one of the shells fired by our Artillery burst right in the wagon & exploded the ammunition & killed 30 Boers. One of the Carabiniers was killed in the above operations. The force was too weak to attack the Boers & returned to Camp.

13th July.

Marched towards Dwarsvlei, 8 miles, & arrived at our camping place at 4 p.m. after marching over very rough ground. One of our chaps found some dynamite in a farmhouse, which was afterwards destroyed.

13th July. Lieut. D. G. Auchinleck

Durban Winter Races. Very jolly day, won some money, about £50 odd. Very good racing.

15th July.

Arrived at Ladysmith 5 a.m. Missed the post cart, drove out to Upper Tugela, 36 miles, in cape cast arriving about 3 p.m. Edie and Gervans look just the same as ever. Very nice wee house, looking forward to an enjoyable leave.

15th July to 26th Aug.

Spent a most enjoyable time in "Erin" but could not get thoroughly rid of dysentery. I could not take any very violent exercise but went for drives etc. and read and wrote a great deal. Gervans wanted me to go home and I went in to consult Maj. Burnside, S. M. O. Ladysmith who advised me the same, so my case was sent to P. M. O. Natal for a decision. Received orders to proceed to convalescent camp, Howick.

16th July. L. J. Bryant

Marched to Kromdraai, 5 miles. The 13 prisoners captured the other day were sent into Krugersdorp this morning & our Cavalry captured 5 more Boers. We also found a box full up with bars of gold which was in a farmhouse, & also a box of ammunition.

18th July.

The Camp Stood. We sent another convoy into Krugersdorp to day, for more provisions. Our Cavalry escorted it & captured 5 more prisoners. One man of "B" Coy. was killed to day at Sterkfontein by the Boers.

19th July.

The Column marched to Vlakplaats (15 miles) this morning via Sterkfontein. A. B. & H Coys. rejoined the Column when we arrived at Sterkfontein.

25th July.

The Camp Stood. A party of ten men from each Coy. went out this morning as a detached post, one man was killed by them. Two Squadrons of the Carbs. & Greys, with Guns, went out to bring in some Boer families. The Boers were sniping into our Camp all day, from the Magaliesberg Ranges, but did no harm.

26th July.

Marched to Doornkloof, 7 miles. We set a trap for the Boers by sending out a part of the Carbs. early this morning & they hid in a farm house. The remainder of the Column then moved off about 4 hours later & as usual a party of Boers came out of their hiding places to snipe at us, the consequence was they got between our Rear Guard & the force hiding in the farm house & so got between two fires. The result was that 2 Boers were killed, 1 wounded & 4 captured. There were no casualties on our side.

30th July.

Marched to Boschfontein, 8 miles.

5th Aug.

The Column marched to Witfontein, 6 miles via Thorndale. Our Segt. Major left the Bn. (Time Expired) for England, the following appeared in our Bn. Orders:- The C.O. wishes it placed on record the regret he feels at the departure of S. M. Martin, for England, at the expiration of his 27 years honourable & faithful service, a regret he knows is shared by all Ranks of the Battn. Sergt. Major Martin has always shown the highest attributes of a good soldier & it is impossible to overestimate what the Bn. owes to him. He hopes to rejoin the Bn. for a year after a well earned holiday at home, but, if not, he carries with him the honour & respect of all ranks & every good wishes for his future welfare.

6th Aug.

D Coy with a force of Cavalry escorted a Convoy through Zeebochock [Zeekoehoek] Pass at 6 a.m. this morning. They took the

Convoy to Krugersdorp for more provisions. The remainder of the Column, marched to Doornkloof, 4 miles, at 10 a.m. A party of Boers are reported to be holding Breedts Nek.

7th Aug.

E. G. & H. Coys. with 400 Cavalry & all the Guns left Camp this morning at 6 a.m. to take possession of Breedts Nek. Col. Kekewichs[4] Column is also operating against Breedts Nek from Krom River north of the Nek, & Gen. Bartons Column is operating against Nooitgedacht, and possibly Groblaars Pass, at the same time. The Boers heard of the movement of our troops & retired last night. The above mentioned forces returned to Camp this afternoon.

8th Aug.

The Column went to Hekpoort, 8 miles. This morning a force of our Cavalry then went out with all the Guns to operate against Damhoek Pass, which the Boers are holding.

9th Aug.

C. E. G. & H. Coys. with a force left Camp at 6 a.m. to take possession of Damhock Pass. The remainder of the Column shifted Camp to Yeomanry Hill, during the day, 6 miles. F. Coy. was sent out early this morning to hold Zeekoehoek Pass whilst the Convoy passed through. D Coy. with the Convoy & F. Coy arrived here during the evening. They were fired on by some Boers & one man of the R. A. was killed. H. Coy. & the Cavalry returned from Damhock this evening about 6 p.m. C. E. & G. Coys. are left at the pass to hold it all night.

10th Aug.

B Coy. & a force of Cavalry went out on a reconnaissance early this morning. The remainder of the Column shifted Camp to Hartebeestefontein near Damhock Pass at 1 p.m., 4 miles.

11th Aug.

A & B Coys. left Camp early this morning to scour the Magaliesburg Ranges of hills from Damhock Pass to Breedts Nek. They will be out 4 days. D. F. & H. Coys. relieved C. E. & G. Coys off the hills at Damhoek Pass. Our Regt. have to hold the hills until further orders.

14th Aug.

A.& B. Coys. rejoined the Bn. to day, as did the men of E. Coy. who were out on Convoy duty. A force of Cavalry left Camp early this morning.

16th Aug.

G Coy proceeded to Nooigedacht early this morning to hold the pass there. They returned to Camp at 6 p.m. The following appeared in Bn. Orders:- Extract from Brigade Orders.

The captures of the Column for the week ending this evening includes:- 4 Boers killed, 8 wounded, 18 prisoners, 28 rifles, 2,500 rounds small arm ammunition & 53 wagons etc. Whilst congratulating all Ranks, on the excellent work, the C. O. Column deeply deplores the loss of the gallant officer of the Carabiniers & the Guides Mc Sweeney, who fell in Action on Wednesday, whilst doing such splendid work. Pte. R. Arnold & Lieut. F. E. Till, were killed. The remaining five wounded.

19th Aug.

Marched to Zilikats (Nitrals) Nek, 4 miles. We fell in again at 10 p.m. & done a night march to Mamagelies Kraal.

20th Aug.

We arrived at Mamagelies Kraals at 12.30 p.m. having been on the march since 10 p.m. last night. We marched about 26 miles altogether. We captured 1 Boer & 2 Kaffirs, also some wagons.

22nd Aug.

Marched to Zand Drift, 14 miles. Twenty eight (28) Boers including a Commandant surrendered to our Column today.

25rd Aug.

Marched to Kaffirs Kraals, 16 miles

27th Aug.

Marched to Zwartz-Kopjes, 20 miles.

28th Aug.

Marched to Roode Kopjes, 7 miles.

29th Aug.

Marched to Rustenburg, 11 miles.

29th Aug. Lieut. D. G. Auchinleck

Presented myself to M. O. i/c C. Camp. Col. Rose by name but apparently took no interest in the case so I don't know what is going to happen. Absolutely nothing to do here and it is miserably uncomfortable. Got a letter from Inkson and wrote to him, Edie, S. E. A. and Proprietor Crown Hotel. Watched a cricket match and tennis for a short time in the afternoon.

31st Aug. L. J. Bryant

Marched to Bosch-hock [Boschhoek], 17 miles.

2nd Sep.

Marched to Kaffir Kraals, 4 miles. The following appeared in Bn. Orders, being an extract from Bge. Orders:- In accordance with attached message (Copy below) from Gen. Featherstone, the Column will move tomorrow, as ordered, all starting at 6 a.m.

Carabiniers from Bulhoek, via Ebenezer Waterval to Koedolsfontein, remainder of Column as to day from present position via Twee River to Koldalsfontein; crossing Selous River by the drift in rear of Camp.

Message to Colonel Allenby.

All the Boers seen to day, seem to be concentrated at Roodeval, therefore, unless they break through during the night, all Columns must start when it is light tomorrow, & converge on that place. Hamilton will move by Waterfall & Spitz Kop, Hickey by Kosterfontein, Allenby by Waterval & Koldalsfontein & Kerewich by Selous Kraal & Doornlaagte. Should enemy have broken through during night, Lord Methuen has undertaken pursuit, in latter case, I will issue orders what to do, as soon as possible.

Sgd. Featherstone, General.

3rd Sept.

We carried out last nights instructions & marched to Koldalsfontein, 18 miles, but the Boers, who were under De la Ray & Kemp, got away during the night. The Carabiniers had one man killed & 2 wounded last night. D. F. & H. Coys rejoined the Column again to day, they have been trekking with Kerewick's Column, this last week.

4th Sept.

The Camp Stood. D. & H. Coys with a force went on a reconnaissance to day, & the Cavalry captured 5 Boers, wounded 1, & wounded a woman accidentally.

8th Sept.

Marched to Boschfontein (Wolhuters Kop), 13 miles.

9th Sept.

Marched to Zandfontein, 7 miles.

10th Sept.

Marched to Black water Spruit, 11 miles.

11th Sept.

Marched to Pretoria, & camped at Inaggi Camp near Proclamation Hill, 13 miles.

12 Sept.

We are now taken off the Mobile column & now form part of the Garrison of Pretoria.

13th Sept.

The following appeared in Bn. Orders:- it is notified for Information that the Battalion has trekked 942 miles since April 30th last. This is from Camp to Camp, & does not count any trips made by Coys. on Convoy duty etc.

16th Sept. Lieut. D. G. Auchinleck

Left for Ladysmith in command of 150 men as escort to Boer prisoners.

17th Sept. L. J. Bryant

The following appeared in Bn. Orders. Viz :- The Bn. takes over the posts of the 1st Yorkshire Regt. tomorrow. Breakfast 5.30 a.m., pack wagons 6 a.m. marching off when ready. A Coy finds 2 Officer & 50 men to proceed to Commando Nek, & one Officer, 3 N.C.Os. & 18 men to proceed to Silverton. B Coy. takes over the post at Koedoespoort & East Redoubt, C. & D. Coys. takes over guarding Boer prisoners, & Blockhouses up to Veterinary Field Hospital. E. Coy takes over posts at Yeomanry Hill. F. G. & H. Coys will be at Head Qtrs at Johnston's Redoubt.

17th Sept. Lieut. D. G. Auchinleck

5.30 a.m. Started with 450 prisoners for Durban, arriving 12 noon.

23rd Sept.

Marked fit and left for Durban to store kit en route for Regiment.

28th Sept.

Got to Pretoria at 3.30 p.m. Found Regt. scattered all over the town, 43 posts. Headquarters at Johnston Redoubt.

29th Sept.

Went down to town with Best to buy clothes. Rode round with Ricardo in the afternoon to see Inkson, Inkson out.

30th Sept.

Inkson and Wilson came to lunch. Inkson, Ricardo and Case say I am to go home. Anyhow I go into hospital tomorrow with a view to my having a board.

1st Oct.

Came into no. 19 General Hospital Pretoria. Everything awfully comfortable and everybody very kind. Looked after by Dr. Hunt, civil surgeon, Sister McCarthy by day and Sister Cowley by night. Maj. Davis in command.

2nd Oct.

Have not got to stay in bed, thank goodness. Hunt examined me very carefully to day and said I was very anaemic. Jeffcoat came to see me in the afternoon.

5th Oct.

Stayed in bed for breakfast as to make the day a bit shorter. Sisters had an "at home" in the afternoon and the band of the Gordons played. Burke turned up to call on me and Davy, Stewart and Best came down to see the "at home".

10th Oct.

Pouring with rain. My Board held to day.

12th Oct.

Davy, Manders and Kenny came to the Hospital to say Good-bye. Started off in an ambulance about 4 p.m. to go on the 'Princess Christian' at Howitzer siding. Held quite a levee as Cox, Davy, Ricardo, Best, Miller, Ridings and Crawford, Inkson and Tyndale were there to see me off and all were full of energy. Slept on train.

13th Oct.

Started off 6 a.m. only one other officer, Lt. Wyllie of the K.F.S. on the train. Very comfortable, bed with spring mattresses etc. Arrived Elandsfontein at 8 a.m. where Rimington and Clarke, 2 more officers joined us. Meals good. Very comfortable on the train. Got to Volkstrust at 7.30, bed 9.

14th Oct.

Got to Glencoe at 4.30 a.m. Started at 8 a.m. Got to Mooi River about 3.30 p.m. amd detrained and went over to the Hospital. Very cold place. Expect to be here upwards of a week.

15th Oct.

Up at 8 a.m. Bowen of the Imperial Yeomanry is the only other officer here in the Mess. Col. Lucas is P. M. O. Lt. Col. Hackett i/c of Officers Ward. Looked after by Sister Todd by day and Sister Burton by night. Received wire from Edie saying she could not stay with me as she had accepted an invitation to the Burnsides. Rather provoking.

21st Oct.

Received letters from Edie and Gervais, 3 days late. Much surprised by Edie turning up at 42 Hospital after lunch. She had sent a wire but I had never received it. Spent a ripping afternoon. Walked up to the top of the big hill and we sat down and talked. Had to fly for our lives from a thunderstorm, which we just escaped. Went up after dinner and sat and chatted for a couple of hours. Am afraid Edie is rather uncomfortable at the Hotel.

22nd Oct.

Spent the whole morning talking. Too cold to go out. Saw Edie off by 1 p.m. train, as she had to get back to the Burnsides. Played Poker in the afternoon.

At this point Lieutenant Auchinleck's diary comes to a close. Never one to record the day by day movements of the Regiment other than when it applied to himself, he does not record when he left for home nor does he record any of the events relating to his passage.

25th Oct. L. J. Bryant

A draft of 54 men joined the Bn. to day.

6th Nov.

Nothing unusual occurred. One Coy. relieves another Coy. off det. at their several places now & again, just for a change of scene etc. We played a Football Match against No. 7 Gen. Hospital & beat them by 3 goals to 0. They beat us hollow at cricket.

9th Nov.

King's Birthday. Sports were held in the town to day to celebrate the King's Birthday. There were 21 events all together, one being a Tug of War. The following sent in teams, Engineers, Transport, Cameron Highlanders, Artillery, Johannesburg Police & we sent in a team. We had to pull against the Engineers in the first heat, & we beat them twice. The Jo'burg Police & The Cameron Highlanders also won their heats. Lots were drawn as to who should enter for the Final & the Camerons entered for it by drawing a Bge. Our team & the Police then pulled in the semi-final. The first pull was stubbornly contested, our team were within an ace of winning, but got tired & were themselves beaten, the Police also beat us in the 2nd pull & so entered the Final. After an hours rest, the Police & the Camerons opposed each other in the Final Round, & after a good deal of excitement the Camerons won by 2 pulls to one.

11th Nov.

Our Regt. having been selected to find the Body Guard for Lord Kitchener, H. Coy. & part of other Coys. were picked out for the duty & left Camp this morning relieving the Gordon Highlanders off that duty. G. Coy. went on detachment to Ouderstepoort near Waterval.

29th Nov.

I proceeded to Ouderstepoort to do duty with G. Coy. who are in Blockhouses there.

25th Dec.

Xmas Day. We got 1 pint of beer, 1 lb. of Xmas pudding & a small parcel of presents given to us to day by the Field Force Canteen.

26th Dec.

We were relieved off Det. to day at 8 a.m. by the Gordon Highlanders & we proceeded to Pretoria by rail about 4 p.m. & joined B. & F. Coys. at the Railway Station. The 3 Coys. then got into the train to proceed to Kroonstaad, Orange River Colony. We slept in the carriages all night at the Station. The remainder of the Bn. left Pretoria a few days ago.

<u>Orange River Colony</u>

27th Dec.

We left Pretoria at 3.45 a.m. & arrived at Kroonstaad at 9.45 p.m. & slept on the platform all night.

28th Dec.

We rose at 3.30 a.m. & then went on fatigue unloading the luggage off the train. We then had our Breakfast & then marched about 2 miles from the Station & pitched our Camp for the day. A line of blockhouses are being built from Kroonstaad to Harrismith, our other 4 Coys. are building some about 50 miles away, & as they are finished, so they are taken over by an N.C.O. & ten men.

29th Dec.

We fell in about 8 a.m. & marched 12 miles towards Lindley to join our other half Battalion.

30th Dec.

Marched 14 miles today.

31st Dec.

Marched 7 miles. Rose at 3.30 a.m. & marched at 5 a.m.

Chapter Eight

1902
Orange River Colony

New Year's Day 1902 found the Royal Inniskilling Fusiliers occupying a series of blockhouses whilst still engaged in the construction of others. As each blockhouse was completed a party, consisting of one NCO and ten ORs, was left to man it whilst the Battalion moved on extending the line. The number of blockhouses eventually constructed by the Inniskillings numbered 128, out of which members of the Regiment eventually manned seventy-six.

The eventual length of the blockhouses manned by the Inniskillings was 20.31 miles. There were two trenches, the length of the first, which measured 5 feet by 4 feet, was 9.62 miles, whilst the second, 3 feet by 5 feet, spanned 12.38 miles. The entanglements west of the fence consisted of a series of barbed wire and stakes measuring 14.06 miles, whilst a corresponding entanglement on the eastern side measured 14.45 miles.

Though this vast network of blockhouses, devised by Lord Kitchener, was intended to wear down and hamper the movement of the Boer commandos, it also had the unfortunate effect of draining the army of valuable troops. The vast numbers needed to man these fortifications were numbers which the army could ill afford. In the case of the Royal Inniskilling Fusiliers, manning seventy-six blockhouses meant in effect taking 836 valuable troops more or less out of the line. Detailed to man these fortifications, the Battalion occupied the blockhouses, after construction, throughout the peace negotiations right up until peace was declared on 31 May, at which time orders were issued to dismantle the line.

As the Inniskillings set about dismantling their section of the line, further orders were received for the Battalion to concentrate at Kroonstad in preparation to entrain for De Aar in Cape Colony. On their arrival they established a temporary camp before proceeding, at the end of July, by rail once more to Naauwpoort, Cape Colony.

The Battalion was engaged upon a variety of duties in and around Naauwpoort until mid-October at which point it marched for Middleburg which was to prove its last assignment in South Africa before returning home. However, not everyone embarked upon the SS *Aurania* on 17 January 1903 bound for Queenstown. A draft of 247 NCOs and ORs were sent to join the 2nd Battalion stationed at Mafeking. Those who did return on the SS *Aurania* numbered fourteen officers, thirty-eight sergeants and 405 rank and file.

1st Jan. L. J. Bryant

New Years Day. We marched to Zuggofontein [Quaggafontein] which is three miles from Lindley & joined our Head Quarter party. We marched 15 miles to day. A. C. D. & E. Coys. are now in blockhouses. We were on fatigue building a Fort from 5.30 p.m. until 7 p.m.

6th Jan.

We have finished the Fort. I got transferred from E. Coy. to G. Coy for duty.

11th Jan.

We were on fatigue daily building Blockhouses. A party of 20 men have to build 1 Blockhouse per day & a man gets 1/- for every B'house he helps to build. B. & F. Coys. are now in B'houses.

If the blockhouses were to be properly protected then it was essential certain key areas in the surrounding countryside should be identified, cleared if necessary, and occupied. The 1st Battalion the Royal Inniskillings Fusiliers joined De Lisle's[1] force in its pursuit of De Wet, who having concentrated his force at Winterhoek was pursued through Slangfontein, half-way between Lindley and Heilbron and driven east to Vecht Kop and Boschkopjes by General Elliot's[2] Column. De Lisle's task was to occupy Kaffir Kop, a one- time favourite haunt of De Wet, and thus safeguard the blockhouse line from Lindley to Bethlehem which would be occupied by the Inniskillings.

12th Jan. L. J. Bryant

G. & H. Coys. left Lindley this morning to proceed to Kaffir Kop with De Lisles Column, to fortify the Kopje, and also to build Blockhouses towards Bethlehem. We marched 20 miles & camped for the night about 3 miles off Kaffir Kop.

13th Jan.

Marched to Kaffir Kop, 3 miles & camped there.

14th Jan.

On fatigue building Blockhouses.

15th Jan.

On the same fatigue. H. Coy. & part of G. Coy. took over Blockhouses to day.

Having been captured on 10 October 1901 by the 10th Hussars the Boer Commandant Scheepers stood trial on a catalogue of charges including murder, train wrecking, arson, ill treatment of prisoners and wounded and other various assorted atrocities. The trial took place at Graaff Reinet on 18 December 1901 and though he protested he was not a bandit but a soldier the court decreed that regardless of how he defined his role nothing excused his conduct.

Though the pro Boer lobby in England, and both the German and Dutch press demanded the death penalty be put aside, Kitchener insisted it go ahead as a warning to others who in the court's opinion flaunted the rules of decency and war. His decision could have been influenced to a certain extent by a proclamation issued by the British Government in August 1901 declaring that all commandos responsible for atrocities should face the death penalty if found guilty. This decree was in direct response to a declaration by Commandant Kritzinger, in which he stated that all kaffirs giving information to the British should be executed. The death sentence on Scheepers was passed in public by Lieutenant-Colonel the Hon. A. Henniker, CB[3] and the following day Scheepers was led out at Graaff Reinet and shot. However it's somewhat ironic that when Kritzinger was tracked down on 16 December 1901 at Hanover Road and subsequently put on trial he was acquitted of any offences against the laws of war.

18th Jan. L. J. Bryant

A. B. C. D. & E. Coys. were relieved from Blockhouses & arrived here to day. F. Coy are still in Blockhouses at Lindley.

26th Jan.

A young Officer of ours & 2 men of this Coy. went out to a farm house some distance away from their Blockhouse to get some firewood & were taken for Boers by some of our Mounted Infantry, who at once opened fire on them. But luckily no one was hit.

27th Jan.

B. Coy. & the remainder of D. Coy returned to Kaffir Kop to day, they have to build Blockhouses towards Lindley & occupy them.

Throughout the construction of the blockhouse line the troops were constantly sniped upon, whilst minor skirmishes took place in and around the surrounding countryside. The line was eventually completed on 29 January 1902 and stretched from Kroonstad to Lindley, from Lindley to Bethlehem and from Bethlehem to Harrismith, a distance of approximately 150 miles. To the north the line from Heilbron through Frankfort to Vrede and Botha's Pass was completed the following week.

1st Feb. L. J. Bryant

A few snipers visited E. Coy. during the night.

2nd Feb.

After being nicely settled down, my Coy. were relieved from these Blockhouses & we had to take over other ones about 7 miles from Kaffir Kop, towards Lindley. We took over these Blockhouses from some Cavalry men who were occupying them & the Houses are only just put up, & only half completed. They are at the extreme left of our line of Blockhouses.

4th Feb.

Having learnt that the Boers were going to make an attempt to cross the Line tonight three men from each Blockhouse had to go out & dig a trench midway between each B'house. Two men & myself from our B'house volunteered for this duty & went into the trench. The Boers under Gen. Prinsloo[1] made an attempt to cross the line about 9.30 p.m. the night was very dark & everything was in their favour. They tried to cross between two of this Coys. Blockhouses, where there was a dip, but not knowing about the trenches midway between the Blockhouses they approached too near to one of the trenches & were immediately challenged by the Sentry who did not know who they were. Instead of challenging them the Sentry should have opened fire on them at once, but he did not do so. The Boers wounded the Sentry in the neck & so alarmed the men in the Blockhouses by their firing

& we at once opened fire on them & they scattered. The firing ceased at 11 p.m. for the night.

5th Feb.

We have to occupy the trenches until the 7th inst. We leave them at daybreak & reoccupy them about 7 p.m. in the night.

6th Feb.

Snipers visited us during the night but did no harm. They opened fire at 1 p.m. & finished at 3 p.m. in the night.

10th Feb.

The Boers again attempted to cross the Line here tonight. They drove a herd of cattle in front of themselves to break down the wire entanglements & also to shield themselves but they were unsuccessful in their attempt to break through. We captured 50 head of cattle early the next morning. I was not in the trench this time.

11th Feb.

A draft of 40 men joined the Bn. today. We heard this morning that Gen. Prinsloo & 30 men crossed the Line on the 4th inst. but that the remainder of his force were driven back by our fire, also that his Adjt. Schoeman was killed & 2 of his men wounded. We had no wire fence on that night between B'houses.

15th Feb.

We recd. a Wire from Lord Kitchener in which he said he hoped we would be on the alert for the next few days, as Columns co-operating with each other, start to day to drive the Boers against the Blockhouse Line.

17th Feb.

Forces of Boers were reported to be moving South West about 2 miles from this Line of Blockhouses very early this morning, but they turned out to be two of our Columns converging on Kaffir Kop.

We heard that the Boers tried to break through the Columns last night, but were repulsed with loss. The driving operations are now over & as far as it is known it was not a successful one, as only one or two Boers & some cattle were captured.

27th Feb.

"B" Coy. who occupy the Blockhouse next to us found 200 rounds of ammunition, some s. a. ammunition & 4 rifles buried in a farm house near one of the blockhouses.

7th Mar.

Another driving operation takes place to day & finishes on the 9th inst. We have occupied the trenches again until it is over. The Boers again attempted to cross the Line here, but failed to do so.

9th Mar.

The drive operations are now over as far as we are concerned, as the Boers have been driven passed our Line of Blockhouses & towards Kroonstaad.

18th Mar.

A party of Boers came within range of one of our Blockhouses but retired as soon as we opened fire on them. We wounded one Boer & killed his horse.

12th Apr.

The boers in small numbers crossed the Line once or twice where B. coy are, as the Blockhouses there are further apart than what they are here & there is a very bad dip there. We have been busy putting up a wire fencing & trip wire etc. between each Blockhouse so as to make it far harder for the Boers to try & cross, & so that they can not get wagons etc. across without giving us an alarm. We have two rifles loaded pointing down on each side of the wire, & we have a wire leading right into the roof of the B'house & a tin is attached to it, so that when it is touched it makes a noise & so gives us the alarm & all the Sentry has to do is to fire each rifle down the wire. We are going to attach the alarm wire onto the triggers of the rifles so that when the wire is tampered with it will pull the trigger & so let the rifles off. We also have to dig a trench between each Blockhouse beside the wire fence, it has to be 5 foot wide at the top, sloping down to one foot wide at the bottom, 3 foot deep, & the length varies according to the distance between each B'house. We are at work on the trench every day from 9 to 12 except Sundays.

14th Apr.

Some of the Boer Leaders are having an Interview with Lord Kitchener, with a view to ending the war.

15th Apr.

We heard that Botha, De Wet [2], De la Ray & Steyn[3] have joined the peace conference.

16th Apr.

Heard that Lord Kitchener has joined the peace conference at Klerksdorp.

17th Apr.

It is rumoured that the Boer Leaders have had terms offered to them & have got to the 21st inst. to say whether they will accept them & surrender.

21ˢᵗ Apr.

It is rumoured here that the Boer Leaders have accepted the terms offered to them at the peace conference, & have joined the field once more to tell their commandos that they have done so & they have got to the 15ᵗʰ May to tell their burghers that they have accepted the terms & to hunt up all stray men & tell them what they intend to do. There was a Total Eclipse of the Moon tonight from 7.30 to 10.30 p.m. We had to post double Sentries in case the Boers tried to break through the Line whilst it was on.

25ᵗʰ Apr.

De Wet paid a friendly visit to Kaffir Kop to day.

4ᵗʰ May.

We are still working like slaves at the trenches between blockhouses. We are only supposed to do a square yard a day each but the Officer in this Coy. makes 2 men do 3 yards between them before he lets them away, & the ground is stony.

5ᵗʰ May.

A small party of Boers crossed the Line between the last Blockhouse of this Company's line & the first one of the West Surreys.

6ᵗʰ May.

A driving operation takes place to day, the Boers are to be driven towards Kroonstaad. Altho' we occupy Blockhouses from 40 to 60 miles from Kroonstaad yet we have to post double Sentries whilst the drive is on, & this Coy. still has to work from 9 to 12 altho' the men on Sentry go 2 hours in the daytime & 4 hours in the night.

11ᵗʰ May.

The drive is now over, & ended in a large capture of Boers. We still have to post double Sentries.

16ᵗʰ May.

We heard an Armistice is on until the 24ᵗʰ inst. so as to give any Boers who wish to come in & surrender time to do so.

17ᵗʰ May.

At last the order for double Sentries at night-time is done away with.

23ʳᵈ May.

One man in my Blockhouse (136) accidentally shot himself in the leg this morning at 11.30 a.m.

26ᵗʰ May.

We are still working at the trench between B'houses.

27ᵗʰ May.

We heard to day that the Boers have now got till the 29ᵗʰ inst. to come in & surrender if they wish to do so.

31ˢᵗ May.
We have nearly got the trench between Blockhouses finished now.

Whilst the blockhouse line and its defences neared completion peace talks had already been held with Boer delegates. On 17 April 1902 Boers meeting at Pretoria asked for an armistice to consult their burghers, but such a move was refused by Kitchener as he viewed their request with suspicion. Eventually, however, on 15 May Boer delegates met at Vereeniging with the result that on the 17ᵗʰ representatives consisting of Botha, De la Rey, Smuts and Hertzog were chosen to negotiate directly with the British.

The first meeting between both sides took place at Pretoria on 19 May 1902. As a result it was agreed that Lord Milner should meet with Smuts and Hertzog on the 20ᵗʰ to draft a joint document acceptable to all. What emerged from such a meeting was a document which was put to the Boers at Vereeniging and accepted. As a result the representatives returned to Pretoria and it was there at Melrose House that the peace was signed at 10.30 p m bringing the war to a close.

The terms of the surrender were as follows:

1.   The burghers in the field were to lay down their arms and surrender guns, rifles, munitions, recognizing King Edward VII as their lawful Sovereign.

2.   All burghers outside the Boer States and all burghers in British prisons, on declaring "their acceptance of the position of subjects of King Edward VII," were to be gradually brought home.

3.   The burghers thus surrendering were not to be punished or deprived of their property.

4.   No proceedings were to be taken against them for any part they had taken in the war, though acts contrary to the laws of war, notice of which had been given to the Boer generals, were to be tried by court-martial.

5.   The Dutch language was to be permitted to be taught in schools where the parents of children desired it, and its use in law courts where necessary "for the better and more effectual administration of justice" was sanctioned.

6.   The possession of rifles by burghers was permitted, where required for protection, and subject to a licence.

7.   Military government was at the earliest possible date to be succeeded by civil government, and as soon as circumstances permitted representative institutions leading to self-government were to be introduced.

8.   Franchise should not be granted to the natives until self-government had been introduced, when the country could settle its own policy.

9.   No special tax was to be imposed upon landed property to pay for the cost of the war.

10.   A commission, on which the local inhabitants were to be represented, was to be appointed at the earliest possible date, in each district of the Boer territories, to restore the people to their homes and to supply those who were destitute, owing to their losses in the war, with seed and implements. To this end the British government promised to place £3,000,000 as a free gift in the hand of the commissioners, and to allow all notes issued by the Boer Governments and all receipts given by officers of the Boer armies in the field to be presented to a judicial commission, and, if it could be shown that they had been issued in return for valuable consideration, to be regarded as evidence of the losses in the war suffered by those to whom they were originally given. The British Government further agreed to make advances on loans free of interest for two years.

Peace Declared

1st June. L. J. Bryant

We received word to day, that peace is declared. Each blockhouse from Lindley to Bethlehem fired one rocket each, one after each other, at 7 p.m. & the men gave 3 cheers to celebrate the occasion. We had a large Bonfire at Kaffir Kop.

2nd June.

To day was observed as a Holiday for our Regt. & we got 1 dram of rum & a dram of whiskey each.

3rd June.

We still have to work 3 hours a day on the trench to keep us in the open air, but we are let off sentry duty in the daytime, except in one or two B'houses which are kept up as observation posts. The remainder only post Sentries from 6 p.m. to 6 a.m.

4th June.

My Coy. was relieved from the Blockhouse by B. Coy. & we concentrated at 128 B'house for the time being. We have to proceed to Kroonstaad for duty there. Twenty-four men of this Coy. (myself included) left by wagon this afternoon at 3 p.m. for Lindley en route for Pretoria, to take part in the Thanksgiving Service for Peace, which is to be held at Pretoria on Sunday. We got to Lindley at 8 p.m.

6th June.

We arrived at Kroonstaad at about 11 this morning & entrained for Pretoria at 2 p.m.

7th June.

We arrived at Pretoria about 9.30 a.m. & we camped with a lot more troops about 4 miles from the Town. We all fell in at 11 a.m. & marched down to the Barracks to rehearse tomorrows service & we returned to camp again about 6 p.m. Marched about 7 miles altogether.

8th June.

The Thanksgiving service for the restoration of Peace took place to day in the Market Square at 10 a.m. The troops in our Camp (1800 all told) fell in at 7 a.m. & marched off to the Market Square, about 3 miles distance. Before the Service started Lord Kitchener distributed a few medals to some men etc.

The Service started about 10 a.m., there was about 4000 Troops taking part in it & a large crowd of civilians assembled to witness the ceremony. We all sang the National Anthem at the end of the Service & gave 3 cheers for the King & 3 more for Lord Kitchener. We then marched back to our respective Camps, arriving there at 3 p.m.

9th June.

We left Pretoria at 8 p.m. to return to Kroonstaad after waiting 5 hours for our train.

10th June.

We arrived at Vereeniging[4] about 2 p.m. & got out of the train & stopped with our 2nd Battn. for the night.

11th June.

We left Vereeniging at 3 p.m. & continued on our journey to Kroonstad.

12th June.

We arrived at Kroonstaad at 5 p.m. & rejoined our Coy. again at East Fort. The Coy. arrived at Kroonstaad on the 9th June. We now have to find 4 guards day & night.

19th June.

A party of men 150 strong left the Bn. to day for England. Time expired.

20th June.

This Coy. is very weak in numbers now & as we have to do such a lot of duty we only get 1 night in bed, now & again we get 2 nights.

21ˢᵗ June.

Lord Kitchener passed through Kroonstaad to day on his way to Cape Town, for England. We were told that any man who wished to go down to the station to give him a parting cheer could do so , without a pass.

As the most of us did not like the idea of walking about two miles just to give a man a send off & as we badly needed a sleep, we of course made up our minds to stay in the Camp, but an order was given out, that any man who was left still in Camp at 2 p.m. would be taken for Fatigue, so a good number of the men went to the Rly. Station, but the Fatigue didn't come off.

23ʳᵈ June.

Our football Team played the Engineers to day in the Kroonstaad tournament & the game ended in a draw, nothing being scored.

26ᵗʰ June.

We were to have had a ceremonial Parade to day in the town owing to the Kings Coronation but the parade was cancelled as we heard that the King was very ill.

28ᵗʰ June.

The Company were relieved off duty at East Fort to day by a Coy. of the Rifle Brigade & we pitched our Camp on East Hill, next to our Details

30ᵗʰ June.

Our Football Team played off their tie with the Engineers before a small crowd. A good game in which we had the best of the game all through, ended in a win for us by 2 goals to one. There are now only three teams left to compiete the Tournament viz:- Royal Artillery, Inniskillings & a team from the R.A.M. Corp. Our team succeeded in drawing a bye & so plays the winners of the R. Artillery V R.A.M.C. match, which comes off to day. The Final takes place on Saturday 5ᵗʰ Inst. The Winners to receive Gold Medals.

5ᵗʰ July.

The Bn. arrived here at 8 a.m. this morning marching from Kaffir Kop in 3 days. The Final of the Football Tournament took place to day at 3 p.m. before a very large assembly of people. Admission 1/-. We were opposed to the Royal Army Medical Corps., whose team was composed of the best players in the Garrison of Kroonstaad. The game was keenly contested all through but our Eleven proved victorious by 2 goals to none. This makes the 2ⁿᵈ Tournament we have won.

6th July.

Had Divine Service in Camp instead of in the Town. A draft of 80 men joined us to day.

-Cape Colony –

7th July.

We left Kroonstaad to day to proceed to De Aar, Cape Colony. The right Half Bn. entrained at 2 p.m. & the Left Half Bn. at 6 p.m. The Bn. Band played us to the station.

8th July.

We arrived at Bloemfontein about 9 a.m. & had our Breakfast & then resumed our journey.

9th July.

We arrived at De Aar at 5 p.m. & pitched our Camp.

12th July.

We played a Friendly Match against the 60th K.R.R.s [King's Royal Rifles] & were beaten by 3 goals to none.

13th July.

H Coy. proceeds to the Rest Camp for duty. Twenty men of G. Coy. (myself included) left De Aar this morning at 7 a.m. for Philips Town for duty. We rode on wagons to Philips Town & arrived there at 4 p.m.

14th July.

We are doing duty over Stores here.

16th July.

A Convoy arrived here to day & we put half the stores on it, for De Aar.

17th July.

We packed the remainder of the stores on the Convoy to day.

18th July.

We left Philips Town to day for De Aar & camped about 7 miles from De Aar for the night.

18th July.

We arrived at De Aar at 9 a.m. & rejoined the Bn. again.

24th July.

Had C.O.s Parade at 10.30 a.m. we played a football match against the Liverpools, the match ended in a draw of 1 goal each.

26th July.

There was Doctors Inspection to day at 9 a.m.

29th July.

The Bn. left De Aar to day for Naaupoort. We left De Aar at 9 a.m. & arrived at Naauport at 2 p.m. & pitched our Camp at 4p.m.

30th July.

We struck our Camp at 2 p.m. & re-pitched it in line at 3.30 p.m.

31st July.

I was admitted into Hospital with Bronchitis.

9th Aug.

"Coronation Day." The whole Garrison at Naauport paraded at 11 a.m. under Gen. Comdg. The District, and at 12 noon our Regt. fired a Feu-de-joie, in Honour of the King being Crowned.

The Troops then marched past & were dismissed. One of the Sisters here in the Hospital very kindly arranged a Small Tea Party for the patients in my ward, which we greatly enjoyed. We then went out to have a look at the Fireworks which were being set off from the different camps.

11th Aug.

A draft of 102 men joined the Bn. to day.

21st Aug.

Besides having Bronchitis, the Doctor here found that my right lung was affected thro' a cold & the P. M. O. [Principal Medical Officer] marked me for Deelfontein, for a change of air.

22nd Aug.

Our Regt. played a Football Match to day against the Grenadier Guards & a good game ended in a draw, nothing being scored. Since this we have played a match with the Town Eleven & they beat us by 4 goals to 2, also one against the 5th Lancers & we beat them by 3 goals to 0. We have also played against the 4th Mounted Battery & got beat the first time by 1 goal to 0, & we beat them the second time. Nothing else occurred.

29th Aug.

Our Football Team travelled to Hanover Road to play a return match against the Grenadier Guards. They beat us by 2 goals to one.

30th Aug.

We played a return match against the Town Eleven here to day & beat them by 7 goals to one.

31st Aug.

Another lot of Reserve men left the Bn. to do for England.

3rd Sept.

I left Naaupoort to day by the Hospital Train for Deelfontein at 3 p.m.

4th Sept.

I arrived at Deelfontein at 12.30 p.m. & went into the Hospital there.

5th Sept.

My disease was changed from Bronchitis to phthisis to day.

At this point, during his spell in hospital, Private Bryant suspended his entries, possibly due to his condition, or the fact that little of significance took place during this period.

22nd Dec.

We started decorating the wards for Xmas day.

25th Dec.

Xmas Day. We each received 1lb. of Xmas pudding from the field Forces Canteen Fund to commemorate Xmas & our Sister very kindly arranged a small tea party for us, which we greatly enjoyed. We also got an extra bottle of stout given to us instead of the usual pint of beer.

1903

1st Jan.

New Years Day. Our Sister was married to day to a Civilian Doctor. The Ceremony took place at the Church here & we all went to witness it. My C.O. applied for me to rejoin the Battn. again, as they were going Home soon, but the Doctors here wrote back to the C.O. & told him that I would be invalided home separately.

14th Jan.

My Regiment passed through Deelfontein this morning on the way to Cape Town. They had plenty of flags flying from the trucks & they sail on Saturday by the S. S. Aurania for England.

3rd Mar.

We received orders at 8.30 p.m. to go to the Stores & draw our kits out & get ready to proceed to Bloemfontein. We had to catch the 9.30 p.m. Mail Train. We proceeded to the Station at 9.30 a.m. & were then told that the train would be 2 hours late & had to go back to our ward again. We then went back to the Station again at 1 a.m. & when the first Mail Train did come in, we were told that we would have to go by the second portion. We were knocking about for over half an hour waiting for the second portion of the Mail to arrive, when we were told that there would be no room for us on the second portion of the Mail Train, as it was already full up, so we had to go back to our wards again & get what little sleep we could.

4th Mar.

We were to have proceeded to Bloemfontein by the Mail Train tonight but we got a rotten order to catch the 2.30 p.m. train, & proceeded to De Aar in a luggage train. We had to sit on top of the luggage & the sun was hot enough to roast us. After waiting at De Aar about 6 hours we had to proceed to Bloemfontein by a Troop Train. We should have travelled to Bloemfontein by the Mail Train, as we had sick men with us, but the Railway Staff Officer at De Aar got a Guards wagon attached to the Troop Train, & packed us & our belongings in that. There were eleven patients & 2 orderlies & we had no room to lay down, let alone sleep.

5th Mar.

We arrived at Naauwpoort very early this morning & after knocking about for a few hours our van was attached to a luggage train & we resumed our journey. We arrived at Norvals Pont about 1.30 p.m. and had our dinner at the Restaurant, we then proceeded on our journey. We arrived at Bloemfontein at 2 a.m. this morning (6th March) & 3 Ambulances met us at the Station & took us to the Military Hospital. We went into three Marquees when we got to the Hospital, 4 men in a Marquee. We were properly tired out when we arrived at the Hospital for the want of sleep.

20th Mar.

I was discharged from Hospital to return to duty again at my own request. I left Bloemfontein Hospital at 2 a.m. & was attached to the S. W. Bs. [South Welsh Borderers] as a Detail.

9th Apr.

I left the Rest Camp at Stellenbosch at 5.30 a.m. to proceed to Cape Town. I left by the 2 p.m. train with a party of Details. We arrived at Cape Town about 5.30 p.m. & embarked on H. M. S. Staffordshire for England. We set sail about 6 p.m.

15th Apr.

We arrived at St. Helena & disembarked about 130 men of the Manchesters & took on some Troops & their families.

25th Apr.

Arrived at Las Palmas & coaled here.

30th Apr.

Arrived at Southampton after a pleasant voyage.

3rd May.

Rejoined the Battalion again.

The End

Chapter Nine

The Return of the
1st Battalion
The Royal Inniskilling Fusiliers

The homecoming of the Royal Inniskilling Fusiliers was even more rapturous than their send off.   Having been away from home for more than three years their return was greeted with jubilation the length and breath of Ireland, from Queenstown to Derry. The flag-waving crowds that had seen them off would prove a mere shadow of what awaited them on their return.

Travelling on the SS *Aurania*, under the captaincy of Captain John Kirk, with a brief stop at St. Vincent en route, the *Aurania* docked at Queenstown on Sunday morning the 8 February 1903 amid tumultuous celebrations. Onboard was a compliment of fourteen Officers, 420 men and one Warrant Officer.

Shortly after disembarkation the Inniskillings boarded a special train bound for Derry with a few scheduled stops along the way. The train departed Queenstown at 10 pm, arriving somewhat later than anticipated on Monday morning at Enniskillen. Greeted by throngs of enthusiastic townspeople, the Inniskillings could make a stop of no more than an hour before heading once more for Omagh where an equally enthusiastic assembly of dignitaries and towns-folk awaited them. The train pulled into Omagh Railway Station at approximately eight minutes to one, running well behind schedule, which was no surprise given the occasion and all that had occurred en route. However, after the obligatory round of welcoming speeches and greetings, it was time to embark once more on the final leg of their journey.

Crowds in Derry had been gathering in the vicinity of the Great Northern Railway Station, Foyle Road and John Street since around two o'clock in the afternoon, eagerly awaiting the arrival of husbands, sons and sweethearts whom they hadn't seen in over three years. The fact that the Inniskillings were delayed did little to dampen their spirits. If anything it allowed time for the crowds to swell to even greater numbers. Heading the civic and military dignitaries awaiting their arrival on the platform were the Duke and Duchess of Abercorn, accompanied by their guests, the wife and daughter of the American Chargé d'Affaires in London.

At approximately two thirty the impending arrival of the train bearing the Inniskillings was indicated by the lowering of the long-distance signal. Five minutes later the explosion of several detonators heralded the train's imminent arrival, causing a spontaneous outburst of cheering from the assembled crowd. As the train pulled into the railway station with the Inniskillings still dressed in their South African khaki uniforms the crowd erupted, as both civilian and military dignitaries tried to make their speeches of welcome. Such was the size of the crowd that eagerly awaited the arrival of the Inniskillings that everyone became intermingled as the Fusiliers made their way, four deep, across Carlisle bridge on their way to Ebrington Barracks. The Regimental band headed the procession, followed by a team of sappers, whilst Colonel Payne and Lieutenant Col. Cox headed the battalion, mounted on two chargers. In the midst of the troops, the Colours were borne by Lieutenant Pike and 2nd Lieutenant Young.

The enthusiasm of the onlookers was the main reason for the slow progress of the Battalion as the troops eventually reached Ebrington Barrack. However, at approximately a quarter to five in the afternoon the Regiment formed up once more in the barrack square and made its way back to the Guildhall Square via Carlisle Bridge, Carlisle Road, the Diamond and Shipquay Street. Again progress was hampered as thousands of cheering, flag-waving onlookers lined the route, buntings and flags bedecking every possible building and lamppost.

On their arrival in the Guildhall Square the Royal Inniskilling Fusiliers formed up before a specially constructed platform prior to receiving their South African Campaign Medals from the Duke of Abercorn. The afternoon light was already beginning to fade as the medal ceremony progressed. Long rows of Fusiliers and recently returned reservists mounted the platform to receive their hard-earned South African campaign medals from the Duke of Abercorn, attended by Major-General Sir H. M'Calmont and Colonel Mellor, Commanding Officer of the 27th Regimental District.

On completion of the presentation of medal ceremony, the troops defiled into the Guildhall where they were guests at a Civic Banquet held in their honour. As the 600 troops dined and listened to various speeches extolling their recent deeds by prominent dignitaries, the enthusiastic crowd that had lined the route and massed around the Guildhall Square waited patiently for the proceedings to conclude.

The evening finally came to a close with a torchlight procession accompanying the Inniskillings on their return across the city to Ebrington Barracks. Headed by the Good Templar Brass Band and 120 torchbearers, who lined the route across the city, the procession made its way, albeit slowly, via Shipquay Street, the Diamond, Ferryquay Street, Carlisle Road, the Bridge, Spencer Road and Clooney Terrace.

So ended a momentous day in the lives of the citizens of Derry and a glorious chapter in the history of the Royal Inniskilling Fusiliers. The Boer War itself may, over the years, have been relegated and superseded by the excesses of the two world wars of the twentieth century, but that cannot alter the bravery and valour of those men who took part in the last great Victorian campaign.

Unfortunately, as we enter the dawn of a new century, a new millennium, so too must we enter a new age of battlefields and relentless warfare. Pessimistic though that prediction may be, nothing is surer. As day follows night, warfare is endemic in the society in which we live. Suffering and death has been the inheritance of man since time immemorial and will continue to be so until the end of time. The greed and intolerance of following generations soon silence the laments and tears for the fallen.

Private Bryant aptly concludes his diary account of the Boer War with the following suitable commemoration of those comrades left behind in the numerous graves that dot the battlefields of the veldt.

"To The Memory of the Dead
Inniskilling Fusiliers."

They rest in peace in a Foreign Land,
Far, far away, from their Native Shore,
We mourn that truly Noble Band,
Who can return to us no more,
In death they were all Soldiers brave,
So let us check the rising tears,
A Victory to our Land they gave,
The Inniskilling Fusiliers.

They knew not fear, they spurned Retreat,
When led by the Colonel they loved so dear,
His voice to their ears was music sweet,
That bound their hearts with its magic spell.
In Death he was a Soldier Brave,
So let us check the rising tear,
On Africa's Soil he met his Doom,
Our Inniskilling Fusilier.

Yes, Killed in action, we hear with woe,
The fate of him who was best of all,
Tho' the Victory's won, he will never know,
And unheeded now is the Bugle Call.
Beside him many a Soldier fell
Whose name will be a Memory dear,
Noble in Life, to Death fought Well,
The Inniskilling Fusilier.

The Regiment hold a record high,
And proud are the men who bear its name,
On them we always may rely,
For Deeds of Valour and Lasting Fame,
So let us all Unite in Praise,
Our Voices in Fearless Manly Cheers,
They've won our Best and Highest Praise,
The Inniskilling Fusiliers.

Epilogue

The amalgam of the diaries in this book give an excellent overview of the campaign in South Africa as it specifically applied to the 1st Battalion the Royal Inniskilling Fusiliers. Though not all of the same calibre, they do supplement and enrich each other. 4445 Private L. J. Bryant's account, whilst displaying a certain degree of humour, is surprisingly more informative in respect of the tactical aspect of the Regiment than either that of Captain Jeffcoat or Lieutenant Auchinleck. Being a considerably more voluminous document than that of the others, he demonstrates a single-minded determination to cover every aspect of life in the Regiment from its departure until its eventual triumphant return.

However, one theme common to all three diarists is their singular determination to avoid self-glorification. Intentionally or otherwise, they avoid the temptation to indulge in a catalogue of self-appreciation which sadly is all too often the case in diaries and memoirs of those of more senior rank. And yet when it seems right and fitting to mention deeds worthy of a mention in despatches and the award of a Distinguished Service Order neither Private Bryant nor Captain Jeffcoat give any indication as to how these honours were achieved.

For the Royal Inniskilling Fusiliers, like so many other regiments who saw action in South Africa during the Boer War, the campaign turned out to be much more costly, in terms of loss of human life, than first envisaged. Some may say it's a soldier's lot to risk life and limb, it's the very nature of his profession. However, what had at first been intended as a relatively short punitive expedition turned into a much more protracted, often demoralizing, affair of the worst kind, a guerrilla war.

In the end the policy drawn up by Kitchener of constructing lines of blockhouses and the burning of farms brought the war to a close. However, one of the more contentious aspects of the war was his adoption of a policy of concentration camps in which civilians, displaced when their farmhouses were burnt, were housed.

Naturally, when we think with our twentieth century knowledge of concentration camps, we automatically visualize the horrors of Bergen-Belsen, Auschwitz, Buchenwald and the numerous other Nazi concentration camps of World War II. During the Boer War, however, the phrase was coined to signify camps in which people were 'concentrated' in one particular area. They should not be confused with Nazi extermination camps. However, unpalatable though the truth may be, these camps were scenes of squalor, filth and death from disease for which Kitchener must take the lion's share of the blame. The Army at the time was ill-equipped to undertake such a monumental task, having little or no experience of catering for such huge numbers. Dysentery and disease were endemic.

Diseases such as dysentery and enteric fever did more than decimate the civilian occupants of the camps, both white and coloured alike, it also laid waste the British Army, unaccustomed as the troops were to life on the veldt. If we take the Inniskillings simply as a microcosm of such a force and examine their casualty rolls we can see that dysentery, enteric fever and septicaemia accounted for a huge percentage of their overall strength.

In the end the peace agreement signed following the conference at Vereeniging was the best settlement both factions could seriously expect. Both sides had suffered appallingly, the Boers in both loss of life and devastation to property, whilst the British escaped with little more than the tattered remnants of their pride. It had been a much more costly venture than the British government had at first calculated both in numbers of troops lost and the huge overall cost to the exchequer.

A consequence of the Boer War, however, was to drag the British Army into the twentieth century, to herald the end of cavalry dominance and set-piece battles fought over relatively short periods. The first great war of the new century, World War I, would demand a completely new strategy from both the British Army and the British Government. No longer could Britain go it alone confident in its "splendid isolation".

However, a much more lasting and damning consequence was the fact that native Africans were overlooked and betrayed by both the Boers and the British Government alike in the eventual peace settlement. Britain succumbed to the Afrikaners' insistence that native black Africans should be denied even limited rights, thus placing their fate firmly in the hands of both civilian and political Afrikaner administrations to come. Britain unwittingly assisted in sowing the very seeds which would eventually grow into Apartheid.

Appendix I

Boer War,
South Africa 1898-1902

It is several years now since I first visited the Royal Inniskilling Fusiliers Regimental Museum at Enniskillen Castle intent upon finding out all I could regarding the service of my wife's two grandfathers, Frederick Lawrence and James Joseph Donnelly, both of whom served with the Regiment and lost their lives during the Great War.

To my surprise, upon making enquiries from the curator, Major George Stephens, and consulting the Roll of Honour of Ireland, no mention of their deaths could be found. It was suggested that they probably numbered among the vast sea of servicemen who lost their lives in action but had no known grave. However, if indeed that were the case, their names would still have been included on the Roll, regardless of whether they had an official grave or not.

On the contrary, however, I was able to inform the Regiment that, indeed, far from having no known grave, they were both buried in military graves within yards of each other in the City Cemetery, Derry. Upon making further enquiries and contacting the Commonwealth War Graves Commission, it was subsequently discovered that both Fusiliers had been wounded, repatriated and died of wounds at home. Thus no record of their deaths ever found its way back to their Regiment, which, with the passage of time, lost track of them.

This experience made me realize that, if it could happen to both my wife's grandfathers, then just how many other relatives are unaware of what actually happened to fathers, brothers or grandfathers. On the whole, tracing soldiers who lost their lives during the Great War and since is not that difficult, given the information and records available. However, records predating the Great War are not so comprehensive and not so readily accessible. In the course of my research I also discovered that my wife's grandfather, Frederick Lawrence, had seen service with the Regiment during the Boer War and taken part in the Relief of

Ladysmith. This again set me wondering just how many families, like my own, have no idea regarding the service details of their grandfathers or great-grandfathers, and in many cases what actually became of them.

As a result I have attempted to compile as thorough an index as possible of those Officers, NCOs and ORs who saw service with the 1st Battalion the Royal Inniskilling Fusiliers during the Boer War 1898-1902 and its immediate aftermath. The index is self-explanatory. Arranged alphabetically, it indicates honours received, if the individual was wounded at any time, and whether he was killed in action, died of wounds or disease during the South African campaign. Or indeed, if he survived, did he subsequently lose his life during the Great War 1914-1918. I have also included Fusiliers with a service number of 7000 and above, even though they did not qualify for the presentation of a South African campaign medal. Given that they served with the Regiment, albeit for a short period, they have been included since the primary purpose of this book is to assist relatives undertaking research into an individual's participation with the Regiment during the South African campaign.

Since the establishment of the Imperial War Graves Commission, later to become the Commonwealth War Graves Commission, by Royal Charter in 1917, it is quite a simple task to trace a relative who died on active service. However, before the Great War, documentation is not so comprehensive and indeed the graves of those servicemen who lost their lives during the Boer War and in earlier campaigns lie for the most part unattended and in neglect.

Moreover, historians are often accused of being dispassionate onlookers, voyeurs reporting on distant events and drawing conclusions with the aid of hindsight, whilst ignoring the smaller more human contributions made by the ordinary individual on the ground. It is for this very reason that I have concentrated on the roll of the Fusilier rather than the overall picture. In a way I may be considered a romantic, in that I have attempted to produce a work which gives the everyday Fusilier some credit and acknowledgement for his achievements, rather than a few individuals whom history so readily accredits, due to rank and social status.

By compiling such an index I hope in some small way to rekindle long-forgotten memories which may have lain dormant for decades. By so doing I hope to go some small way to enable an individual's name to live on when most certainly it would have been lost in the mists of time.

Appendix II

Roll of Officers & Warrant Officers, 1st Battalion Royal Inniskilling Fusiliers

The following Appendix is dedicated to the Officers and Warrant Officer of the 1st Battalion the Royal Inniskilling Fusiliers who served with the Regiment during the Boer War 1899-1902. It is also a casualty roll for both the Boer War and World War I, and as such is self-explanatory. Bold lettering denotes the individual was killed in action or subsequently died of wounds or disease.

Second-Lieutenant C. Alexander   Served with 1st Battalion the Leicestershire Regiment.

Major J. L. Armitage

Second-Lieutenant J. A. Armstrong

Captain E. W. Atkinson

Lieutenant D. G. Auchinleck   Son of Major Thomas Auchinleck of Crevenagh, Omagh Co. Tyrone: Husband of Madoline Auchinleck, Captain, 2nd Battalion Royal Inniskilling Fusiliers, Killed in Action, 20th Oct. 1914, Aged 37, Interred Strand Military Cemetery 13 Klm South of Ieper, Grave Ref. VIII. Q. 6.

Captain R. G. Bell   Wounded, (Right Shoulder, Left Leg, Left Thigh, Foot Amputated) 23rd Feb. 1900, Inniskilling Hill, Relief of Ladysmith, Leinster Regiment.

Lieutenant T. A. D. Best   Wounded Battle of Colenso, 15th Dec. 1899 Wounded Inniskilling Hill, 23rd Feb. 1900.   MID (4th September 1901), Boer War, Major, DSO and Bar. (Lieutenant-Colonerl) World War I, Wounded in Action Gallipoli 1915, Son of William J.& Annie Best, Malabar Hill Bombay,   Husband of Amy M. Best, Anneville, Clonmel, Co. Tipperary. Native of Scotland, Killed in Action Monday 20th Nov1917, Aged 38, World War I,   Interred Ruyaulcourt Military Cemetery, Grave Ref. F. 8.

Captain P. S. Beves

Major E. B. Blennerhassett

Captain F. O. Bowen   3rd Battalion The Connaught Rangers.

Major Brannigan — Wounded 15th Dec. 1899, Battle of Colenso, Boer War, Royal Army Medical Corps.

Captain L. E. Buchanan — 4th Battalion Royal Inniskilling Fusiliers, (The Royal Tyrone Regiment),

Captain E. J. Buckley — Wounded 15th Dec. 1899, Battle of Colenso, Boer War, MID (Twice) (30th March 1900 & 4th September 1901).

Lieutenant A. Bull — 3rd Battalion Royal Inniskilling Fusiliers, From Wandsworth Rd. Belfast, Died of Wounds, Pylkop, Boer War, 12th Apr.1902

Captain J.N.H. Burke — 3rd Battalion The Connaught Rangers.

Lieutenant A. Byrne — Born Derry, Wounded 15th Dec. 1899, Battle of Colenso, Boer War, Brigadier General, Assistant Adjutant General May 1916 World War I.

Second Lieutenant R. A. Challoner — Died of Wounds, Rooiwal, Boer War, 21st Apr. 1902 Interred Coligny Graveyard Grave No. 26

Second-Lieutenant C. W. Chaloner — Served with Remount Depot.

Major J. F.W. Charley — Killed in Action, Battle of Colenso, 15th Dec. 1899.

Major R. C. Cox — Commanding Officer 27th Jan 1904, exchanged with Colonel Mackenzie to command 2nd Battalion May 1905, Born 12th Nov. 1857, Commissioned in the 27th Foot (from Militia), Commanded 1st Battalion in South Africa 3rd Mar 1901-8th Mar. 1902 when appointed Commandant at Lindley, MID, (23rd June 1902), Boer War, Promoted Brevet Lieutenant-Colonel Boer War, Retired 27th Jan. 1908, Commanded the 7th Royal Inniskilling Fusiliers and Royal Irish Regiment during World War I.

Captain J. N. Crawford — Wounded 23rd Feb. 1900, Inniskilling Hill, Relief of Ladysmith, Boer War.

Lieutenant J. G. Devenish — Wounded 15th Dec. 1899, Battle of Colenso, Wounded 23rd Feb. 1900, Inniskilling Hill, Relief of Ladysmith, MID, (4th September 1901),Boer War,

Second-Lieutenant T. F. Dunbar

Captain J. Evans — Wounded (Chest, Right Arm, Right Hand, Buttock, Right Leg, Left Leg), Inniskilling Hill, Relief of Ladysmith, 23rd Feb 1900.

Captain R. M. Foot — Wounded 23rd Feb. 1900, Inniskilling Hill,Relief of Ladysmith, Boer War, Brigadier-General during World War I, awarded DSO.

Second-Lieutenant A. M. Forteath — MID, (4th September 1901), Promoted Brevet Major Boer War.

Captain W. L. P. Gibton Commanding Officer 24th Feb.-12th Mar. 1900,
Died of Disease (Dysentery), Ladysmith, Boer War, 19th Mar. 1900.
Lieutenant R. B. Goodden   3rd Battalion The Dorset Regiment.
Lieutenant A. J. M. Gordon   Dysentery.
Major A. J. Hancocks   Commanding Officer 22nd Nov. 1910,
       Born 13th Sept. 1864, Wounded Battle of Colenso, 15th Dec. 1899,
                                                Retired 19th Feb. 1914.
Second-Lieutenant H. A. Harris
Captain W. F. Hessey   Wounded 15th Dec. 1899, Battle of Colenso,
MID (30th March 1900, 9th Nov. 1900 & 4th September 1901), Boer War,
Brevet Lieutenant-Colonel temp. Brigadier-General (World War I) MID.
Major H. O. D. Hickman   Commanding Oficer 27th Jan. 1908, Born
13th Nov. 1860, Commissioned in the 19th Foot 14th Jan. 1880, Joined
Royal Inniskilling Fusiliers 8th Jan. 1890. Employed in the Egyptian
Army 25th Sept. 1885 - 8th Sept. 1889, Assistant Military Secretary and
Aide-de-Camp to the Governor of Bermuda 24th June 1896 - 24th Feb.
1900, Second in Command Royal Military College 19th Feb. 1910, War
Office Staff 9th Apr. 1912, Retired 2nd Jul. 1913, Re-employed during
World War I, retired with honorary Brigadier-General 9th Feb. 1918.
Second Lieutenant A. H.Hutton   Died of Disease, (Enteric Fever),
                                Ladysmith, Boer War, 14th Apr. 1900.
Colonel E. T. Inkson VC   Born Naini Tal, India 5th April 1872,
                                Attd., Royal Inniskilling Fusiliers,
During the attack on Hart's Hill(Inniskilling Hill), during the Relief of
Ladysmith Colonel Inkson carried 2nd Lieutenant Devenish, Royal
Inniskilling Fusiliers, who had been seriously wounded, to safety. For this
he was awarded the Victoria Cross.   Died Chichester Sussex 19th
February 1947, also awarded DSO.
Captain A. C. Jeffcoat, MID, (13th September 1900), & DSO Boer War.
Captain R. W. Johnston   MID, (Boer War), Res. Of Officers
                  Attd. 1st Battalion Royal Inniskilling Fusiliers
Captain F. G. Jones   Commanding Officer 19th Feb. 1914, Born 8th
Apr. 1864, Commissioned in Royal Inniskilling Fusiliers (from Militia)
16th Dec. 1885, Wounded (Broken arm), Inniskilling Hill, Relief of
Ladysmith, 23rd Feb. 1900. MID, (Twice) (30th March 1900 & 4th
September 1901), Boer War, Promoted Brevet Major Boer War,
Lieutenant-Colonfel, Son of Rev. Edward G. and Eliza W. Jones, of
Cecilstown Lodge, Mallow, Co. Cork, Died of Wounds Tuesday 9th May
1915 Gallipoli, World War I, Aged 51, No Known Grave,
Commerated Helles Memorial, Gallipoli Peninsula, Panels 97-101.

Captain G. W. Kenney

Second-Lieutenant W. D. Kenney

Lieutenant W. A. C. Kinsman   Wounded 8th Apr. 1902, Boer War.

Captain H. A. Leverson   Wounded 15th Dec. 1899, Battle of Colenso.

Lieutenant N. H. Lincoln   MID, Boer War , Killed, Boer War,
8th Apr. 1902, Interred Pietersberg Cemetery (Military Plot) Row No. 6-1
Originally Interred, Malipspoort.

Major C. J. Lloyd Davidson, DSO   Commanding Officer 3rd Nov. 1906,
Born 6th Oct. 1858, Eglinton Co. Derry, Commissioned in the 27th Foot
13th Aug. 1879 Wounded Inniskilling Hill, Relief of Ladysmith, 23rd/24th
Feb. 1900,   MID (Twice) (13th December 1900 & 4th September 1901),
DSO Boer War, Retired 3rd Nov. 1910, Died 15th Mar. 1941,
interred St Canice's Church Eglinton.

Colonel R. Lloyd Payne, DSO   Commanding Officer 27nd Apr. 1900 on
promotion from the Somerset Light Infantry, Born 24th May 1854,
Commissioned in 105th Foot (Militia) 5th Jan 1876, joined 13th Foot 19th
Jan. 1876,   DSO, Boer War, MID (Twice) (13th September 1900 & 9th
November 1900) Boer War,   Promoted Brevet Colonel Boer War 29th
Nov. 1900, Colonel of the 13th Foot 5th April 1914,
Retired 23rd July 1917, Died 20th Dec. 1921.

Captain F. C. Loftus   Died of Wounds,
Battle of Colenso, 15th Dec. 1899.

Lieutenant J. T. Lowry Died as result of an accident at Frere, Boer War.

Lieutenant-Colonel G. M. Mackenzie   Commanding Officer (29th Oct.
1902), Appointed to 2nd Battalion on exchange with Cox, May 1905,
Born 6th Jun 1860, Commissioned in 108th Foot 13th Aug 1879, MID,
Boer War. Retired 3rd Nov. 1906,
Commanded 1st London Infantry Brigade (T.A.) 1908-1912,
Retired with honorary rank of Brigadier-General 16th Feb. 1918.

Captain D. MacLachlan   Wounded 21st Jan. 1900 Relief of Ladysmith,
Died of Wounds, Venter's Spruit west of Spion Kop, 31th Jan. 1900.

Captain L. A. McClintock   MID, (Boer War),
3rd Battalion Royal Inniskilling Fusiliers.

Lieutenant J. H. W. Makin

Lieutenant E. I. Manders

Captain H. T. Manley

Captain L. H. Martineau   3rd Battalion Northampton Regiment.

Lieutenant W. W. Meldon   Wounded 15th Dec. 1899, Battle of Colenso.

Second Lieutenant A. R. Miller   Died of Disease, (Dysentery),
Ladysmith, Boer War, 15th May 1902.

Captain L. Moore   4th Battalion Royal Inniskilling Fusiliers.
(The Royal Tyrone Regiment), Served with Northumberland Fusiliers.
Captain G. W. Morley   Died of Disease, (Enteric Fever),
Ladysmith, 10th Apr. 1900.
Lieutenant A. J. Murray   Wounded 8th Apr. 1902, Boer War.
Second-Lieutenant C. S. Page
Lieutenant & Quartermaster J. A. Page
Lieutenant W. Pike   Son of Major Richard James Pike
(1st Battalion Suffolk Regiment.)
& Mary Emily Todd Pike of Glendaray, Achill Sound, Co. Mayo,
Ireland,Capt., Killed in Action, Friday 21st Aug. 1915,
Aged 34, No Known Grave,
Commemorated Helles Memorial, Gallipoli Peninsula, Panels 97-101.
Lieutenant H. P. Potts   Wounded 23rd Feb. 1900,
Inniskilling Hill, Relief of Ladysmith, Boer War.
Captain C. S. Owen   4th Battalion Royal Inniskilling Fusiliers,
(The Royal Tyrone Regiment).
Lieutenant D. de la C. Ray
Lieutenant C. Ridings   Wounded 23rd Feb. 1900,
Inniskilling Hill, Relief of Ladysmith, Boer War.
Lieutenant P. L. Rivis   5th Battalion Royal Inniskilling Fusiliers,
(The Royal Donegal Regiment).
Major F. A. Sanders   MID, (30th March 1900), Boer War,
Killed in Action,   Inniskilling Hill, Relief of Ladysmith, 23rd Feb. 1900.
Lieutenant R. C. Smythe
Second-Lieutenant C.G. Stewart
Major C. P. Stewart
Lieutenant G. R. V. Stewart   Wounded 27rd Feb. 1900,
Inniskilling Hill, Relief of Ladysmith, Boer War.
Captain A. St. Ricardo, DSO   From Sion Mills Co. Tyrone,
MID, (Thrice) (13th September 1900, 4th September 1901 & 23rd June
1902), Boer War, DSO Boer War,
Captain temporary Brigadier-General (World War I) MID.
Lieutenant W O. Stuart   From Omagh, Co. Tyrone, Killed in Action,
Inniskilling Hill, Relief of Ladysmith, Boer War, 23rd Feb. 1900.
Lieutenant-Colonel T. M. G. Thackeray   Commanding Officer
(1st Feb. 1897), Born, 23rd June 1849, Commissioned in 16th Foot, Joined
West India Regiment 5th Jan. 1881, Joined 27th Foot 23rd Mar. 1881 MID
(30th March 1900), Boer War, Killed in Action, Inniskilling Hill, Relief
of Ladysmith, Natal, Boer War, 23rd Feb. 1900.
Lieutenant W. P. Thompson   Wounded 8th Apr. 1902, Boer War.

Second-Lieutenant E. F. Traill

Second Lieutenant C. R. J. Walker Killed, Boer War, 19th Feb. 1902, Lichtenburg Cemetery, Grave No. 82.

Captain M.H.E. Welch Dysentery, 18th Royal Irish Regiment.

Second-Lieutenant J. L. Weston MID, (4th September 1901), Boer War, 5th Battalion Royal Dublin Fusiliers.

Lieutenant T. W. Whiffen Wounded 15th Dec. 1899, Battle of Colenso.

Second-Lieutenant H. N. Young Husband of Mrs. A. Young of Craigantaggart, Dunkeld, Perthshire, Wounded Rustenburg & Magaliesburg area between June & September 1901, World War I Major (Acting Ltieutenant Colonel) DSO, Attached 11th Battalion Sherwood Foresters (Notts & Derby Regtiment) Killed in Action, 25th Oct. 1918, World War I,

Interred Pommereuil British cemetery, Nord, France, Grave Ref. E. 7.

Lieutenant R. A. B. Young MID, (Twice) (30th March 1900 & 4th September 1901), Boer War, awarded OBE during World War I.

0606 Sergeant-Major G. Bleakley Awarded MC during World War I.

2117 Regimental Sergeant Major Martin MID, (Twice) (30th March 1900 & 13th September 1900) & DCM, Boer War.

Band-Master A. Turner

Appendix III

Roll of NCO & Other Ranks
1st Battalion
Royal Inniskilling Fusiliers

The following Appendix is dedicated to the Non-Commissioned Officers and Other Ranks of the 1st Battalion the Royal Inniskilling Fusiliers who served with the Regiment during the South African Campaign, 1899-1902 and its immediate aftermath. Amongst its many facets, it is also a casualty roll for both the Boer War and World War I, and as such is self-explanatory. Bold lettering denotes the individual was killed in action or subsequently died of wounds or disease.

A

3221 Corporal R. Adair — Wounded, 23rd Feb. 1900, Inniskilling Hill, Relief of Ladysmith, Boer War.

1342 Private J. Adams — Wounded, 23rd Feb. 1900, Inniskilling Hill, Relief of Ladysmith, Boer War.

299 Private J. Aiken — 4th Battalion Royal Inniskilling Fusiliers, (The Royal Tyrone Regiment), Boer War.

1995 Private J. Allen — 4th Battalion Royal Inniskilling Fusiliers, (The Royal Tyrone Regiment), Boer War.

4212 Sergeant G.W. Anderson — Wounded 23rd Feb. 1900, Inniskilling Hill, Relief of Ladysmith, Boer War.

1602 Private T. Anderson — 4th Battalion Royal Inniskilling Fusiliers, (The Royal Tyrone Regiment), Boer War.

3407 Private W. Andrews — Wounded 15th Dec. 1899, Battle of Colenso,

3446 Private G. Appleton — Wounded 23rd Feb. 1900, Inniskilling Hill, Relief of Ladysmith, Boer War.

629 Private P. Armstrong — Wounded 23rd Feb. 1900, Inniskilling Hill, Relief of Ladysmith, Boer War.

771 Private T. Armstrong — Died of Wounds, Gunshot wound to the abdomen, Base Hospital Martizburg, Inniskilling Hill, Relief of Ladysmith, Boer War, 27th Feb. 1900.

3752 Private G.E. Arthur — Killed in Action, Inniskilling Hill, Relief of Ladysmith, Boer War, 23rd Feb. 1900.

3764 Sergeant J.S. Arthur — Wounded 23rd Feb. 1900, Inniskilling Hill, Relief of Ladysmith, Boer War.

5589 Boy R.H. Arthur   5th Battalion Royal Inniskilling Fusiliers
(The Royal Donegal Regiment), Died of Disease, (Enteric Fever),
Boer War, 23rd Aug. 1901.
6137 Private J. Atkinson   Wounded 23rd Feb. 1900,
Inniskilling Hill, Relief of Ladysmith, Boer War.

B

947 Private J. Baird   4th Battalion Royal Inniskilling Fusiliers
(The Royal Tyrone Regiment), Killed in Action, Nooitgedacht
13th Dec. 1900, Served with Northumberland Fusiliers, Boer War.
1420 Private W. Barnett   Died of Disease, (Dysentery), 3rd Jan. 1901,
Interred Pretoria Cemetery (Church of England) Grave No. 351.
6034 Private W. Barrett   3rd Battalion Royal Inniskilling Fusiliers,
Died of Wounds, Kaffir Kop, Boer War, 15th Apr. 1902.
4379 Private C. Barry   Killed in Action,
Inniskilling Hill, Relief of Ladysmith, Boer War, 23rd Feb. 1900.
416 Private J. Baxter   4th Battalion Royal Inniskilling Fusiliers,
(The Royal Tyrone Regiment)
Died of Disease (Dysentery), Ladysmith, 8th Jun. 1900.
3295 Drummer J. Beattie   Wounded 15th Dec. 1899, Battle Of Colenso,
1598 Private W. Beck   4th Battalion Royal Inniskilling Fusiliers,
(The Royal Tyrone Regiment), Boer War.
1422 Private A. Bell   4th Battalion Royal Inniskilling Fusiliers,
(The Royal Tyrone Regiment), Boer War.
6958 Private J. Bell Son of Sarah Bell of 3, Cowan St. Newry Co. Down
2nd Battalion Royal Inniskilling Fusiliers, World War I, Killed in Action,
France & Flanders, 21st Mar. 1918, World War I, No Known Grave,
Poziéres Memorial, Somme, France, Panel 38 to 40.
3321 Private J. Bennett   Wounded 23rd Feb. 1900,
Inniskilling Hill, Relief of Ladysmith, Boer War.
4837 Private H. Bingham   Wounded 16th Apr. 1902, (forehead),
Kaffir Kop, Blockhouse Duty, Boer War.
3363 Sergeant B. Binfield   Died of Disease, (Enteric Fever),
Relief of Ladysmith, Boer War, 21st Jan. 1900.
5746 Private J. Black   Reported Missing in Action
after Battle of Inniskilling Hill, Relief of Ladysmith, 23rd/24th Feb. 1900
1202 Private J. Blearney   4th Battalion Royal Inniskilling Fusiliers,
(The Royal Tyrone Regiment), Boer War.
2705 Private W. Boylan   Wounded 15th Dec. 1899, Battle of Colenso,
1500 Private J. Boyle   Reported Missing in Action
after Battle of Inniskilling Hill, Relief of Ladysmith, 23rd/24th Feb. 1900

6142 Private R. Boyle   Wounded 8th Dec. 1901, Boer War.
896 Private W. Boyle   4th Battalion Royal Inniskilling Fusiliers,
(The Royal Tyrone Regiment), Boer War.
6075 Private J. Brady   Wounded 23rd Feb. 1900,
Inniskilling Hill, Relief of Ladysmith, Boer War.
6016 Private F. Bramwell   Wounded 15th Dec. 1899, Battle of Colenso,
Wounded 23rd Feb. 1900, Inniskilling Hill, Relief of Ladysmith,
3661 Sergeant R. Branagh   MID (4th September 1901), Boer War.
6687 Private R. Branagh   Born Shankill, Co. Antrim,
2nd Battalion Royal Inniskilling Fusiliers, World War I,
Killed in Action, France & Flanders Monday 6th Jul. 1917, World War I,
No Known Grave, Commerated Le Touret Memorial,
Le Touret Military Cemetery Panel 16, 17.
6914 Private J. Brawley   Born Derry City, Husband of Annie Brawley,
47 Cown St., Glasgow, Died of Wounds, France & Flanders, 23rd Aug.
1914, World War I,   Interred St. Germain-en-Laye Cemetery, Yvelines,
France, Military Plot I.
794 Private W. Brennan   5thBattalion Royal Inniskilling Fusiliers,
(The Royal Donegal Regiment), Died of Disease, (Enteric Fever), Boer
War, 2nd Feb. 1901,   Interred Pretoria Cemetery (Roman Catholic)
Grave No. 82.
5830 Corporal J.A. Bridgett   Died as result of an accident,
Boer War, 28th Mar. 1900, Interred Middleburg Cemetery, Grave No. 9.
4500 Private M. Brogden   Wounded 23rd Feb. 1900,
Inniskilling Hill, Relief of Ladysmith, Boer War.
5042 Private Private J. Brown   Died of Wounds,
Inniskilling Hill, Relief of Ladysmith, Boer War, 23rd Feb. 1900.
3101 Quartermaster-Sergeant J. S. Brown   Died of Disease,
(Enteric Fever), Boer War, 6th Mar. 1902.
730 Sergeant W. Brown   3rd Battalion, Royal Inniskilling Fusiliers,
Died of Disease, (Enteric Fever) at Ladysmith, Boer War, 21st Apr. 1900.
3131 Private W.J. Brown   Wounded 9th Sept. 1900, Boer War.
5654 Private R. Brownlee   Wounded 23rd Feb. 1900,
Inniskilling Hill, Relief of Ladysmith, invalided home on SS *Galatea*.
5834 Private R. Brownlee   Wounded (Right Arm & Chest),
23rd/24th Feb. 1900, Inniskilling Hill, Relief of Ladysmith, Boer War.
3120 Private W.J. Brunnen   Wounded 23rd Feb. 1900,
Inniskilling Hill, Relief of Ladysmith, Boer War.
2855 Private A. Bryan   Wounded 15th Dec. 1899,
Battle of Colenso,

4445 Private L. J. Bryant   Born Leytonstone, Essex,
MID (4th Sept. 1901), Boer War,
2nd Battalion Royal Inniskilling Fusiliers, Sergeant World War I,
Regimental Band, Died at Home, Saturday 6th Jul. 1919, Interred
Brookwood Military Cemetery, Woking Surrey, Grave Ref. VI. H. 8A.

2934 Private P. Burke   Wounded 23rd Feb. 1900,
Inniskilling Hill, Relief of Ladysmith Boer War,
invalided home on SS. *Galatea*.

2703 Private P. Burke   Killed, Boer War.

771 Private P. Burke   Killed, Boer War.

1653 Private T. Burke   4th Battalion Royal Inniskilling Fusiliers,
(The Royal Tyrone Regiment), Boer War.

3351 Private T.L. Burke   Killed in Action,
Battle of Colenso, Boer War, 15th Dec 1899.

4155 Sergeant H. Burkett   Killed in Action,
Inniskilling Hill, Relief of Ladysmith, Boer War, 23rd Feb. 1900.

6213 Private M. Burns   Died as result of an accident,
Boer War, 13th Jan. 1901.

4312 Private G. Button   Wounded (Left Thigh, both Arms & Right
Shoulder), 23rd/24th Feb. 1900, Inniskilling Hill, Relief of Ladysmith.

C

1349 Private J. Callan   4th Battalion Royal Inniskilling Fusiliers,
(The Royal Tyrone Regiment), Boer War.

6172 Private J. Callan   Killed in Action,
Inniskilling Hill, Relief of Ladysmith, Boer War, 23rd Feb. 1900.

622 Private T. Callan   4th Battalion Royal Inniskilling Fusiliers,
(The Royal Tyrone Regiment), Boer War.

1528 Private A. Camley   Wounded 23rd Aug. 1900,
Operations leading to action at Geluk on 25th, 26th & 27th Aug 1900,

2279 Private J. Campbell   Wounded 15th Dec. 1899, Battle of Colenso,

5800 Private J. Campbell   Killed in Action,
Inniskilling Hill, Relief of Ladysmith, Boer War, 23rd Feb. 1900.

6716 Private J. Campbell   Died of Disease, (Dysentery),
Boer War, 24th May 1901.

1489 Private D. Canavan   4th Battalion Royal Inniskilling Fusiliers,
(The Royal Tyrone Regiment),
Served with Northumberland Fusiliers, Boer War.

6182 Private J. Carr   Born Downpatrick, Co. Down, Son of
William Carr Husband of Annie Carr of John St. Downpatrick Co. Down,
2nd Battalion Royal Inniskilling Fusiliers, World War I,
Killed in Action, France & Flanders, 26th Aug. 1914, World War I,
No Known Grave,
Commemorated La Ferte-Sous-Jouarre Memorial, Seine-et-Marne,
3460 Private B. Carroll   MID (13th September 1900), Boer War.

6868 Private S.A. Carson   Born Drumagh, Co. Tyrone, CSM,
Killed in Action, France & Flanders, Saturday 28th Jan. 1917,
DCM World War I, No Known Grave,
Commemorated Thiepval Memorial, Pier & Face 4 D 5 B
4819 Lance-Sergeant L. Case   Wounded 20th Jan. 1900,
Spermans Drift, Relief of Ladysmith, Boer War.
6154 Private B. Cassidy   Wounded 23rd Feb. 1900,
Inniskilling Hill, Relief of Ladysmith, Boer War.
2552 Sergeant H.R. Castle   Wounded 23rd Feb. 1900,
Inniskilling Hill, Relief of Ladysmith, Boer War,
invalided home on SS *Galatea*.

549 Private H. Caulfield   3rd Battalion Royal Inniskilling Fusiliers,
Died of Disease, (Enteric Fever), Ladysmith, Boer War, 25th May 1900.
427 Private W. Caulfield   Wounded 15th Dec. 1899, Battle of Colenso,
3556 Corporal H. Chambers   'C' Coy.Wounded 15th Dec. 1899,
(foot & knee), Battle of Colenso, Boer War.
1667 Private W. Chambers   4th Battalion Royal Inniskilling Fusiliers,
(The Royal Tyrone Regiment), Boer War.

5914 Corporal D. Clarke   Died of Disease, (Enteric Fever),
Station Hospital, Middelburg 10th Dec. 1900,
Interred Middelburg Cemetery, Grave No. B18.
5180 Private J. Clarke   Wounded 23rd Feb. 1900,
Inniskilling Hill, Relief of Ladysmith, Boer War.

6133 Private J. Clarke   Died of Disease, (Enteric Fever),
Boer War, 26th Feb. 1902.

5341 Sergeant T.A. Clarke   Died of Disease, (Enteric Fever),
Boer War, 22nd Nov. 1900, Interred Middelburg Cemetery, Grave No. B6.
1834 Private W. Clarke   4th Battalion Royal Inniskilling Fusiliers,
(The Royal Tyrone Regiment), Boer War.

6386 Private W. Clarke   Born Shankill, Co. Antrim.
1st Battalion Royal Inniskilling Fusiliers, World War I, Killed in Action
France & Flanders,   Friday 1st Jul 1916,   World War I, No Known
Grave,   Commemorated Thiepval Memorial Pier & Face 4 D 5 B.

3108 Sergeant J. Clelland   MID (30th March 1900), Boer War. DCM, Killed in Action, 8th May 1901, Interred Middleburg Cemetery, Grave No. P15.

7035 Private R. Coates   Born Ballymacarett, Co. Down, Son of Robert & Annie Coates, A/C.S.M., Died of Wounds at Sea, Returning from Gallipoli, Thursday 26th Aug. 1915, Aged 32, Commemorated Helles Memorial Gallipoli Peninsula Panels 97-101

903 Private J. Coleman   4th Battion Royal Inniskilling Fusiliers, (The Royal Tyrone Regiment), Boer War.

6940 Private J. Coleman   Born Kingstown, Co. Dublin, 2nd Battalion Royal Inniskilling Fusiliers, World War I, Died of Wounds at Home in Derry (Ebrington Barracks), 9th Nov. 1915, Interred City Cemetery Derry Military Section G, World War I.

3481 Private W. Coleman   Wounded Reported Missing in Action after Battle of Inniskilling Hill, Relief of Ladysmith, 23rd/24th Feb. 1900.

6019 Private S. Collins   Died of Disease, (Enteric Fever), Ladysmith, Boer War, 19th Apr. 1900.

1528 Private A. Combey   4th Battalion Royal Inniskilling Fusiliers, (The Royal Tyrone Regiment), Boer War.

2711 Private J. Commons   Wounded 15th Dec. 1899, Battle of Colenso,

1819 Private C. Connaghan   4th Battalion Royal Inniskilling Fusiliers, (The Royal Tyrone Regiment), Boer War.

5618 Private C. Connell   Wounded 23rd Feb. 1900, Inniskilling Hill, Relief of Ladysmith, Boer War.

977 Private W. Connelly   Wounded 23rd Feb. 1900, Inniskilling Hill, Relief of Ladysmith, Boer War.

5919 Sergeant D. Connors   Wounded 23rd Feb. 1900, Inniskilling Hill, Relief of Ladysmith, Boer War.

3163 Sergeant C. Conway   Wounded 15th Dec. 1899, Battle of Colenso,

6146 Private J. Coote   Wounded 27th Aug. 1900, Bergendal Farm (Major-Geneneral Kitchener's Seventh Brigade).

2864 Private R. Cotter   Wounded 15th Dec. 1899, Battle of Colenso,

1095 Private W. Cotter   Died of Wounds Bergendal, Transvaal, Boer War, 6th Jan. 1901, Interred Belfast Town Cemetery,Military Grave No. 203.

5257 Drummer C. Couchman   MID (4th September 1901), Boer War.

1932 Private J. Coyle   4th Battalion Royal Inniskilling Fusiliers, (The Royal Tyrone Regiment), Served with Northumberland Fusiliers, Boer War.

1655 Private P. Coyle   4th Battalion Royal Inniskilling Fusiliers,
(The Royal Tyrone Regiment)
Served with Northumberland Fusiliers, Boer War.

1101 Private D. Craig   3rd Battalion Royal Inniskilling Fusiliers,
Killed in Action, Inniskilling Hill, Relief of Ladysmith, 23rd Feb. 1900.

3087 Private R. Craig   Wounded 23rd Feb. 1900,
Inniskilling Hill, Relief of Ladysmith, Boer War.

3965 Sergeant W. Craig   MID, (Twice) (13th September 1900
& 4th September 1901) & DCM, Boer War.

1255 Private G. Cranston   Wounded 23rd Feb. 1900,
Inniskilling Hill, Relief of Ladysmith, Boer War.

1412 Private W. Crawford   4th Battalion Royal Inniskilling Fusiliers,
(The Royal Tyrone Regiment), Boer War.

2606 Private J. Crawle   Died of Disease, (Enteric Fever),
Boer War, 15th Mar. 1901.

6622 Private S. Cree   Son of Mary Gee of Belfast & William Cree,
Husband of Agnes Cree, 3 Druse St., Belfast, Born Shankill, Co. Antrim,
2nd Battalion Royal Inniskilling Fusiliers, World War I, Sergeant.
Died France & Flanders, Monday, 15th Dec. 1914, Aged 30,
Interred Ste. Marie Cemetery, Le Havre, Grave Ref. 14. G. 5.

6011 Private J. Cribbin   Died of Wounds,
Battle of Colenso, 16th Dec. 1899.

2612 Private C. Critcher   Wounded 20th Jan. 1900,
Spion Kop, Relief of Ladysmith.

3087 Private D. Crothers   Wounded 23rd Feb. 1900,
Inniskilling Hill, Relief of Ladysmith, Boer War.

1445 Private G. Crowe   4th Battalion Royal Inniskilling Fusiliers,
(The Royal Tyrone Regiment),Boer War.

5263 Private G. Crozier   Wounded 8th Apr. 1902, Blockhouse Duty,

3562 Private J. Cubbinson   Killed in Action,
Inniskilling Hill, Relief of Ladysmith, Boer War, 23rd Feb. 1900.

1755 Private F. Cullen   4th Battalion Royal Inniskilling Fusiliers,
(The Royal Tyrone Regiment), Boer War.

2899 Private E. Cully   Wounded (Abdomen & Right Foot),
Died of Wounds, Inniskilling Hill, Relief of Ladysmith, 27th Feb. 1900.

2419 Private J. Curran   Wounded 15th Dec. 1899 Battle of Colenso,

3286 Private J. Curran   Wounded 23rd Feb. 1900,
Inniskilling Hill, Relief of Ladysmith, Boer War.

2464 Private H. Curran   Wounded 23rd Feb. 1900,
Inniskilling Hill, Relief of Ladysmith, Boer War.

3645 Private P. Curran — Wounded 23rd Feb. 1900, Inniskilling Hill, Relief of Ladysmith, Boer War.

1101 Private G. Currans — 4th Battalion Royal Inniskilling Fusiliers, (The Royal Tyrone Regiment), Served with Northumberland Fusiliers.

D

3048 Private W. Darcey — Wounded (Both Legs), 23rd/24th Feb. 1900, Inniskilling Hill, Relief of Ladysmith, Boer War.

3320 Private J. Darley — Died as result of an accident, 20th Mar. 1900.

1486 Private A. Daragh — 4th Battalion Royal Inniskilling Fusiliers, (The Royal Tyrone Regiment), Served with Northumberland Fusiliers.

1354 Private J. Darragh — 4th Battalion Royal Inniskilling Fusiliers, (The Royal Tyrone Regiment), Boer War.

3312 Private C. Davis — Wounded 23rd Feb. 1900, Inniskilling Hill, Relief of Ladysmith, Boer War.

3694 Corporal F. Davis — Wounded 23rd Feb. 1900, Inniskilling Hill, Relief of Ladysmith, Boer War.

4527 Private T. Davis — Wounded 15th Dec. 1899, Battle of Colenso.

5299 Private A. Dawson — Died of Disease, at Frere (Dysentery), No Date.

7044 Private W. Deery — Son of Michael & Bridget Deery of Derry, Born Templemore, Co. Derry, "A" Coy. 2nd Battalion Royal Inniskilling Fusiliers, World War I, Killed in Action, France & Flanders, Tuesday 1st Sept. 1914, Aged 33, World War I, Interred Verberie Communal Cemetery, 11 km. south-east of Compiègne, Grave Ref 9.

2543 Corporal K. Delaney — Wounded 15th Dec. 1900, Battle of Colenso.

1064 Colour-Sergeant M. Delaney — Wounded 23rd Feb. 1900, Inniskilling Hill, Relief of Ladysmith, Boer War, MID(4th September 1901)

2226 Private P. Devenney — Killed in Action, 12th Oct. 1900, Witpoort, N.E. Transvaal, Boer War.

5542 Private P. Devenney — Killed in Action, Spion Kop, Natal, 23rd Jan. 1900.

1336 Private P. Devenney — 4th Battalion Royal Inniskilling Fusiliers, (The Royal Tyrone Regiment) Killed in Action Mooi River 22nd Mar 1900.

3469 Private S. Devenney — Wounded (Shell wound to left leg, Right Shoulder, Face & compound fracture to Left Arm), 23rd/24th Feb. 1900, Inniskilling Hill, Relief of Ladysmith, Boer War.

4328 Lance-Corporal W. Devin — Died of Wounds, Inniskilling Hill, Relief of Ladysmith, Boer War, 24th Feb 1900.

6103 Private J. Devlin Killed in Action, Inniskilling Hill, Relief of Ladysmith, Boer War, 23rd Feb. 1900.

2675 Private W. Devlin Wounded (Both Thighs), 23rd/24th Feb. 1900, Inniskilling Hill, Relief of Ladysmith, Boer War.

5212 Drummer J. Dillon 5th Battalion Royal Inniskilling Fusiliers, (The Royal Donegal Regiment) Died of Disease, (Enteric Fever),15th June 1900.

3604 Private W. Dixon Wounded (Left Leg & Right Arm), 23rd / 24th Feb. 1900, Inniskilling Hill, Relief of Ladysmith, Boer War.

6935 Lance-Corporal J. Doak Born Lurgan Co. Antrim, Son of John & Susan Doak of Portadown, Husband of Alice Jane Doak of 25 Mournview St., Portadown, 2nd Battalion Royal Inniskilling Fusiliers, Sergeant, Died of Wounds, France & Flanders, 15th Jul. 1916, Aged 32, Interred Warloy-Baillon Communal Cemetery Extension, 21 km., north-east of Amiens, Grave Ref. III. E. 25.

3729 Lance-Corporal S. Dobbin Killed in Action, Battle of Colenso 15th Dec. 1899.

3222 Private J. Dodds Wounded 15th Dec. 1899, Battle of Colenso.

6945 Private J. Dodds Born Lisburn Co. Down, Died of Wounds, Gallipoli, 31st Aug. 1915, World War I, Interred Cairo War Memorial Cemetery, Egypt, Grave Reference D. 74.

2024 Private E. Doherty Killed in Action, Inniskilling Hill, Relief of Ladysmith, Boer War, 23rd Feb. 1900.

5758 Private J. Doherty Born Letterkenny Co. Donegal, A/CQMS, Killed in Action, France & Flanders, 22nd Mar. 1918, World War I, MM, No Known Grave, Commermorated Pozières Memorial, Somme, France Panel 38-40.

953 Private M. Doherty 4th Battalion Royal Inniskilling Fusiliers, (The Royal Tyrone Regiment), Boer War.

3356 Drummer P. T. Doherty Wounded 15th Dec. 1899 Battle of Colenso.

1484 Private W. Doherty 4th Battalion Royal Inniskilling Fusiliers, (The Royal Tyrone Regiment), Boer War.

3230 Private W. Doherty Died of Disease, (Enteric Fever), Station Hospital Middleburg, Struck off Roll 1st Dec. 1900, Boer War.

1854 Private F. Donaghy 4th Battalion Royal Inniskilling Fusiliers, (The Royal Tyrone Regiment), Boer War.

5932 Private W. Donegan Died of Wounds, Boer War, 3rd July 1901Interred Krugersdorp Cemetery, Grave No. 24.

2461 Private J. Donnelly Wounded 15th Dec. 1899, Battle of Colenso.

4358 Private P. Donnelly   4th Battalion Royal Inniskilling Fusiliers,
(The Royal Tyrone Regiment), Boer War.

5761 Private J. Dougan   Killed in Action,
Inniskilling Hill, Relief of Ladysmith, 23rd Feb. 1900, Boer War.

3230 Private W. Dougherty   Died of Disease, (Enteric Fever),
Boer War, 2nd Dec.1900, Interred Middleburg Cemetery, Grave No. B13.

6077 Private Dowds   Reported Missing in Action
after Battle of Inniskilling Hill, Relief of Ladysmith, 23rd/24th Feb. 1900,
Killed, Inniskilling Hill, 23rd/24th Feb. 1900, Boer War.

2361 Private J. Doyle   Wounded 23rd Feb. 1900,
Inniskilling Hill, Relief of Ladysmith, Boer War.

6064 Private P. Doyle   2nd Battalion Royal Inniskilling Fusiliers,
World War I, Died France & Flanders, 16th May 1915,
Commemorated Le Touret Memorial, Pas de Calais, France, Panel 16-17.

2165 Drummer W. Dudley   from Annahoe, Co. Tyrone.

1908 Private P. Duffy   Died of Wounds, Major-General W. Kitchener's
Seventh Brigade, Bergendal Farm, Boer War, 27th Aug. 1900.

6067 Private E. Duncan   Wounded 19th Dec. 1900,
Thorndale, Boer War.

E

4498 Lance-Corporal C. Eddiker   Wounded 23rd Feb. 1900,
Inniskilling Hill, Relief of Ladysmith, Boer War.

5388 Private W. Erwin   Reported Missing in Action
after Battle of Inniskilling Hill, Relief of Ladysnith, 23rd/24th Feb. 1900.

5715 Private W. Espey   Killed in Action,
Inniskilling Hill, Relief of Ladysmith 23rd Feb. 1900, Boer War.

3463 Private D. Evans   Wounded 15th Dec. 1899, Battle of Colenso.

6714 Private J. Ewart   Son of Thomas & Annie Ewart,
2nd Battalion Royal Inniskilling Fusiliers, World War I,
Died of Wounds France & Flanders, Tuesday 6th Oct. 1914, Aged 43
Cairo Memorial Cemetery, Grave Ref. B. 113.

F

2432 Private J. Farmer   Wounded 15th Dec. 1899, Battle of Colenso.

6707 Private J. Farnen   Killed, Boer War.

2348 Private J. Farrell   Wounded 23rd Feb. 1900,
Inniskilling Hill, Relief of Ladysmith, Boer War.

7139 Private W. Farren   Son of John & Lettie Farren, of Monellan,
Co. Donegal, Husband of Mary A. Farren, 27 Florence St., Waterside
Derry, "C" Coy. 2nd Battalion Royal Inniskilling Fusiliers, World War I,
Killed in Action, Wednesday 21st Oct. 1914, Aged 31, No Known Grave,
Commemorated Ploegsteert Memorial Panel 5,
Berks Cemetery Extension, South of Ieper.

6164 Private J. Feeley   Killed in Action,
Inniskilling Hill, Relief of Ladysmith 23rd Feb. 1900, Boer War.

5625 Private W. Ferguson   Wounded 15th Dec. 1899, Battle of Colenso.

5693 Private W. Ferguson   Wounded 23rd Feb. 1900,
Inniskilling Hill, Relief of Ladysmith, Boer War.

751 Private P. Finlay   4th Battalion Royal Inniskilling Fusiliers,
(The Royal Tyrone Regiment), Boer War.

1241 Private J. Finney   Killed, Boer War, 26th Feb. 1901,
Interred Pretoria Cemetery (Roman Catholic), Grave No. 87.

5019 Corporal B Fitzgerald   Drummer Promoted Corporal
for Gallantry in the Field (26th December 1899)
MID (30th March 1900) & DCM. Boer War.

6033 Private O. Fitzgibbon   Wounded in thigh 12th Oct. 1900,
Witkloof enroute to Middleburg, Boer War.

3602 Private D. Fitzpatrick   Wounded 23rd Feb. 1900,
Inniskilling Hill, Relief of Ladysmith, Boer War.

6201 Corporal H. Fitzsimmons   Died of Disease, (Enteric Fever),
Boer War, 21st Feb. 1901 Interred Elandsfontein Cemetery,Grave No.79.

407 Private C. Flannagan   4th Battalion Royal Inniskilling Fusiliers,
(The Royal Tyrone Regiment), Boer War.

952 Lance-Corporal E. Flannagan   Wounded 23rd Feb. 1900,
Inniskilling Hill, Relief of Ladysmith, Boer War.

6017 Private F. Flannagan   Wounded 15th Dec. 1899,
Battle of Colenso.

1218 Corporal W. Flannagan   4th Battalion Royal Inniskilling Fusiliers,
(The Royal Tyrone Regiment), Boer War.

2586 Private M. Flood   Wounded (Chest & Right Arm),
23rd / 24th Feb. 1900, Inniskilling Hill, Relief of Ladysmith, Boer War.

3213 Private J. Flynn   Wounded (Right Arm & Left Chest),
23rd / 24th Feb. 1900, Inniskilling Hill, Relief of Ladysmith, Boer War.

5424 Private J. Flynn   Killed in Action,
Inniskilling Hill, Relief of Ladysmith 23rd Feb. 1900, Boer War.

2884 Corporal M. Forbes   Wounded 23rd Feb. 1900,
Inniskilling Hill, Relief of Ladysmith, Wounded 27th Aug. 1900,
Bergendal Farm Major-General W Kitchener's Seventh Brigade.

5899 Private H. Forsythe   Wounded (Left Arm & Hip),
23rd / 24th Feb. 1900, Inniskilling Hill, Relief of Ladysmith, Boer War.
3090 Private R. Fowler   Wounded 23rd Feb. 1900,
Inniskilling Hill, Relief of Ladysmdith, Boer War.
1022 Private J. Fox   4th Battalion Royal Inniskilling Fusiliers.
(The Royal Tyrone Regiment), Served with Northumberland Fusiliers.
2574 Private W. Fox   Wounded 23rd Feb. 1900,
Inniskilling Hill, Relief of Ladysmith, Boer War.
4591 Colour-Sergeant G.E. Framingham   MID, (4th September 1901),
Boer War later RSM & QM of the 1st Battalion; awarded MBE & MC.
2660 Private W. Frazer   Wounded 23rd Feb. 1900,
Inniskilling Hill, Relief of Ladysmith, Boer War,
invalided home on SS Galatea.

G

6275 Private E. Gallagher   Wounded (Back & Shoulder),
Inniskilling Hill, Relief of Ladysmith, 23rd / 24th Feb. 1900.
Died of Wounds, Norts Hill 25th Feb. 1900, Boer War.
92 Sergeant J. Gallagher   4th Battalion Royal Inniskilling Fusiliers,
(The Royal Tyrone Regiment), Boer War.
1884 Private J. Gallagher   5th Battalion Royal Inniskilling Fusiliers,
(The Royal Donegal Regiment), Boer War.
5928 Private J. Gallagher   4th Battalion Royal Inniskilling Fusiliers,
(The Royal Tyrone Regiment), Boer War.
4943 Lance/Corporal J. Gallagher   5th Battalion Royal Inniskilling
Fusiliers, (The Royal Donegal Regiment) Regt. Band, Wounded
(Chest & lung), 23rd/24th Feb. 1900 Inniskilling Hill, Relief of Ladysmith,
Died of Wounds, Mooi River, 21st. Mar. 1900.
3329 Private P. Gallagher   Wounded 15th Dec. 1899,
Battle of Colenso, Boer War.
6108 Private P Gallagher   Wounded Reported Missing in Action
after Battle of Inniskilling Hill, Relief of Ladysmith, 23rd/24th Feb. 1900
2799 Private T. Gallagher   Wounded 12th Dec. 1900, Boer War.
5918 Lance-Corporal D. Gamble   Wounded (Bullet wounds,
compound fracture of left thigh, right arm, chest and neck),
23rd / 24th Feb. 1900,Inniskilling Hill, Relief of Ladysmith, Boer War.
4621 Lance-Corporal J.A. Gardner   MID, (Twice), (13th September 1900
& 4th September 1901), Boer War.
2686 Private J. Gavan   Wounded 16th Dec. 1900,
Thorndale, Boer War.

6445 Private W. Gentles 2nd Battalion Royal Inniskilling Fusiliers,
World War I, Killed in Action, France & Flanders, Saturday7[th] Nov. 1914
No Known Grave, Commemorated Ploegesteert Memorial Panel 5,
Berks Cemetery Extension South of Ieper.

1657 Corporal J. Gibbings 4th Battalion Royal Inniskilling Fusiliers,
(The Royal Tyrone Regiment), Boer War.

2407 Private J. Gillespie Wounded (Both Legs),
23rd/24th Feb. 1900, Inniskilling Hill, Relief of Ladysmith, Boer War.

5755 Lance-Corporal T. Gilligan Died of Wounds,
Inniskilling Hill, Relief of Ladysmith, Boer War, 23rd Feb. 1900.

2791 Private J. Gilmore Wounded 15th Dec. 1899,
Battle of Colenso, Boer War.

1533 Private M. Girr 4th Battalion Royal Inniskilling Fusiliers,
(The Royal Tyrone Regiment), Boer War.

3913 Private W. Goldsmith Wounded (Right Arm & Abdomen),
23rd / 24th Feb. 1900, Inniskilling Hill, Relief of Ladysmith, Boer War.

2993 Colour-Sergeant A.E. Goodall Wounded 23rd Feb. 1900,
Inniskilling Hill, Relief of Ladysmith, Boer War.

5892 Private T. Goodman Died of Disease,
(Enteric Fever), Mooi River, Boer War.

2567 Private M. Gordon Wounded 23rd Feb. 1900,
Inniskilling Hill, Relief of Ladysmith, Boer War.

3794 Private W.J. Gordon Killed in Action,
Inniskilling Hill, Relief of Ladysmith, Boer War, 23rd Feb. 1900.

5923 Sergeant J. Gore Wounded 15th Dec. 1899,
Battle of Colenso, Boer War.

5962 Private J. Gourley Wounded 23rd Feb. 1900,
Inniskilling Hill, Relief of Ladysmith, Boer War.

7091 Private J. Gourley Died as a result of Meningitis, Boer War.

3738 Private H. Grace Invalided home on SS *Galatea.*

5511 Corporal J. Graham Wounded 15th Dec. 1899,
Battle of Colenso, Boer War.

4457 Private W.J. Graham Died of Wounds,
Thorndale, Boer War, 16th Dec. 1900.

950 Corporal D. Green 4th Battalion Royal Inniskilling Fusiliers,
(The Royal Tyrone Regiment), Boer War.

2347 Private T. Green Wounded 23rd Feb. 1900,
Inniskilling Hill, Relief of Ladysmith, Boer War.

2480 Private T. Grenfield Wounded 23rd Feb. 1900,
Inniskilling Hill, Relief of Ladysmith, Boer War.

3428 Private J. Gribbon   Wounded 15th Dec. 1899,
Battle of Colenso, Boer War.
3372 Corporal W. Griffin   Wounded 23rd Feb. 1900,
Inniskilling Hill,Relief of Ladysmith, Boer War.
3455 Private D. Guy   Killed in Action,
Inniskilling Hill, Relief of Ladysmith, Boer War, 23rd Feb. 1900.

H

5005 Serjeant A. Hall   Husband of Annie Hall,
of 14 Wellington Place, Enniskillen, Co. Fermangh
4th Battalion Royal Inniskilling Fusiliers (The Royal Tyrone Regiment),
World War I, CSM, Died of wounds at Home, Tuesday 23rd June 1915,
Aged 39, Interred Enniskillen Roman Catholic Cemetery.
3773 Private A. Hamilton   Wounded 15th Dec. 1899,
Battle of Colenso, Boer War.
1046 Private G. Hamilton   4th Battalion Royal Inniskilling Fusiliers,
(The Royal Tyrone Regiment), Boer War.
3511 Private R. Hamilton   Wounded (Abdomen & Right Side),
23rd / 24th Feb. 1900, Inniskilling Hill Relief of Ladysmith,
Died of wounds, Boer War.
6703 Private T. Hamilton   2nd Battalion Royal Inniskilling Fusiliers,
World War I, Killed in Action, Thursday 30th Nov. 1917,
No Known Grave,
Commemorated Tyne Cot Cemetery, Memorial Panel 70 – 72.
6414 Private G. Hampsey   Died of Disease, (Enteric Fever),
Boer War, 3rd Feb. 1901, Middleburg Cemetery, Grave No. D6.
3482 Private J. Hanley   Wounded 15th Dec. 1899,
Battle of Colenso, Boer War.
993 Private S. Hanna   4th Battalion Royal Inniskilling Fusiliers,
(The Royal Tyrone Regiment), Boer War.
890 Private J. Haren   Wounded (Head & Right Shoulder),
23rd/24th Feb. 1900, Inniskilling Hill, Relief of Ladysmith, Boer War.
3170 Sergeant J. Harrison   Killed in Action,
Inniskilling Hill, Relief of Ladysmith, Boer War, 23rd Feb. 1900.
6686 Private J. Harvey   Died of Wounds,
Gallipoli, Friday 5th June 1915, World War I,
Interred Twelve Trees Copse Cemetery, Helles area, Sp. Mem. C. 333.
2640 Private J. Hatton   Wounded 15th Dec. 1899,
Battle of Colenso, Boer War.
2473 Private J. Hayes   Wounded 23rd Feb. 1900,
Inniskilling Hill, Relief of Ladysmith, Boer War.

3381 Private J. Healy   Wounded (Both Legs),
23rd/24th Feb. 1900, Inniskilling Hill, Relief of Ladysmith, Boer War.

4467 Drummer F. Hearn   Wounded 15th Dec. 1899,
Battle of Colenso, Boer War.

4322 Private J. Henderson   Killed in Action,
Thorndale, Boer War, 15th Dec. 1900.

6080 Private J. Henderson   Wounded 23rd Feb. 1900,
Inniskilling Hill, Relief of Ladysmith, Boer War.

6202 Private R. Henderson   Killed In Action,
Inniskilling Hill, Relief of Ladysmith, Boer War, 23rd Feb. 1900.

264 Private W. Henderson   Wounded 23rd Feb. 1900,
Inniskilling Hill, Relief of Ladysmith, Boer War.

2726 Private J. Hickey   Died of Wounds, Boer War, 13th Jan. 1900.

2425 Corporal M. Hickey   Wounded 15th Dec. 1899,
Battle of Colenso, Boer War.

3219 Private T. Hider   Wounded 23rd Feb. 1900,
Inniskilling Hill, Relief of Ladysmith, Boer War

1325 Private H. Hill   4th Battalion Royal Inniskilling Fusiliers,
(The Royal Tyrone Regiment), Boer War.

7185 Private M. Hill   Son of Patrick & Ellen Hill,
Native of Widnes 2nd Battalion Royal Inniskilling Fusiliers World War I
Killed in Action France & Flanders, Thursday 22nd Jul. 1915 Aged 33,
Interred Bethune Town Cemetery, Grave Ref. IV. D. 21.

4370 Private W. Hill   Wounded 15th Dec. 1899,
Battle of Colenso, Boer War, Died of Wounds, 19th Dec. 1899.

5779 Private W. Hillier   Killed in Action,
Inniskilling Hill, Relief of Ladysmith, Boer War, 23rd/24th Feb. 1900.

5027 Private A.S. Holden   Wounded 23rd Feb. 1900,
Inniskilling Hill, Relief of Ladysmith, Boer War.

1065 Private W. Hollywood   Wounded 23rd Feb. 1900,
Inniskilling Hill, Relief of Ladysmith, Boer War.

4060 Colour/Sergeant G. Holmes   Wounded 15th Dec. 1899,
Battle of Colenso, Boer War.

4021 Lance-Sergeant T. Hood   Killed in Action,
Inniskilling Hill, Relief of Ladysmith, Boer War, 23rd Feb. 1900.

890 Private J.Horen   Wounded Reported Missing in Action
after Battle of Inniskilling Hill, Relief of Ladysmith, 23rd/24th Feb. 1900

4284 Private P. Howard   Wounded 22nd Jan. 1900,
Spion Kop, MID (4th September 1901) & DCM, Boer War.

2168 Private M. Hughes Died of Disease, (Enteric Fever), Boer War, 10th Jul. 1901.

6239 Private J. Hull Wounded Reported Missing in Action after Battle of Inniskilling Hill, Relief of Ladysmith, 23rd/24th Feb. 1900

5587 Private J. Humphries Killed in Action, Inniskilling Hill, Relief of Ladysmith, Boer War, 23rd Feb. 1900.

4999 Corporal R.S. Hunt Wounded 23rd Feb. 1900, Inniskilling Hill, Relief of Ladysmith, Boer War.

1540 Private J. Hyndsman Died of Disease, (Enteric Fever), 17th May 1900.

6934 Private R. Hyndsman Son of William & Mary Hyndsman, Omagh, Co. Tyrone, Husband of Mary Hyndsman, 9 Kennedy St., Strabane,Died of Wounds, Gallipoli, Thursday 17th Dec. 1915, Aged 33 World War I, Interred Lancashire Landing Cemetery, 11 km. west of Sedd el Bahr, Gallipoli Peninsula, Grave Ref. H. 78.

5088 Private J. Hynes Wounded 23rd Feb. 1900, Inniskilling Hill, Relief of Ladysmith, Boer War.

I

5816 Private G. Ingram. Wounded 15th Dec. 1899, Battle of Colenso, Boer War.

2968 Sergeant J. Ireland Killed in Action, Battle of Colenso, Boer War,15th Dec. 1899.

2683 Private T.H. Irvine Wounded 23rd Jan. 1900, Spion Kop, Boer War.

2700 Private W. Irwin Killed in Action, Inniskilling Hill, Relief of Ladysmith, Boer War.

J

6011 Private J. Jenkins Wounded 4th Feb. 1902, Boer War.

3580 Private A. Johnston Wounded 23rd Feb. 1900, Inniskilling Hill, Relief of Ladysmith, Boer War.

2628 Private J. Johnston Wounded 23rd Feb. 1900, Inniskilling Hill, Relief of Ladysmith, Boer War.

3096 Private J. Johnston Wounded 23rd Feb. 1900, Inniskilling Hill, Relief of Ladysmith, Boer War.

7138 Private J. Johnston Son of Mrs. Mary Johnston, Anney Cottage, Breagh, Co. Tyrone, 2nd Battalion Royal Inniskilling Fusiliers, World War I, Killed in Action, France & Flanders, 21st Oct. 1914, No Known Grave, Commerated Ploegsteert Memorial Panel 5.

1047 Private J. Johnstone   4th Battalion Royal Inniskilling Fusiliers,
(The Royal Tyrone Regiment), Boer War.

3305 Private W.J. Jones   Died of Wounds,
Inniskilling Hill, Relief of Ladysmith, Boer War, 23rd Feb. 1900.

2746 Private J. Joyce   Killed in Action,
Inniskilling Hill, Relief of Ladysmith, Boer War, 23rd Feb. 1900.

6176 Private J. Joyce   2nd Battalion Royal Inniskilling Fusiliers,
World War I, Killed in Action, France & Flanders, Thursday 2nd Apr.
1915,   No Known Grave, Commemorated Le Touret Memorial,
Panel 16 & 17, Le Touret Military Cemetery.

487 Sergeant F. Judge   4th Battalion Royal Inniskilling Fusiliers,
(The Royal Tyrone Regiment), Boer War.

1189 Corporal W. Judge   4th Battalion Royal Inniskilling Fusiliers,
(The Royal Tyrone Regiment), Boer War.

K

2695 Private M. Kavanagh   Died of Disease,
(Dysentery), 26th Dec. 1899.

5771 Private M. Kavanagh   Died of Disease,
(Dysentery), 8th Jun. 1900.

2601 Private P. Kavanagh   Killed in Action,
Inniskilling Hill, Relief of Ladysmith, Boer War, 23rd/24th Feb. 1900.

6256 Private T. Kealey   2nd Battalion Royal Inniskilling Fusiliers,
World War I , Killed in Action, France & Flanders
Saturday 16th May 1915, No Known Grave Le Touret Memorial,
Le Touret Military Cemetery, Panel 16 & 17.

2044 Private D. Keegan   Killed in Action,
Nooitgedacht 13th Dec. 1900, Served with Northumberland Fusiliers.

6697 Private J. Keegan   Killed in Action, Boer War, 18th Jul. 1901.

3605 Sergeant B. Keenan   Wounded 23rd Feb. 1900,
Inniskilling Hill, Relief of Ladysmith, Boer War.

2927 Private F. Keeping   Wounded 15th Dec. 1899,
Battle of Colenso, Boer War.

3044 Corporal T. Keeping   Wounded (Abdomen, Thigh & Arm),
23rd / 24th Feb. 1900, Inniskilling Hill, Relief of Ladysmith, Boer War.

6059 Private D. Kelly   Wounded 23rd Feb. 1900,
Inniskilling Hill, Relief of Ladysmith, Boer War.

705 Private E. Kelly — Wounded Reported Missing in Action after Battle of Inniskilling Hill, Relief of Ladysmith, 23rd/24th Feb. 1900 Wounded 23rd Feb. 1900, Inniskilling Hill, Relief of Ladysmith,

2886 Private J. Kelly — Wounded 22nd Jan. 1900, Spion Kop, Boer War.

6053 Private J. Kelly — Wounded 15th Dec. 1899, Battle of Colenso, Boer War.

3536 Sergeant J.A. Kelly — MID (4th September 1901) & DCM, Boer War.

4194 Private S. Kelly — Promoted Corporal by Lord Kitchener for Gallantry in the Field (23rd April 1901), Boer War.

3179 Lance-Corporal T. Kelly — from 11 Disraeli Street, Belfast, Killed in Action, Battle of Colenso, 15th Dec. 1899.

2765 Private W. Kelly — Invalided home on SS *Galatea*.

2372 Private T. Kempton — Wounded 23rd Feb. 1900, Inniskilling Hill, Relief of Ladysmith, Boer War.

484 Private H. Kennedy — 4th Battalion Royal Inniskilling Fusiliers, (The Royal Tyrone Regiment), Boer War.

4750 Private M. Kennedy — Wounded 15th Dec. 1899, Battle of Colenso, Boer War, Died of Wounds 16th Dec. 1899.

4237 Private P. Kennedy — Wounded 15th Dec. 1899, Battle of Colenso, Boer War.

5687 Private P. Kennedy — Wounded 23rd Feb. 1900, Inniskilling Hill, Relief of Ladysmith, Boer War.

5233 Private J. Kenny — Killed, Boer War, 6th Sept. 1903, Interred Pretoria Cemetery (Roman Catholic).

6412 Private J. Keown — 2nd Battalion Royal Inniskilling Fusiliers, Killed in Action, France & Flanders, Tuesday 26th Aug. 1914, Interred Esnes Communal Cemetery, Grave Ref. I.

1804 Private P. Kerrigan — Wounded 23rd Feb. 1900, Inniskilling Hill, Relief of Ladysmith, Boer War.

3049 Private T. Kerrigan — Wounded 23rd Feb. 1900, Inniskilling Hill, Relief of Ladysmith, Boer War.

5988 Private W. Kidd — Wounded 23rd Feb. 1900, Inniskilling Hill, Relief of Ladysmith, Boer War.

995 Private D. Kincaid — Killed in Action, Battle of Colenso, 15th Dec. 1899, Boer War.

3079 Private T. Kinnon — Wounded 23rd Feb. 1900, Inniskilling Hill, Relief of Ladysmith, Boer War.

3155 Corporal W. Kyle — Wounded 23rd Aug. 1900, Geluk, Boer War.

L

6902 Private C. Lavery Killed in Action,
France & Flanders, 16th May 1915, World War I, No Known Grave,
Commemorated Le Touret Memorial Le Touret Military Cemetery,
Panel 16-17.

1094 Private C. Lawless 4th Battalion Royal Inniskilling Fusiliers,
(The Royal Tyrone Regiment), Boer War.

5955 Private F. Lawrence Born Kusauli, India,
Son of Frederick Lawrence of Ipswich,
Husband of Margret Lawrence of 2 Orchard Lane, Derry,
Died of Wounds at Home, Ebrington Barracks Derry, 9th Mar. 1915,
Aged 38, Interred Derry City Cemetery,
Plot M, Row D, Grave No. 589, World War I.

5017 Private D. Leahy Died of Disease, (Enteric Fever), Boer War.

6284 Private P. Ledwidge Died, France & Flanders,
31st Aug 1916, World War I,
Interred Ste. Marie Cemetery, Le Havre, Grave Ref. Div. 3. E. 8.

3571 Colour-Sergeant A. R. Lee MID, (Twice) (13th September 1900
& 4th September 1901) & DCM, Boer War.

3419 Private J. Lee Wounded 23rd Feb. 1900,
Inniskilling Hill, Relief of Ladysmith, Boer War.

5999 Private H. Leith Killed in Action,
Battle of Colenso, 15th Dec. 1899, Boer War.

725 Private J. Leonard Wounded 23rd Feb. 1900,
Inniskilling Hill, Relief of Ladysmith, Boer War.

1672 Private F. Lewis 4th Battalion Royal Inniskilling Fusiliers,
(The Royal Tyrone Regiment) Served with Northumberland Fusiliers,
Boer War.

1198 Private T. Lindsay 4th Battalion Royal Inniskilling Fusiliers,
(The Royal Tyrone Regiment), Boer War.

213 Private W. Lindsay 4th Battalion Royal Inniskilling Fusiliers,
(The Royal Tyrone Regiment), Boer War.

5621 Private G. Linton Killed in Action,
Inniskilling Hill, Relief of Ladysmith, Boer War, 23rd Feb. 1900.

4256 Private P. Little Wounded 8th Apr. 1902, Boer War.

1542 Private C. Loughlin 4th Battalion Royal Inniskilling Fusiliers,
Died of Disease, (Enteric Fever), Boer War, 15th Jun. 1900.

70 Private J. Loughran 4th Battalion Royal Inniskilling Fusiliers,
(The Royal Tyrone Regiment), Boer War.

1709 Private P. Loughran   4th Battalion Royal Inniskilling Fusiliers,
(The Royal Tyrone Regiment), Boer War.

1277 Lance-Corporal C. Lunney   Wounded 23rd Feb. 1900,
Inniskilling Hill, Relief of Ladysmith, Boer War.

3999 Private J. Luthell   Killed in Action, Boer War, 29th Aug. 1902,
Interred Elandsfontein Cemetery, Grave No. 372.

2796 Private T. Lynch   Wounded 15th Dec. 1899, Battle of Colenso,
Wounded 23rd Feb. 1900, Inniskilling Hill, Relief of Ladysmith.

M

3470 Private A. Mackey   Wounded, 23rd/24th Feb. 1900,
Inniskilling Hill, Relief of Ladysmith, Boer War,
Reported Missing in Action,

6279 Private R. A. Mackey   Sergeant, World War I,
Killed in Action, Gallipoli, 21st Aug 1915, World War I.

2620 Private A Magee   Killed, Boer War, 8th Jan. 1901,
Interred Pretoria Cemetery (Church of England), Grave No. 494.

2617 Sergeant J. Magee   Wounded (Back & Chest),
23rd/24th Feb. 1900, Inniskilling Hill, Relief of Ladysmith, Boer War.

1231 Private M. Magee   4th Battalion Royal Inniskilling Fusiliers,
(The Royal Tyrone Regiment) Served with Northumberland Fusiliers,
Boer War.

6666 Lance-Sergeant W. J. Magee   Son of Francis James
& Louisa F. Magee, of 80 Kimberley St., Ballynafeigh, Belfast,
"G" Coy. 1st Battalion Royal Inniskilling Fusiliers CSM,
Killed in Action, Gallipoli, 17th May 1915, DCM, World War I,
Interred Twelve Tree Copse Cemetery 1 km. south-west of Krithia
in the Helles area, Grave Ref. Sp. Mem.C. 174.

968 Private J. Magnes   4th Battalion Royal Inniskilling Fusiliers,
(The Royal Tyrone Regiment) Served with Northumberland Fusiliers,
Boer War.

13 Private J. Maguire   Wounded 20th Jan. 1900, Spion Kop, Boer War.

3037 Private J. Maguire   Killed in Action,
Inniskilling Hill, Relief of Ladysmith,Boer War, 23rd Feb.1900.

6310 Private J.S. Maguire   Died of Disease,
(Enteric Fever), 28th May 1901.

2847 Private T. Mahon   Wounded 23rd Feb. 1900, Inniskilling
Hill, Relief of Ladysmith, Died of Wounds, Bergendal Farm,
Major-General Kitchener's Seventh Brigade,
Boer War, 27th Aug. 1900.

2935 Private R. Mahoney   Killed in Action,
Inniskilling Hill, Relief of Ladysmith, Boer War,23rd Feb. 1900.

2534 Private J. Malone   Killed in Action,
Inniskilling Hill, Relief of Ladysmith, Boer War, 23rd Feb. 1900.

2925 Private J. Meehan   5th Battalion Royal Inniskilling Fusiliers,
Killed in Action,
Inniskilling Hill, Relief of Ladymith, Boer War, 23rd Feb. 1900.

6977 Private L. Meenagh   Killed in Action,
France & Flanders, Friday 1st Jul. 1916,
Interred "Y" Ravine Cemetery Beaumont-Hamel, South of Auchonvillers
Grave Ref. D. 103.

5496 Private E. Mernor   Wounded 23rd Feb. 1900,
Inniskilling Hill, Relief of Ladysmith, Boer War.

1135 Private D. Milligan   Wounded 23rd Feb. 1900,
Inniskilling Hill, Relief of Ladysmith, Boer War.

3231 Private J. Milligan   Wounded 15th Dec. 1899,
Battle of Colenso, Boer War.

870 Private W. Milligan   3rd Battalion Royal Inniskilling Fusiliers,
Killed in Action,
Inniskilling Hill, Relief of Ladysmith Boer War 23rd Feb. 1900.

2970 Private A. Mills   from 26 Orchard Row, Derry,
MID (4th September 1901) & DCM, Boer War.

4231 Lance-Corporal J. Mitchell   Wounded 8th Apr. 1902,
Blockhouse duty betweenn Kroonstadt-Lindley-Bethlehem.

3130 Private W. Mitchell   Wounded 15th Dec. 1899, Battle of Colenso.

3617 Sergeant P. Mooney   Wounded 15th Dec. 1899, Battle of Colenso,
Died of Disease,(Enteric Fever), Boer War 12th June. 1900.

2537 Private D. Moore   Invalided home of SS *Galatea*.

1529 Private J. Moore   4th Battalion Royal Inniskilling Fusiliers,
(The Royal Tyrone Regiment), Served with Northumberland Fusiliers.

6204 Private T. Moore   Killed in Action,
Inniskilling Hill, Relief of Ladysmith, Boer War, 23rd Feb. 1900.

3297 Private W. Moore   Wounded 23rd Feb. 1900,
Inniskilling Hill, Relief of Ladysmith, Boer War.

5905 Private J. Moorhead   Died of Disease,
(Dysentery), 18th May 1900.

1827 Private G. Morris   4th Battalion Royal Inniskilling Fusiliers,
(The Royal Tyrone Regiment), Served with Northumberland Fusiliers,

3168 Private J. Morrison   Wounded 15th Dec. 1899, Battle of Colenso, Wounded Reported Missing in Action after Battle of Inniskilling Hill, 23rd/24th Feb. 1900, Died of Wounds Inniskilling Hill, Relief of Ladysmith,   23rd/24th Feb. 1900.

5922 Private R. Morrison   Wounded 23rd Feb. 1900, Inniskilling Hill, Relief of Ladysmith, Boer War.

3457 Private S. Morton   Wounded 16th Dec., Boer War.

596 Corporal J. Muldoon   4th Battalion Royal Inniskilling Fusiliers, (The Royal Tyrone Regiment), Boer War.

2909 Private W. Muldoon   Died of Disease, (Pneumonia), 19th Oct. 1901, Boer War,Interred Pretoria Cemetery (Roman Catholic), Grave No. 113.

6265 Private R. Mulholland   Died of Disease, (Dysentery), 14th Feb. 1900.

783 Private T. Mulholland   Wounded (Buttock & Left Hip), 23rd/24th Feb. 1900, Inniskilling Hill, Relief of Ladysmith, Boer War.

5501 Lance-Corporal J. Mullan   Killed In Action, Inniskilling Hill, Relief of Ladysmith, Boer War, 23rd Feb. 1900.

3303 Private T. Mullan   Died of Wounds, Inniskilling Hill, Relief of Ladysmith, Boer War, 23rd Feb. 1900.

3503 Private J. Mullen.   Wounded 15th Dec. 1899, Battle of Colenso, Died of Wounds, Inniskilling Hill, Relief of Ladysmith, 23rd/24th Feb. 1900.

1304 Private J. Murdoch   4th Battalion Royal Inniskilling Fusiliers, (The Royal Tyrone Regiment), Served with Northumberland Fusiliers.

5859 Private R. Murdock   Wounded (Chest & Left Arm), 23rd/24th Feb. 1900, Inniskilling Hill, Relief of Ladysmith, Boer War.

2524 Private C. Murphy   Killed in Action, Boer War, 8th Nov. 1900.

2936 Lance-Corporal H. Murphy   Wounded 15th Dec. 1899, Battle of Colenso, Boer War.

6177 Private J. Murphy   Son of John & Kate Murphy of Killree St., Bagenalstown, Husband of Mary Murphy of 3 Philip St. Bagenalstown, Co. Carlow, 2nd Battalion Royal Inniskilling Fusiliers, World War I, Killed in Action, Saturday 1st November 1914 Aged 42, France & Flanders, No Known Grave, Commemorated Ploegsteert Memorial, Berks Cemetery Extension South of Ieper, Panel 5.

3281 Private S. Murphy   Wounded (Both Buttocks), 23rd/24th Feb. 1900, Inniskilling Hill, Relief of Ladysmith, Boer War.

7100 Private T. Murray 2nd Battalion Royal Inniskilling Fusiliers,
Killed in Action,
France & Flanders, Tuesday 26th Aug. 1914, World War I,
No Known Grave, La Ferté-sous-Jouarre Memorial 66 km. East of Paris.

Mc

1342 Private J. McAdam Wounded,
(Left Arm Amputated, caused by explosives),
Inniskilling Hill Relief of Ladysmith, Boer War, 23rd/24th Feb. 1900.

212 Private J. McAleer 4th Battalion Royal Inniskilling Fusiliers,
(The Royal Tyrone Regiment), Boer War.

4995 Private J. McArthur Wounded 23rd Dec. 1900,
MID (4th September 1901).

305 Private J. McAshee 4th Battalion Royal Inniskilling Fusiliers,
(The Royal Tyrone Regiment) Served with Northumberland Fusiliers,
Boer War.

6223 Private T. McAvinney Died of Disease,
(Dysentery) at Ladysmith, 5th Mar. 1900.

5624 Private S. McBriars Killed in Action,
Inniskilling Hill, Relief of Ladysmith, Boer War, 23rd Feb. 1900.

739 Private F. McBride 4th Battalion Royal Inniskilling Fusiliers,
(The Royal Tyrone Regiment), Boer War.

5975 Private F. McBride Wounded 21st Jan. 1900,
Spion Kop, Boer War.

1162 Private J. McBride 5th Battalion Royal Inniskilling Fusiliers,
(The Royal Donegal Regiment),
Died of Disease, (Pneumonia), 5th Sept. 1901

881 Private J. McBryde 4th Battalion Royal Inniskilling Fusiliers,
(The Royal Tyrone Regiment) Served with Northumberland Fusiliers,
Boer War.

5603 Private J. McCabe Wounded 23rd Feb. 1900,
Inniskilling Hill, Relief of Ladysmith, Boer War.

6654 Private R. McCabe 2nd Battalion Royal Inniskilling Fusiliers,
Sergeant, World War I.
Killed in Action, France & Flanders, 27th Mar. 1918, World War I,
Interred Serre Road Cemetery No. 2, Grave Ref. IX. A. 6.

6089 Private J. McCafferty Wounded 8th Apr. 1902,
Blockhouse Duty, Kroonstadt-Lindley-Bethlehem, Boer War.

4502 Private O. McCann   4th Battalion Royal Inniskilling Fusiliers, (The Royal Tyrone Regiment), Boer War, Killed in Action, No Known Grave Commemorated Helles Memorial Panel 97-101Gallipoli, 26th Apr. 1915 World War I.

6040 Private A. McCartney   Died of Wounds, Bergendal, 27th Aug. 1900.

536 Private. F. McCauley   from Enniskillen, Co. Fermanagh.

1106 Private G. McCauley   4th Battalion Royal Inniskilling Fusiliers, (The Royal Tyrone Regiment) Served with Northumberland Fusiliers, Boer War.

6114 Private R. McCauley   Killed in Action, Battle of Colenso, 15th Dec. 1899.

3932 Private J. McClaren   Wounded Reported Missing in Action after Battle of Inniskilling Hill, Relief of Ladysmith, 23rd/24th Feb. 1900

5674 Private J. McClelland   Killed in Action, Inniskilling Hill, Relief of Ladysmith, Boer War, 23rd Feb. 1900.

2410 Private W. McClenaghan   Wounded 23rd Feb. 1900, Inniskilling Hill, Relief of Ladysmith, Boer War.

5664 Private W. McClure   Killed in Action, Inniskilling Hill, Relief of Ladysmith, Boer War, 23rd Feb. 1900.

1702 Private P.McConnell   4th Battalion Royal Inniskilling Fusiliers, (The Royal Tyrone Regiment), Boer War.

3412 Private C. McCoo   Wounded 15th Dec. 1899, Battle of Colenso.

3643 Private J. McCormick   Wounded 23rd Feb. 1900, Inniskilling Hill, Relief of Ladysmith, Boer War.

6476 Private J. McCormick   Killed as result of an accident, (Drowned), Boer War, (No Date).

3092 Private S. McCormick   MID, (twice), (13th September 1900 & 4th September 1901), Boer War.

1566 Private T. McCrea   4th Battalion Royal Inniskilling Fusiliers, (The Royal Tyrone Regiment), Boer War, Died of wounds at Belfast, South Africa, Bergendal Farm, Major-General W. Kitchener's Seventh Brigade,   27th Aug. 1900,

1155 Private J. McCready   4th Battalion Royal Inniskilling Fusiliers, (The Royal Tyrone Regiment), Served with Northumberland Fusiliers, Died of Disease, (Dysentery) at Station Hospital, Middleburg, Boer War, 20th Dec. 1900, Interred Middleburg Cemetery, Grave No. B26.

6109 Private H. McCue   Wounded 29th May 1901, Colonel E.H.H. Allenby's Column, Operations North of the Pretoria-Delagoa railway line, Boer War.

7196 Private H. McCullagh   Killed, Boer War.
1671 Sergeant R. McCutcheon   4th Battalion Royal Inniskilling Fusiliers,
                      (The Royal Tyrone Regiment), Boer War.
884 Private J. McDaid   Wounded 23rd Feb. 1900,
                  Inniskilling Hill, Relief of Ladysmith, Boer War.
6196 Private J. McDaid   Killed in Action,
        Inniskilling Hill, Relief of Ladysmith, Boer War, 23rd Feb. 1900.
4268 Private P. McDowell   Killed in Action,
        Inniskilling Hill, Relief of Ladysmith, Boer War, 23rd Feb. 1900.
967 Private P. McElhatton   4th Battalion Royal Inniskilling Fusiliers,
                      (The Royal Tyrone Regiment), Boer War.
2702 Private J. McElhenny   Wounded 15th Dec. 1899,
                          Battle of Colenso, Boer War.
5373 Private D. McEvoy   Wounded 23rd Feb. 1900,
                  Inniskilling Hill, Relief of Ladysmith, Boer War.
3234 Private R. McEvoy   Killed in Action,
        Inniskilling Hill, Relief of Ladysmith, Boer War, 23rd Feb. 1900.
825 Corporal J. McFarland   4th Battalion Royal Inniskilling Fusiliers,
                      (The Royal Tyrone Regiment), Boer War.
4588 Sergeant J. McFarland   Wounded 23rd Feb. 1900,
                  Inniskilling Hill,Relief of Ladysmith, Boer War.
810 Private M. McGale   Wounded 27th Dec. 1900,
                          Thorndale, Boer War.
2386 Private W. McGarrity   Wounded 15th Dec. 1899,
                          Battle of Colenso, Boer War.
5960 Private J. McGarry   Died of Wounds,
                  16th Dec. 1899, Battle of Colenso.
640 Private W. McGarry   3rd Battalion Royal Inniskilling Fusiliers,
          Died of Disease, (Septicaemia), Boer War, 29th Oct. 1900.
5893 Private R. McGeown   Wounded Reported Missing in Action
        after Battle of Inniskilling Hill, Relief of Ladysmith, 23rd/24th Feb. 1900
2630 Private A. McGhee   Wounded 15th Dec. 1899,
                          Battle of Colenso, Boer War.

3364 Sergeant J. McGhee   Killed in Action,
                  Battle of Colenso, 15th Dec. 1899.

1496 Private J. McGriffen   Died of Disease, Boer War.
5709 Private J. McGilton   Died of Wounds,
                  Bergendal, Boer War, 27th Aug. 1900.
2976 Private E. McGinney   Wounded 5th Sept. 1901, Boer War.
5743 Private McGinty   Died of Wounds,
                  Battle of Colenso, 16th Dec. 1899.

5948 Sergeant G. McGlade   Wounded (Right Foot & Left Thigh), 23rd/24th Feb. 1900, Inniskilling Hill, Relief of Ladysmith, Boer War.

4331 Private J. McGlinchey   Wounded 15th Dec. 1899, Battle of Colenso, Boer War.

2798 Private J. McGowan   Wounded Reported Missing in Action after Battle of Inniskilling Hill, Relief of Ladysmith, 23rd/24th Feb. 1900

3371 Private P. McGrath   Killed in Action, Inniskilling Hill, Relief of Ladysmith, Boer War, 23rd Feb. 1900.

5691 Private R. McGrath   Wounded 15th Dec. 1899, Battle of Colenso, Boer War.

2033 Private T. McGrogarty   Wounded (Compound fracture left leg), 23rd/24th Feb. 1900, Inniskilling Hill, Relief of Ladysmith, Boer War.

1057 Private J. McGuigan   4th Battalion Royal Inniskilling Fusiliers, (The Royal Tyrone Regiment), Boer War.

5998 Private J. McGuigan   Wounded 15th Dec. 1899, Battle of Colenso, Boer War.

661 Private W. Mcguigan   4th Battalion Royal Inniskilling Fusiliers, (The Royal Tyrone Regiment), Boer War.

2455 Private C. McGuinness   Wounded 23rd Feb. 1900, Inniskilling Hill, Relief of Ladysmith, Boer War.

3055 Private J. McHugh   Wounded 23rd Feb. 1900, Inniskilling Hill, Relief of Ladysmith, Boer War.

6998 Private W. McHugh   Son Andrew & Barbara McHugh, 2nd Battalion Royal Inniskilling Fusiliers World War I, Killed inAction, France & Flanders, Saturday 16th May 1915, No Known Grave, Commemorated Le Touret Memorial Panel 16 –17, Le Touret Military Cemetery

5040 Lance-Sergeant P McIntyre   Wounded 5th Mar. 1902, Blockhouse Duty Kroonstadt-Lindley-Bethlehem, Boer War.

2086 Private J. McIvor   4th Battalion Royal Inniskilling Fusiliers (The Royal Tyrone Regiment), Boer War.

3470 Private A. McKay   Wounded Reported Missing in Action after Battle of Inniskilling Hill, Relief of Ladysmith, 23rd/24th Feb. 1900

1953 Private J. McKeegan   4th Battalion Royal Inniskilling Fusiliers (The Royal Tyrone Regiment), Boer War.

207 Private P. McKeevor   4th Battalion Royal Inniskilling Fusiliers, (The Royal Tyrone Regiment), Boer War.

5583 Private D. McKendrick   from Ramelton, Co. Donegal.

3283 Private E. McKenna   Wounded 15th Dec. 1899, Battle of Colenso, Wounded 23rd Feb. 1900, Inniskilling Hill, Relief of Ladysmith.

2429 Private J. McKenna   Wounded Reported Missing in Action
after Battle of Inniskilling Hill, Relief of Ladysmith, 23rd/24th Feb. 1900
3998 Private T. McKeown   Wounded 23rd Feb. 1900,
   Inniskilling Hill, Relief of Ladysmith, Boer War.
4635 Private W. McKey   Wounded 23rd Feb. 1900,
   Inniskilling Hill, Relief of Ladysmith, Boer War.
6051 Private H. McKinney   Wounded 23rd Feb. 1900,
   Inniskilling Hill, Relief of Ladysmith, Boer War.
3147 Sergeant W. McKinstry   Wounded 23rd Feb. 1900,
   Inniskilling Hill, Relief of Ladysmith, Boer War.
2932 Private J. McLaren   Died of Wounds,
   Inniskilling Hill, Relief of Ladysmith, Boer War, 24th Feb. 1900.
5801 Private J. McLaren   Wounded 11th Apr. 1902, Boer War.
5989 Private J. McLaren   Wounded 15th Dec. 1899,
   Battle of Colenso, Boer War.
4674 Private J. McLelland   Wounded 15th Dec. 1899,
   Battle of Colenso, Boer War.
1583 Private F. McLoughlin   Wounded (Both Hips),
23rd / 24th Feb. 1900, Inniskilling Hill, Relief of Ladysmith, Boer War.
1116 Private J. McLoughlin   Wounded 19th Dec. 1900,
   Major-General R.A.P Clements Column in action against
   De La Ray at Thorndale, Boer War.
4733 Private P. McLoughlin   Wounded (Head & Back),
23rd/24th Feb. 1900, Inniskilling Hill, Relief of Ladysmith, Boer War.
5865 Private P. McLoughlin   Wounded 23rd Feb. 1900,
   Inniskilling Hill, Relief of Ladysmith, Boer War.
6486 Private J. McMahon   2nd Battalion Royal Inniskilling Fusiliers,
Died of Wounds at Home, 8th Nov. 1914, World War I, Interred Netley
   Military Cemetery, attached to Royal Victoria Hospital, Netley,
   Grave Ref. C. E. 1629.
5855 Private E. McManus   Died of Disease,
   (Dysentery), Boer War, (No Date).
133 Private J. McManus   Wounded 23rd May 1902, Boer War.
1551 Private J. McManus   Killed in Action, Boer War, 7th Dec. 1900.
5748 Private J. McManus   Wounded 15th Dec. 1899,
   Battle of Colenso, Boer War.
2989 Private T. McManus   Wounded, Reported Missing in Action,
   Inniskilling Hill, Relief of Ladysmith, 23rd/24th Feb. 1900, Boer War.
6145 Private J. McMullen   Died of Wounds,
   Battle of Colenso, Boer War. 16th Dec. 1899.

1449 Quartermaster-Sergeant M. McMurran Reported Missing in Action
after Battle of Inniskilling Hill, 23rd/24th Feb.1900,
MID (4th September 1901) & DCM,BoerWar.

2484 Private T. McNeill Wounded 23rd Feb. 1900,
Inniskilling Hill, Relief of Ladysmith, Boer War.

5828 Private R. McNulty Wounded 23rd Feb. 1900,
Inniskilling Hill, Relief of Ladysmith, Boer War.

677 Corporal P. McPhillips 4th Battalion Royal Inniskilling Fusiliers,
(The Royal Tyrone Regiment), Boer War.

1214 Private J. McPike 4th Battalion Royal Inniskilling Fusiliers,
(The Royal Tyrone Regiment), Boer War.

884 Private J. McQuade Reported Missing in Action
after Battle of Inniskilling Hill, 23rd/24th Feb. 1900.

2857 Private J. McQuillan Died of Wounds,
Battle of Colenso, 16th Dec. 1899.

5909 Private J. McShane Wounded 15th Dec. 1899,
Battle of Colenso, Boer War.

3065 Private R. McShane From Sugarhouse Lane, L'Derry,
Wounded 23rd Feb.1900,Inniskilling Hill, Relief of Ladysmith,
Died of Disease,(Dysentery) Station Hospital Middleburg 27th Nov. 1900,
Interred Middleburg Cemetery, Grave No. B.9.

104 Private C. McSorley 4th Battalion Royal Inniskilling Fusiliers
(The Royal Tyrone Regiment), Boer War.

1440 Private J. McSorley 4th Battalion Royal Inniskilling Fusiliers,
(The Royal Tyrone Regiment), Boer War.

1511 Private B. McSwiggan 4th Battalion Royal Inniskilling Fusiliers,
(The Royal Tyrone Regiment), Boer War.

978 Private J. McSwiggan 4th Battalion Royal Inniskilling Fusiliers,
(The Royal Tyrone Regiment) Served with Northumberland Fusiliers,
Boer War.

N

2031 Private L. Nash Died of Disease, (Enteric Fever),
Blockhouse Duty, Kroonstadt-Lindley-Bethlehem, 2nd Apr. 1902.

2559 Private R. Nash Reported Missing in Action
after Battle of Inniskilling Hill, 23rd/24th Feb. 1900.

4492 Private T. G. Neal Wounded 23rd Feb. 1900,
Inniskilling Hill, Relief of Ladysmith, Boer War.

425 Private R. Nelson 4th Battalion Royal Inniskilling Fusiliers,
(The Royal Tyrone Regiment), Boer War.

3335 Private G. Nesbitt   Died of Wounds,
Inniskilling Hill, Relief of Ladysmith, Boer War, 24th Feb. 1900.
3880 Private J. Nesbitt   Wounded 23rd Feb. 1900,
Inniskilling Hill, Relief of Ladysmith, Boer War.
3116 Private S. Newell   Wounded 15th Dec. 1899,
Battle of Colenso, Boer War.
1721 Private J. Nicholl   4th Battalion Royal Inniskilling Fusiliers,
(The Royal Tyrone Regiment), Boer War.
1696 Private J. Nixon   4th Battalion Royal Inniskilling Fusiliers,
(The Royal Tyrone Regiment), Boer War.
4551 Private W. Nixon   Died of Disease,
(Dysentery), at Ladysmith, 7th May 1900.
3368 Private J. Noble   Wounded 23rd Dec. 1900.
Major-General R.A.P. Clements Column against De La Rey at Thorndale,
6098 Private J. Noble   Died of Disease (Enteric Fever),
at Ladysmith, 15th Apr. 1900.
2889 Private H. Nolan   Wounded 15th Dec. 1899,
Battle of Colenso Boer War.
2141 Private H. Nolan   4th Battalion Royal Inniskilling Fusiliers,
(The Royal Tyrone Regiment), Boer War.
1183 Private W. Nolan   3rd Battalion Royal Inniskilling Fusiliers,
Died of Disease, (Enteric Fever), at Ladysmith, Boer War, 3rd Apr. 1900.
375 Private J. Nugent   4th Battalion Royal Inniskilling Fusiliers,
(The Royal Tyrone Regiment) Served with Northumberland Fusiliers,
Boer War.

O

5500 Private T. Oakley   Wounded 15th Dec. 1899,
Battle of Colenso, Boer War.
5787 Private J. Oliver   Wounded 23rd Feb. 1900,
Inniskilling Hill, Relief of Ladysmith, Boer War.
1040 Private J. Orr   Killed in Action,
Inniskilling Hill, Relief of Ladysmith, Boer War, 23rd Feb. 1900.
1121 Private E. Owens   Died of Wounds,
Inniskilling Hill, Relief of Ladysmith, Boer War, 23rd Feb. 1900.
6220 Private R. Owens   Born St. Michan's Dublin, Sergeant,
2nd Battalion Royal Inniskilling Fusiliers, World War I, No Known Grave
Commemorated Pozières Memorial, Somme, France, Panel 38-40.

O'

5699 Private C. O'Brien — Wounded 15th Dec. 1899, Battle of Colenso, Boer War.

1597 Private J. O'Brien — Died of Disease, (Dysentery), 28th Mar. 1901, Interred Middelburg (Transvaal) Cemetery, Grave No. 13.

3302 Private W. O'Brien — Killed in Action, Inniskilling Hill, Relief of Ladysmith, Boer War, 23rd Feb. 1900.

5097 Private W. O'Brien — Died of Wounds, Boer War, 28th Mar. 1901.

5769 Private J. O'Connor — Wounded 15th Dec. 1899, Battle of Colenso, Boer War.

5043 Private B. O'Loan — Died of Disease, (Pneumonia), Relief of Ladysmith, Mooi River, Boer War, 27th Jan. 1900.

1731 Private J. O'Loan — 4th Battalion Royal Inniskilling Fusiliers, (The Royal Tyrone Regiment), Boer War.

1537 Private O. O'Lone — 4th Battalion Royal Inniskilling Fusiliers, (The Royal Tyrone Regiment), Boer War.

3471 Private A. O'Nell — Wounded 23rd Feb. 1900, Inniskilling Hill, Relief of Ladysmith, Boer War.

663 Sergeant J. O'Neill — Wounded 15th Dec. 1899, Battle of Colenso, Boer War.

3793 Private J. O'Toole — Wounded 23rd Feb. 1900, Inniskilling Hill, Relief of Ladysmith, Boer War.

P

4911 Corporal J. Parker — Killed in Action, Inniskilling Hill, Relief of Ladysmith, Boer War, 23rd Feb. 1900.

6236 Corporal D. Parks — Killed in action, Inniskilling Hill, Relief of Ladysmith, Boer War, 24th Feb 1900.

4238 Private J. Patterson — Wounded 12th Feb. 1901, Boer War.

473 Private J. Paul — 4th Battalion Royal Inniskilling Fusiliers, (The Royal Tyrone Regiment), Boer War.

3126 Private F. Payne — Killed in Action, Inniskilling Hill, Relief of Ladysmith, Boer War, 23rd Feb. 1900.

2448 Sergeant W. Payne — Wounded 15th Dec. 1899, Battle of Colenso, Boer War.

1043 Private J. Pearson — 4th Battalion Royal Inniskilling Fusiliers, (The Royal Tyrone Regiment), Boer War.

2400 Private A. Pendry — Wounded 23rd Feb. 1900, Inniskilling Hill, Relief of Ladysmith, Boer War.

6751 Private J. Pollock   Husband of Jane Pollock of 76, McLean St.,
Plantation, Glasgow, 2nd Battalion Royal Inniskilling Fusiliers,
Killed in Action,
France & Flanders, 14th Sept. 1914, World War I, No Known Grave,
Commemorated La Ferté-sous-Jouarre Memorial,   66 km East of Paris

6567 Private T. Porter   2nd Battalion Royal Inniskilling Fusiliers,
World War I, Killed in Action, France & Flanders, 16th May 1915,
No Known Grave, Commemorated Le Touret Memorial,
Le Touret Military Cemetery Panels 16- 17.

5037 Private C. Poulton   Reported Missing, Died of Wounds,
Inniskilling Hill, Relief of Ladysmith, Boer War, 23rd Feb. 1900.

6291 Sergeant J. Power   Son P. F. Power,
(Late Colour-Sergeant 2nd Battalion Royal Inniskilling Fusiliers)
& Anastasia Mary Power, 1 & 2 St. George's Circus Southwark London,
Native of Kilkenny 2nd Battalion Royal Inniskilling Fusiliers
Colour-Sergeant
World War I, Died of Wounds, France & Flanders, 13th Jul 1917,
Interred Coxyde Military Cemetery near Koksijde, Grave Ref. 1. E. 12.

990 Private C. Preston   4th Battalion Royal Inniskilling Fusiliers,
(The Royal Tyrone Regiment), Boer War.

3867 Private S. Prior   Died of Disease, (Enteric Fever),
at Ladysmith, 2nd May 1900.

898 Private B. Purvis   4th Battalion Royal Inniskilling Fusiliers,
(The Royal Tyrone Regiment), Boer War.

Q

1122 Private F. Quinn   Wounded 27th Dec. 1900,
Major-General R.A.P. Clements Column
against De La Rey at Thorndale.

1603 Private J. Quinn   4th Battalion Royal Inniskilling Fusiliers,
(The Royal Tyrone Regiment), Died of Disease, (Dysentery),
at Ladysmith, Boer War, 5th Jun. 1900.

2960 Private J.P. Quinn   Wounded 15th Dec. 1899, Battle of Colenso,
Wounded 23rd Feb. 1900, Inniskilling Hill, Relief of Ladysmith.

1436 Corporal P. Quinn   4th Battalion Royal Inniskilling Fusiliers,
(The Royal Tyrone Regiment), Boer War.

6835 Private P. Quinn   Died of Disease, (Dysentery),
Blockhouse Duty, Kroonstadt-Lindley-Bethlehem,
Boer War, 16th Mar. 1902.

R

5605 Private J. Raleigh Died of Wounds,
Inniskilling Hill, Relief of Ladysmith, Boer War, 23rd Feb. 1900.
971 Private J. Ramsey Wounded 23rd Dec. 1900,
Major-General R.A.P. Clement's Column
against De La Rey at Thorndale,
2980 Colour-Sergeant J.S. Rattenberry Wounded 23rd Feb. 1900,
Inniskilling Hill, Relief of Ladysmith, Boer War.
948 Private D. Reed 4th Battalion Royal Inniskilling Fusiliers,
(The Royal Tyrone Regiment), Boer War.
3239 Private J. Reehel Wounded 23rd Feb. 1900,
Inniskilling Hill, Relief of Ladysmith, Boer War.
6419 Corporal A. Reid 2nd Battalion Royal Inniskilling Fusiliers,
World War I, Killed in Action, France & Flanders,
Wednesday 21st Mar. 1918, No Known Grave,
Commemorated Pozières Memorial North-East of Albert, Panels 38-40.
3479 Quartermaster-Sergeant W. Reid MID (23rd June 1902)
& DCM, Boer War.
6007 Private W. Reid 2nd Battalion Royal Inniskilling Fusiliers,
World War I, Killed in Action, France & Flanders,
7th Nov. 1914, No Known Grave, Commemorated Ploegsteert Memorial
Berks Cemetery, south of Ieper Panel 5
19 Private P. Reilly Wounded 23rd Feb. 1900, (chest & back),
Inniskilling Hill, Relief of Ladysmith, Boer War.
4309 Private B. Reynolds Died of Wounds,
Inniskilling Hill, Relief of Ladysmith, Boer War, 27rd Feb. 1900.
3504 Private P. Rider Wounded 23rd Feb. 1900,
Inniskilling Hill, Relief of Ladysmith, Boer War.
4956 Sergeant C.J. Ripsher Wounded 15th Dec. 1899,
Battle of Colenso, Boer War.
2026 Private M. Roach 4th Battalion Royal Inniskilling Fusiliers,
(The Royal Tyrone Regiment) Served with Northumberland Fusiliers,
Boer War.
3606 Private A. Roberts Wounded 15th Dec. 1899,
Battle of Colenso, Boer War.
5686 Private K. Robinson Wounded 11th Apr. 1902,
Blockhouse Duty, Kroonstadt-Lindley-Bethlehem, Boer War.
4330 Private S.P. Robinson Wounded 23rd Feb. 1900,
Inniskilling Hill, Relief of Ladysmith, Boer War.

111 Sergeant T. Robinson Born Castlebar,
Son of John & Ellen Robinson, Killen Castlederg,
Husband of Martha Robinson, 12 Orchard Street, Derry,
Wounded 15th Dec. 1899, Battle of Colenso, Boer War,
Served with Worcestershire Regiment (Service Number 12095) during
World War I, Died at Home, Derry (Ebrington Barracks),
Saturday 27th Mar. 1920 aged 57,
Interred City Cemetery Derry, Section S, Row B, Grave No. 609.

4243 Sergeant F. Rodgers Killed in Action,
Inniskilling Hill, Relief of Ladysmith, Boer War, 23rd Feb. 1900.

3474 Private H. Rooney Wounded (Arm & Thigh),
23rd / 24th Feb. 1900, Inniskilling Hill, Relief of Ladysmith, Boer War.

1981 Private R. Rorrison Wounded 15th Dec. 1899,
Battle of Colenso, Died of Wounds, Boer War, 17th Dec. 1899.

2143 Private G.A. Rowe MID (23rd June 1902) & DCM, Boer War.

3475 Private J. Rowe From Lisnaskea Co. Fermanagh,
Died of Wounds, Battle of Colenso, 15th Dec. 1899.

5276 Private R. Rowe Killed, in Action,
Colonel E.H.H. Allenby's Column in operations north of the
Pretoria-Delagoa railway line,Boer War, 6th Mar. 1901.

5832 Private J.H. Rowley Wounded 23rd Feb. 1900,
Inniskilling Hill, Relief of Ladysmith, Boer War.

2413 Private R. Russell Died of Wounds,
Battle of Colenso, 16th Dec. 1899.

S

2997 Sergeant F.W. Salter Wounded 23rd Feb. 1900,
Inniskilling Hill, Relief of Ladysmith, Boer War.

3228 Private P. Scanlon Wounded 23rd Feb. 1900,
Inniskilling Hill, Relief of Ladysmith, Boer War.

6064 Private J. Scott Wounded (Left Thigh & Right Arm),
23rd/24th Feb. 1900, Inniskilling Hill, Relief of Ladysmith, Boer War.

3613 Private R. Scott Wounded 23rd Feb. 1900,
Inniskilling Hill, Relief of Ladysmith, Boer War.

1495 Private K. Semple 4th Battalion Royal Inniskilling Fusiliers,
(The Royal Tyrone Regiment), Boer War.

4310 Private W. Shannon Wounded 23rd Feb. 1900,
Inniskilling Hill, Relief of Ladysmith, Boer War.

4113 Private J. Shea Wounded 15th Dec. 1899,
Battle of Colenso, Boer War.

5012 Lance-Sergeant E. Shepperd — Wounded 23rd Feb. 1900, Inniskilling Hill, Relief of Ladysmith, Boer War.

3022 Private T. Sheridan — Wounded 9th Dec. 1900, Middelburg, Transvaal,

5760 Private J. Sherman — Killed in Action, Inniskilling Hill, Relief of Ladysmith, Boer War, 23rd Feb. 1900.

5885 Private J. Shields — Wounded 23rd/24th Feb. 1900, Inniskilling Hill, Relief of Ladysmith, Boer War.

5889 Private M. Shields — Wounded 15th Dec. 1899, Battle of Colenso, Wounded 23rd Feb. 1900, Inniskilling Hill, Relief of Ladysmith.

5301 Private J. Singleton — Killed in Action, Inniskilling Hill, Relief of Ladysmith, Boer War, 23rd Feb. 1900.

2342 Private P. Skelly — Died of Wounds, Inniskilling Hill, Relief of Ladysmith, Boer War, 23rd Feb. 1900.

3376 Private J. Slawson — MID (4th September 1901), Boer War.

2802 Private A. Smith — Wounded 15th Dec. 1899, Battle of Colenso, Boer War.

2439 Private A. Smith — Killed in Action, Inniskilling Hill, Relief of Ladysmith, Boer War, 23rd Feb. 1900.

6219 Private S. Smith — 2nd Battalion Royal Inniskilling Fusiliers, World War I, Killed in Action, France & Flanders, 21st Oct. 1914, No Known Grave Commemorated Ploegsteert Memorial Berks Cemetery, south of Ieper Panel 5

3635 Private T. Smith — Wounded 15th Dec. 1899, Battle of Colenso, Boer War.

3960 Private W. Smith — Killed in Action, Battle of Colenso, 15th Dec. 1899.

5535 Private W. Smith — Wounded 15th Dec. 1899, Battle of Colenso, Boer War.

5971 Private R. Snodgrass — Wounded 23rd Feb. 1900, Inniskilling Hill, Relief of Ladysmith, Boer War.

5594 Private O. Somers — Killed in Action, Blockhouse Duty Kroonstadt-Lindley-Bethlehem, Boer War, 11th Apr. 1902.

4763 Private R. Sproule — Wounded 15th Dec. 1899, Battle of Colenso Boer War.

6311 Private T. Sproule   Son of James & Jane Sproule of Coolaness, Irvinestown Co. Fermanagh, Husband of Ellzabeth Sproule of Newton Cunningham Co. Donegal 2nd Battalion Royal Inniskilling Fusiliers, World War I,   Killed in Action, France & Flanders, 16th May 1915, No Known Grave, Commemorated Le Touret Memorial, Le Touret Military Cemetery Panels 16-17.

2776 Private W. Steele   Wounded 16th Dec. 1899, Battle of Colenso, Boer War.

6115 Private J. Stephenson   2nd Battalion Royal Inniskilling Fusiliers, World War I,Killed in Action, France & Flanders Tuesday 21st Oct. 1914, No Known Grave, Commemorated Ploegsteert Memorial, Berks Cemetery Extension South of Ieper, Panel 5.

1266 Private T. Stewart   4th Battalion Royal Inniskilling Fusiliers, (The Royal Tyrone Regiment), Boer War.

2608 Sergeant R. Storer   MID, (23rd June 1902), Boer War.

3566 Private H. Stote   Wounded 23rd Feb. 1900, Inniskilling Hill, Relief of Ladysmith, Boer War.

4810 Private W. Sullivan   Reported Missing in Action after Battle of Inniskilling Hill, Relief of Ladysmith, 23rd/24th Feb. 1900

4650 Private W. Supple   2nd Battalion Royal Inniskilling Fusiliers, World War I, Killed in Action France & Flanders, Monday 1st Sept. 1914, Interred Verberie Communal Cemetery, Verberie, Grave Ref. 5.

3141 Drummer J. Swann   Wounded (Right Thigh & Hip), 23rd/24th Feb. 1900, Inniskilling Hill, Relief of Ladysmith, MID, (Twice) (13th September 1900 & 4th September 1901), Boer War.

T

3496 Private F. Talmage   Died of Disease, (Enteric Fever), 26th Feb. 1901. Interred Middleburg Cemetery,Grave No. 26a.

563 Sergeant C. Tanner   Wounded 15th Dec. 1899, Battle of Colenso, Boer War.

1756 Private W. Tate   4th Battalion Royal Inniskilling Fusiliers, (The Royal Tyrone Regiment), Boer War.

1746 Private J. Tatlor   4th Battalion Royal Inniskilling Fusiliers, (The Royal Tyrone Regiment) Served with Northumberland Fusiliers, Boer War.

5871 Corporal T. Taylor   Reported Missing in Action after Battle of Inniskilling Hill, Relief of Ladysmith, 23rd/24th Feb. 1900.

3410 Private A. Thompson — Wounded 23rd Feb. 1900, Inniskilling Hill, Relief of Ladysmith, Boer War.

3640 Private A. Thompson — MID (30th March 1900) & DCM, Boer War.

1335 Private T. Thompson — 4th Battalion Royal Inniskilling Fusiliers, (The Royal Tyrone Regiment), Boer War.

1363 Corporal W. Thompson — Wounded 9th Dec. 1900, Middelburg Transvaal.

3373 Corporal W. Thompson — Wounded 15th Dec. 1899, Battle of Colenso.

3634 Private W. Thompson — Wounded 15th Dec. 1899, Battle of Colenso.

6994 Private W. Thompson Son of John and Margaret Foy Thompson, 544 Princess St., Kingston, Ontario, Canada, Born Belfast, Died of Wounds at Home, Ebrington Barracks Derry, Wednesday 13th Dec. 1916 aged 33. Sergeant, World War I, Interred City Cemetery Derry Military Plot Section G.

2621 Private J. Thornbury — Wounded 23rd Feb. 1900, Inniskilling Hill, Relief of Ladysmith, Boer War.

5930 Private E. Thornton Killed in Action, Major-General R.A.P. Clements' Column in action against De La Rey at Thorndale, N. Transvaal, Boer War, 19th Dec. 1900.

1709 Private T. Tierney Killed in Action, Boer War, 17th Jun. 1900.

1241 Private J. Tinney Died of Disease, (Dysentery), Middelburg, Transvaal, Boer War, 26th Feb. 1901.

994 Private W. Tomb — 4th Battalion Royal Inniskilling Fusiliers, (The Royal Tyrone Regiment), Boer War.

3357 Private E. Toner — Wounded 23rd Feb. 1900, Inniskilling Hill, Relief of Ladysmith, Boer War.

1478 Private M. Toy — 4th Battalion Royal Inniskilling Fusiliers, (The Royal Tyrone Regiment), Boer War.

5891 Private P. Trainor — Wounded 23rd Feb. 1900, Inniskilling Hill, Relief of Ladysmith, Boer War.

5688 Corporal W. Treacey — Reported Missing in Action after Battle of Inniskilling Hill, Relief of Ladysmith, 23rd/24th Feb. 1900

1587 Private A. Trimble — 4th Battalion Royal Inniskilling Fusiliers, (The Royal Tyrone Regiment), Boer War.

3119 Private J. Tully — Wounded (Abdomen, foot & leg), 23rd/24th Feb. !900, Inniskilling Hill, Relief of Ladysmith, Boer War.

3667 Private A. Tumilty — Wounded 15th Dec. 1899, Battle of Colenso, Boer War.

1971 Private J. Turbitt 4th Battalion Royal Inniskilling Fusiliers, (The Royal Tyrone Regiment), Boer War.

3028 Sergeant H. Turner Died of Wounds, Inniskilling Hill, Relief of Ladysmith, Boer War, 23rd Feb. 1900.

3025 Private P. Twohey Wounded 8th Apr. 1902, Blockhouse Duty Kroonstadt-Lindley-Bethlehem, Boer War.

495 Private P. Tyre Died of Wounds, Boer War, 13th Jul. 1900.

V

609 Private D. Vallely 4th Battalion Royal Inniskilling Fusiliers, (The Royal Tyrone Regiment), Boer War.

1369 Sergeant J. Vauls 4th Battalion Royal Inniskilling Fusiliers, (The Royal Tyrone Regiment), Boer War.

W

5814 Private J. Wadsworth Killed in Action, Inniskilling Hill, Relief of Ladysmith, Boer War, 23rd Feb. 1900.

5675 Private A. Wakefield Wounded 15th Dec. 1899, Battle of Colenso, Boer War.

4010 Private W.H. Walker Died of Disease, (Dysentery), 20th Dec.1901, Interred Pretoria Cemetery (Church of England),Grave No. 977.

3919 Private J. Wallace Killed in Action, Battle of Colenso, 15th Dec. 1899.

5651 Private W. Wallace Wounded 23rd Feb. 1900, Inniskilling Hill, Relief of Ladysmith, Boer War.

3121 Private J. Walls Wounded 23rd Feb. 1900, Inniskilling Hill, Relief of Ladysmith, Boer War.

3675 Lance-Corporal J. Walsh Wounded (Right hand, shell wound right thigh), 23rd/24th Feb. 1900, Inniskilling Hill, Relief of Ladysmith, Boer War.

5332 Private T. Walsh Killed in Action, Inniskilling Hill, Relief of Ladysmith, Boer War, 23rd Feb. 1900.

2767 Private P. Ward Wounded Reported Missing in Action 23rd/24th Feb. 1900, Inniskilling Hill, Relief of Ladysmith, Boer War.

6699 Private W. Warnock Born Newtonards Co. Down, Son of James & Sarah Warnock of 1 Richmond St. Belfast, Co Antrim. Killed in Action France & Flanders Wednesday 26th Aug. 1914 Aged 32, No Known Grave, Commerated La Ferté-sous-Jourre Memorial, 66 km East of Paris.

5631 Private J. Warren Wounded 23rd Feb. 1900, Inniskilling Hill, Relief of Ladysmith, Boer War.

2681 Sergeant T. Waters   Killed in Action, Boer War, (No Date).

964 Lance-Corporal H. Watson   Killed in Action,
Inniskilling Hill, Relief of Ladysmith, Boer War, 23rd Feb. 1900.
1350 Private T. Watson   4th Battalion Royal Inniskilling Fusiliers,
(The Royal Tyrone Regiment), Boer War.
2463 Private G. Weir   Wounded 23rd Feb. 1900,
Inniskilling Hill, Relief of Ladysmith, Boer War.
6655 Private G. Weir   Died of Disease, (Enteric Fever),
Relief of Ladysmith, , 2nd Feb. 1900.
4608 Private C. West   Wounded 21st Jan. 1900, Spion Kop, Boer War.
5271 Private T. Whelan   Wounded 16th Apr. 1902,
Blockhouse Duty Kroonstadt-Lindley-Bethlehem, Boer War.
4416 Lance-Corporal M.E. White   from 3 Ferndale Villas,
Carlton Road, New Southgate, North London.
Died of Disease, (Enteric Fever),
Boer War, 9th Apr. 1901. Interred Middelburg Cemetery, Grave No. E17.
5357 Private J. Whitehouse   Died of Disease, (Enteric Fever),
Blockhouse Duty Kroonstadt-Lindley-Bethlehem,
Boer War, 8th Mar. 1902.
2415 Private J. T. Whitters   Wounded 20th Jan. 1900,
Spion Kop, Boer War,
invalided home on SS *Galatea.*
4303 Private J. Wiggins   Wounded 21st Jan. 1900,
Spion Kop, Boer War.
1699 Private R. Wilkinson   4th Battalion Royal Inniskilling Fusiliers,
(The Royal Tyrone Regiment), Boer War.
1040 Private W. Wilkinson   4th Battalion Royal Inniskilling Fusiliers,
(The Royal Tyrone Regiment) Served with Northumberland Fusiliers,
Boer War.
2998 Private F. Williams   Killed in Action,
Battle of Colenso, 15th Dec. 1899.
4823 Sergeant A. J. Windrum   Son of Captain W. Windrum
ex-Royal Inniskilling Fusiliers,
Died of Disease, (Enteric Fever), at Ladysmith 6th Apr. 1900.
5882 Private J. Winter   Wounded (Both thighs & right shoulder),
23rd/24th Feb. 1900, Inniskilling Hill, Relief of Ladysmith, Boer War.
1548 Corporal G. Winters   4th Battalion Royal Inniskilling Fusiliers,
(The Royal Tyrone Regiment), Boer War.
503 Private W. Wisoner   4th Battalion Royal Inniskilling Fusiliers,
(The Royal Tyrone Regiment), Boer War.

3252 Private J. Woods — Wounded 15th Dec. 1899, Battle of Colenso Boer War.

3982 Sergeant J. Wright — Wounded 23rd Feb. 1900, Inniskilling Hill, Relief of Ladysmith, Boer War.

6312 Private J. Wright — Died of Disease, (Enteric Fever), Boer War, 1st Jan 1901, Interred Middelburg Cemetery, Grave No. C6.

3454 Sergeant T. Wright — Died of Disease, (Enteric Fever), 1st Jul. 1900, Boer War.

5084 Private W. Wright — Killed in Action, Battle of Colenso, 15th Dec. 1899.

2577 Sergeant R. Wylie — Killed in Action, 15th Dec. 1899, Battle of Colenso.

3290 Corporal J. Wyth — Killed in Action, Inniskilling Hill, Relief of Ladysmith, Boer War, 23rd Feb. 1900.

Y

5895 Private W. Young — Wounded 23rd Feb. 1900, Inniskilling Hill, Relief of Ladysmith, Boer War.

APPENDIX IV

Roll of NCO & Other Ranks
1st Battalion Royal Inniskilling Fusiliers
South Africa
Boer War 1899-1902.

This Appendix is an index of all those NCOs and ORs who served with the 1st Battalion during the Boer War and which are not to be found under the heading of the previous Appendix.

A

5926 Private J. Abraham
4929 Coporal G. Acheson
6009 Private A. Adams
914 Private P. Adams
6691 Corporal S. Adams
6898 Private J. Agnew
4279 Private T. Agnew
6196 Private W. Agnew
2689 Private C. Aldridge
6581 Private F. Allen
7106 Private G. Allen
3098 Private J. Allen
7088 Private J. Allen
6532 Private J. Allen
6272 Private W. Allen
6259 Boy W. Ames
5676 Private J. Anderson
7176 Private R. Anderson
6319 Private S. Anderson
6436 Private C. Annon
5273 Private. E. M. Arbuckle
4880 Sergeant J. Arbuckle
6602 Private H. Archibald
6440 Private D. Armstrong
6355 Private J. Armstrong
1102 Private W. Armstrong
3199 Private W. Armstrong
3199 Private W. Armstrong
3186 Private J. Arthur
3565 Corporal W. Arthur
2958 Lance/Sergeant F. Ashby

6589 Drummer G.W. Ash
6696 Lance/Corporal A. Atcheson
3036 Sergeant O. Athelston
2104 Sergeant J. Austin
5468 Private W. Ayers

B

3284 Sergeant J. Baker
1952 Private A Ball
6826 Private S. Balmer
6366 Private W. Balmer
6806 Private J. Barbour
496 Lance/Sergeant. D.S. Barnett
2210 Sergeant G. Barnett
6027 Private G. Barrett
6812 Private J. Bates
1006 Private W. Bates
3409 Sergeant P. Beattie
6116 Private T. Beattie
3383 Lance/Corporal W. Beck
2888 Private J. Becker
3524 Private J. Bedder
1532 Private M. Beggs
5663 Private A. Bell
2625 Private A. Bell
3586 Private W. Bell
5902 Private J. Best
5187 Corporal W. Bew
6551 Private J. Bickerstaff
3704 Private A. Binfield

7136 Private R. Birnie
5646 Private J. Black
7048 Private R. Blake
6727 Private S. Blakey
3890 Corporal A. Bleakley
 983 Private J. Bleakley
3692 Private H.A. Boak
6585 Corporal A. Boal
3653 Private H. Boal
6376 Private H Bond
2633 Private G. Bonnett
6991 Private D. Boomer
6656 Private A. Boreland
6588 Private J. Bothwell
6333 Private P. Bowdrie
 629 Private F. Bowey
1846 Private H. Boyce
6895 Private J. Boyd
6247 Private J. Boyde
5868 Private J. Boyle
1094 Private J. Boyle
4754 Private J. Boyle
2343 Private P. Boyle
6313 Drummer P. Boyle
 52 Private T. Boyle
3355 Private J. Bracken
3106 Private T. Brackenridge
5549 Private W.J Bradford
 482 Private W. Brady
5784 Private J. Bradley
2797 Private W. Branter
6238 Private J. Brawl
1328 Private J. Breen
1357 Private J. Breen
 856 Private J. Breen
6635 Corporal B Brennan
2515 Private E. Brennan
6562 Private H. Brennan
2540 Private M. Brennan
1317 Private C. Brewer
1715 Private W. Brewer
4797 Private W.R. Bridgett
7090 Private W. Briggs
1068 Private P. Britton
6309 Private J. Brolly
1192 Private W. Brooks
6205 Private T. Brophy

7187 Private C. Brown
1546 Private C. Brown
5772 Private D. Brown
3615 Private J. Brown
4648 Private J. Brown
6721 Private J. Brown
1806 Private J. Brown
 720 Private J. Brown
6328 Private T. Brown
3698 Sergeant V.D. Brown
6633 Private W. Brown
6504 Private W. Brown
3854 Private W. Brown
1313 Private W. Brown
1792 Corporal J. Bryson
4484 Private G. Buckner
2890 Private M. Burke
 884 Private T. Burke
6559 Private W.J. Burke
6770 Private E. Burley
6984 Corporal J. Burnett
6428 Corporal C. Burns
7182 Private J. Burns
1562 Private J. Burns
5692 Private P. Burns
6776 Corporal J. Burnside
7009 Private J. Burrell
6657 Private H. Burrows
7065 Private J. Butler
2732 Private J. Byrne
1074 Private J. Byrne
 785 Private M. Byrne
2294 Lance/Corporal M. Byrne
1433 Private M. Byrne
1536 Private T. Byrne
4730 Private W. Byrne
4273 Private W. Byrne
4174 Private W. Byrne
5230 Private W.V. Byrne

C

5384 Private E. Caffrey
6158 Private J. Caffrey
3243 Private J. Cahill
6337 Private J. Cairns
3301 Private J. Callaghan

1299 Private P. Callaghan
1198 Corporal A. Campbell
2433 Private C. Campbell
6127 Private G. Campbell
2752 Private J. Campbell
1918 Private J. Campbell
6045 Private J. Campbell
962 Private J. Campbell
877 Private J. Campbell
1110 Private T. Campbell
1319 Private W. Campbell
1051 Private G. Canavan
0841 Private T. Canavan
4589 Private T. Canning
6597 Private E. Carlin
6054 Private J. Carney
1080 Private J. Carney
2690 Private W. Carr
1839 Private J. Carroll
6641 Private J. Carroll
1566 Private P Carroll
2862 Private W. Carroll
6575 Private E. Carson
6643 Private G. Carson
2849 Private A. Carter
766 Private W. Casey
453 Private J. Cassidy
6456 Private J. Cassidy
1701 Private J. Cassidy
718 Private P. Cassidy
5644 Private C. Catlin
1590 Private J. Cauldwell
434 Private O. Caulfield
4640 Private J. Caveney
6200 Private J. Chambers
4201 Lance/Corporal J. Chambers
4398 Private J. Chaplin
6683 Private W. Chaplin
6231 Private T. Chivers
6141 Private J. Church
3483 Private C.C. Clarke
4065 Private J. Clarke
7051 Private J. Clarke
6101 Private J. Clarke
2584 Private M. Clarke
6106 Private W. Clarke
6933 Private J. Clegg

6678 Private R. Clelland
6794 Lance/Corporal R. Clelland
6610 Private F. Clery
5547 Private C. Clifford
2426 Private W. Clifford
3511 Private E. Climpson
6535 Private C. Coates
6022 Private R. Coburn
5876 Private J. Coieman
5983 Private M. Coleman
4317 Sergeant D. Collum
3612 Private. M. Commons
7026 Private J. Conaghan
3461 Private P. Condrew
6042 Private C. Connaghan
2728 Drummer S.P. Connell
419 Private H. Connelly
0405 Private J. Connelly
5072 Private J. Connelly
6370 Private J. Connelly
6660 Lance/Corporal P. Connelly
2704 Private E. Connor
3006 Private P. Connor
2768 Private P. Connor
425 Private P. Connors
6358 Private T. Connors
5807 Private F. Convey
4282 Private J. Convoy
4873 Private P. Conway
4026 Private P. Coogan
2856 Sergeant J.C. Cook
6001 Private W. Cook
6492 Private R. Cook
3819 Private W. Cooke
7085 Private R. Cooper
6519 Private T. Cooper
6758 Boy A. Cope
6422 Private W. Corbett
6974 Private J. Cornwrath
6157 Private M. Corrigan
6546 Private J. Costello
2864 Private R. Cotter
801 Private C. Coulter
5798 Private R. Coulter
6071 Private E. Courtney
6921 Private J. Coventry
7045 Private R. Cowan

2590 Private J. Cowell
3005 Private J. Cox
5092 Private B. Coyle
1856 Private .Coyle
7097 Private P. Coyle
5057 Sergeant J. Cradden
4678 Sergeant G.W. Craddock
6778 Private H. Craig
7078 Private J. Craig
7142 Private J. Craig
3672 Private J. Craig
4887 Private W. Craig
5995 Private W. Craig
6595 Private R. Cranston
3180 Private D. Crawford
6681 Private G. Crawford
7190 Private J. Crawford
6742 Private J. Crawford
5890 Sergeant R. Crawford
2869 Private W. Crawford
6587 Private R. Cree
6698 Private C.R. Creegan
6396 Private R. Creighton
5942 Sergeant W. Crook
6571 Private W. Crooks
3579 Private W. Crooks
1346 Lance/Corporal T. Crowe
2099 Private B. Crumley
3664 Private J. Cullen
1950 Private G. Cummings
6342 Private J. Cummings
7201 Private J. Cunningham
6649 Lance/Corporal J Cunningham
6076 Private R. Cunningham
5969 Private S. Cunningham
5334 Private F. Curran
2694 Private W. Curran
2388 Private W. Curran
937 Private F. Curry
5306 Private J. Cusack

D

6392 Private J. Dalton
3206 Private T. Daly
3244 Private P. Dalzell
3467 Private L. Darcey

6340 Private P. Dardis
3154 Private J. Davey
6324 Private A. Davidson
6171 Private J. Davidson
2151 Private J. Davidson
3665 Private J. Davis
6760 Private J. Davis
5629 Private J. Davis
2171 Private W.E. Davis
1016 Private B. Davies
4110 Private G. Davies
4511 Private E.C. Day
6187 Private J. Day
4154 Lance/Corporal F. Deane
4295 Lance/Corporal A. Deighan
5229 Private P. Dempsey
5945 Lance/Sergeant W. Denton
6021 Private L. Devereaux
2334 Private C. Devlin
6871 Private G. Devlin
114 Private J. Devlin
3309 Private J. Dickson
7167 Private J. Dillon
3367 Private J. W. Diver
3717 Private T. Diver
7018 Private H. Dobbyn
5908 Sergeant W.J. Dobbyn
6226 Private R. Docherty
6897 Private C. Dodds
6913 Private D. Dodds
5020 Private A.C. Doe
0540 Private B. Doherty
0588 Private B. Doherty
6766 Private D. Doherty
3739 Private F. Doherty
7109 Private H. Doherty
2745 Private J. Doherty
3559 Private J. Doherty
5696 Private J. Doherty
1111 Private J. Doherty
2191 Private M. Doherty
4135 Private P. Doherty
5957 Private W. Doherty
1725 Private W. Doherty
1543 Private W. Doherty
1148 Private H. Dolan
6904 Private P. Dolan

5805 Lance/Corporal R. Dolan
3639 Corporal W. Donaghy
3343 Private H. Donegan
3224 Private J. Donnelly
1376 Private J. Donnelly
 939 Private R. Dooley
6211 Private T. Doran
6965 Lance/Corporal J. Dornan
6457 Private J. Dorrington
1068 Private H. Dougan
1957 Private J. Dougan
6550 Private J. Dougan
7077 Private W. Dougan
3331 Private W. Dougan
6537 Private E. Dougherty
6224 Private J. Douglas
5958 Private W. Dowell
6095 Private T. Dowling
2719 Private D. Downey
5987 Private J. Downey
6380 Private J. Downey
4276 Private J. Doyle
2306 Private J. Doyle
6938 Private P. Doyle
2297 Private P. Doyle
2160 Private P. Doyle
1303 Private P. Drumin
3023 Private G. Duffy
6354 Private W.H. Duffy
7135 Private W.J. Duffy
3149 Colour-Sergeant W.J. Dugan
6391 Private R. Duke
 680 Private F. Dundas
7059 Private T.H. Dundas
 488 Private J. Dunleary
2376 Private J. Dunnan
2786 Private P. Dunnan
5756 Private J. Dunne
6543 Private J. Dunne
4939 Sergeant J. Dunne
1393 Private J.J. Dunne
2742 Private P. Dunne
5852 Private R. Dunne
5035 Private F. Dunning

E

6645 Private T. Edgar
5804 Private T. Edmondson
5861 Private T. Edwards
3452 Private J. Elder
3434 Private F. Eldon
 719 Private J. Elliott
6514 Private W. Elliott
5034 Sergeant G. Elsworth
6556 Private S.Emerson
1476 Private J. Emery
5876 Private R. English
6369 Private M. Ennis
3249 Private W. Evans

F

4326 Private J. Fagan
4473 Private W. Fairs
6036 Private P. Fallon
7110 Private H. Farrell
6195 Private P. Farrelly
6174 Private T. Farrelly
 758 Private E. Farrington
 734 Private S. Farrington
5683 Private J. Faulkner
3316 Private A. Fee
3948 Corporal W. Fee
6554 Private D. Feeney
3449 Lance/Corporal J. Ferguson
6584 Private S. Ferguson
5126 Private J. Ferrier
0996 Private J. Ferris
3189 Private J. Finlay
 978 Private W. Finlay
 953 Private C. Finnigan
4277 Private J. Fisher
6190 Private F. Fitzpatrick
1557 Corporal J. Fitzsimmons
6679 Private J. Fitzsimmons
6631 Private J. Flack
6132 Private J. Flagg
5862 Private J. Flannagan
5496 Corporal T.H. Flavelle

6096 Private H. Fleming
5153 Private J. Fleming
6267 Private S. Fleming
2382 Private G. Flood
6750 Private J. Flood
2281 Private J. Flood
4271 Private P. Flood
1301 Private R. Flood
1501 Private W. Flynn
3319 Private P. Foote
6970 Private S. Forde
4340 Private J. Forsythe
2775 Private R. Foster
 812 Private P. Fox
0795 Private J. Franey
2477 Lance/Corporal H. Frankland
2290 Private J. Free
3505 Lance/Corporal J. Fullerton
5735 Private R. Fullerton
1310 Private H. Fulton

G

6416 Private B. Gaffney
6603 Private R. Gaffney
6717 Private D. Gallagher
 916 Private E. Gallagher
6450 Private H. Gallagher
2479 Private J. Gallagher
5717 Sergeant P. Gallagher
6068 Private P. Gallagher
1831 Private P. Gallagher
5817 Private P. Gallagher
2065 Private W. Gallagher
6967 Private J. Gallon
7178 Private R. Gallon
1299 Private W. Gardner
6730 Private W. Gardner
5907 Private J. Gately
3917 Private A. Gates
6629 Private C. Gates
3248 Private J. Gates
3595 Private T. Gates
6430 Private R. Getty
6461 Private R. Gibney
3361 Private E. Gibson
6344 Private J. Gibson

6877 Private J. Gibson
 566 Private J. Gildea
6113 Corporal R. Gildea
6480 Private J. Gillen
6992 Private R. Gillespie
3459 Corporal W. Gillespie
5965 Private P. Gillis
2859 Private J. Gillon
6112 Private J. Gillon
6431 Private D. Gilvarry
3417 Lance/Sergeant J.W. Ginman
5700 Private P. Girr
7491 Private J. Glackin
3567 Corporal S.H. Glanville
6890 Private J. Glass
1353 Lance/Corporal.J Goodfellow
3117 Private J. Goodfellow
5963 Private J. Goodfellow
6435 Private J. Gordon
4334 Private W. Gordon
6642 Private F. Gorman
2351 Private C. Gould
3548 Private H. Gover
5903 Private T. Gracey
6349 Private J. Graham
6953 Private J. Graham
6061 Private W. Graham
2327 Private J. Grant
1381 Private G. Gray
6614 Private J. Gray
6144 Private R. Gray
6368 Private S. Gray
3984 Private W. Gray
7096 Private J. Green
7204 Private J. Green
2971 Private J. Green
2530 Private T. Green
2352 Lance/Corporal W. Green
3856 Private W. Green
3641 Private W. Green
 931 Sergeant J. Greenfield
6674 Private T. Greer
2898 Private J. Gregan
7002 Private S. Grey
6500 Private J. Gribbon
6320 Private N. Gribbon
3654 Private W. Gribbon

2509 Private B. Grimly
5977 Lance/Corporal T. Grundel
6901 Corporal J. Guerin
2995 Private H. Gwalter

H

6896 Private F. Hagan
6964 Private J. Halliday
5156 Private J. Halpin
1582 Private F. Hamill
5978 Private J. Hamill
3526 Private C. Hamilton
1629 Private J. Hamilton
6420 Corporal R. Hamilton
5789 Private W. Hamilton
3195 Sergeant J. Hampson
4514 Private H. Hanlin
5934 Private R. Hanna
6453 Private G. Hanning
6617 Private D. Harbinson
 891 Private F. Haren
5087 Private H. Haren
6099 Private H. Haren
3443 Pte. F. Hargardon
1760 Private J. Harkin
3676 Private J. Harper
4091 Sergeant J. Harper
1786 Private C.H. Harris
 502 Colour-Sergeant. W. A. Harris
6894 Private J. Harrison
6561 Private R. Harrison
6662 Private T. Harrison
4188 Private W. Harrison
6896 Private N. Hart
4856 Private J. Harte
1464 Lance/Corporal. W. J. Harte
6572 Private W.J. Hassell
4668 Private C. Haswell
6757 Boy C. Hatchard
2205 Private T. Haughey
4218 Private F. Hawkins
3172 Private J. Hayes
3064 Private W. Hazlett
1249 Sergeant P. Healey
6162 Private F. Heaney
3294 Private W. Heaney

6710 Private H. Hearty
7041 Private J. Hector
5196 Corporal F.R. Hedges
 977 Private C. Hegarty
2140 Private A. Henderson
1136 Private J. Henderson
 339 Private W. Henderson
4324 Private J. Hendry
6915 Corporal C. Henery
3336 Private P. Henry
1570 Private C. Herald
5467 Private G.P. Herbert
3095 Private T. Herdman
5105 Corporal R. Hermin
4727 Private P. Herlihy
 508 Sergeant W. Herivan
6910 Private J. Hetherington
2504 Private D. Heyslip
1603 Private J. Higgins
2712 Private L. Higgins
3027 Corporal J. Higging
 577 Private C. Higgins
6249 Private T. Higgins
6484 Private J. Higginson
6769 Boy C. Hill
3174 Private J. Hill
6398 Corporal A. Hillis
4552 Lance/Sergeant. A. Hillman
2986 Private G. Hockley
3589 Private R. Holden
6252 Private G. Holmes
5661 Private G. Hookway
1812 Private P. Horan
6515 Lance/Sergeant A. Horner
3576 Private C.J. Horton
3527 Private W. House
5931 Private R. Houston
7199 Lance/Corporal J. H. Howe
6479 Private W. Howlett
3182 Private W. Huddelston
6387 Private M. Huggard
6472 Private D. Hughes
1162 Private J. Hughes
 329 Private P. Hughes
6088 Private J. Humphreys
1624 Private E. Hunter
6892 Private N. Hunter

4989 Sergeant F.C. Hurley
6441 Private J. Huston
1925 Private M. Hutton
2402 Private R. Hydes
6702 Private F. Hyland
4907 Private W. Hyndsman
0803 Private J. Hynes

I

2649 Serjeant W. Iliffe
7130 Private B. Irvine
 786 Private J. Irvine
 716 Private R. Irvine
2142 Private W. Irvine
2460 Private W. Irvine
6924 Private R. Irwin
5388 Private W. Irwin
6506 Private W. Irwin

J

1613 Private H. Jameson
6477 Private H. Jameson
6379 Private J. Jameson
6102 Private M. Jameson
2963 Drummer J. J. Jenner
4653 Private S.T. Jenning
3480 Private W. Jennings
5981 Private A. Jess
6502 Private H. Johnston
6627 Private H. Johnston
 101 Private J. Johnston
2354 Private J. Johnston
6634 Private J. Johnston
6294 Private J. Johnston
4652 Private P. Johnston
1471 Private R. Johnston
6706 Private R. Johnston
5483 Sergeant T. Johnston
6989 Private T. Johnston
1291 Private W. Johnston
6619 Private W. Johnston
7064 Private W. Johnston
 551 Private J. Jones
1015 Private J. Jones

1443 Sergeant J. Jones
6541 Private M. Jordan
6378 Private T. Judson

K

 644 Private J. Kane
5349 Private J. Kane
5856 Private J.S. Kane
7033 Private E. Kavanagh
2468 Private H. Kavanagh
3782 Private J. Keane
5997 Private M. Keane
1252 Private P. Keaney
3554 Lance/Corporal J. Kearney
5553 Drummer P. Kearney
6222 Private P. Kearney
4274 Private H. Keating
5296 Lance/sergeant J. Keating
2677 Corporal W.J. Kee
4559 Sergeant S. Keefe
2860 Private M. Keegan
5551 Private M. Keenan
6620 Private W. Kennan
2472 Private T. Kehoe
6343 Private B. Kelly
6035 Private J. Kelly
 718 Private J. Kelly
2747 Private J. Kelly
6228 Private J. Kelly
5796 Private J. Kelly
6544 Private R. Kelly
6331 Private T. Kelly
2531 Private T. Kelly
6055 Private W. Kelm
0941 Private J. Kelpie
2717 Private W.J. Kempton
2957 Private W. Kendrick
7148 Private H. Kennedy
 421 Private J. Kennedy
6105 Private J. Kennedy
6947 Private J. Kennedy
3992 Lance/Corporal T. Kennedy
7112 Private T. Kennedy
6235 Private J. Kenny
6288 Private J. Keoghan
 361 Private R. Kernaghan

1584 Private J. Kerr
7155 Private W. Kerr
6682 Private W. Kerridge
6460 Private C.W. Key
5648 Private J. Keys
2084 Private H. Kidd
6090 Private E. Kilday
1208 Private P. Kilduff
5732 Private J. Kilgallon
6540 Private J. Kilmurry
2565 Corporal E. M. Kincaid
5834 Private S. Kinney
5870 Private J. Kinsella
1490 Private P. Kinsella
4891 Private B. Kinsley
6459 Private S. H. Kirby
6023 Private W. J. Kirk
1143 Private W. Kirkpatrick
3494 Private L.W. Knott
1239 Private P. Knox
3139 Private J. Kyle

L

1482 Lance/Corporal W. Lackey
4228 Private P. Laird
1636 Privarte J. Lally
1746 Private M. Lane
6327 Private J. Larmour
6557 Private S. Larmour
1780 Private W.J. Larmour
5213 Private J. Larner
5872 Private J. Larkin
6893 Private J. Larkin
6074 Private J. Lavelle
6393 Private G. Lavery
2615 Private H. Lavery
6862 Private H. Lavery
 554 Private J. Lavery
6518 Private S.A. Lavery
1538 Private G. Law
2350 Private W. Lawrence
4146 Private A. Lay
2476 Private J. Lay
5894 Private R. Lecky
3362 Band-Sergeant A. Lee
3835 Private E. Leggett

5074 Private T. Leggett
3404 Private J. Leith
1004 Private Lenaghan
1254 Private J. Leonard
6583 Private J. Leonard
2328 Private T. Leonatd
6381 Private H. Letson
5652 Private J. Lewis
6944 Private J. Lewis
7024 Private T. Leyham
4389 Private J. Lillis
3620 Private P. Lillis
3272 Private W. Lillywhite
6352 Private D. Lindsay
6062 Private J. Lindsay
6725 Private J. Lindsay
6037 Private T. Lismore
6072 Corporal H. Loane
6473 Private S. H. Loane
6591 Private H. Logan
1686 Private W. Logue
1851 Private H. Long
1277 Private C. Lonney
6536 Private P. Lopeman
2795 Private J. Loughlin
6951 Private F. Loughran
3093 Private J. Loughran
3122 Private M. Loughrey
1529 Private J. Love
1292 Private R. Love
 739 Private W. Love
6482 Private F. Lowe
1635 Private W. Lunny
1141 Private E. Lynch
 912 Private J. Lynch
5947 Private J. J. Lynch
1320 Sergeant Lynch
6791 Private W. Lynn
6100 Private T. Lyons

M

1284 Private T. Mack
2525 Private M. Mackey
4635 Private W. Mackey
 762 Private J. Mackill
 948 Private H. Madden

6692 Private J. Madden
4768 Private W. Madden
1910 Lance/Corporal H. Magee
6462 Private H. Magee
1877 Private J. Magee
6316 Private P. Magee
6644 Private T. Magee
6163 Private J. Magorian
1660 Private T. Magowan
6183 Private F. Maguire
303 Private J. Maguire
3359 Private J. Maguire
5808 Private J. Maguire
6410 Private J. Maguire
6365 Private J. Maguire
779 Private P. Maguire
1884 Private P. Maguire
4045 Private P. Maguire
4304 Private P. Maguire
4376 Private P. Maguire
953 Private R. Maguire
242 Private T. Maguire
4974 Sergeant T. Maguire
5411 Private J. Maher
2730 Private J. Mahon
3838 Private M. Mahon
1118 Private T. Mahon
4104 Private W.J. Mahon
6130 Private J. Mallon
1233 Corporal P. Maloney
3781 Private T. Maloney
963 Private J. Mangon
6143 Lance/Corporal J. Manley
6209 Private P. Manning
7014 Corporal J. Mannix
6726 Private S. Mark
5773 Private R. Mars
6593 Private E.H. Marsland
4501 Private E. Martin
6447 Private G. Martin
6648 Private H. Martin
5815 Private J. Martin
3337 Private J. Martin
6799 Private O. Martin
3038 Private P. Martin
5493 Sergeant F. Matthews
6454 Private J. Matthews

4167 Private J. Maxwell
968 Private J. Maynes
6221 Private J. Meredith
4962 Private J. Michael
516 Private W. Middleton
5211 Private A. Miles
6611 Private A. Millar
5693 Private C. Millar
6576 Drummer H. Millar
4618 Sergeant S. H. Millar
6469 Private T. Millar
7168 Lance/Corporal J. Miller
7038 Private J. Milligan
1481 Sergeant W.B Millington
401 Private H. H. Milward
4409 Sergeant F.E. Minns
6908 Private C. Mitchell
6471 Private W. Mitchell
6747 Private W. Mitchell
6179 Private H. Moffett
3086 Private A. Molloy
6455 Private A. Molloy
6501 Private H. Molloy
1551 Private P. Molloy
4818 Private W. Molyneaux
5944 Lance/corporal G Monaghan
4997 Lance/Corporal R.Monaghan
3354 Private H.A. Monk
5811 Sergeant J. Montague
1713 Private B. Monteith
3210 Private A. Montgomery
856 Private W Montgomery
1400 Private W Montgomery
6987 Private A Moody
5244 Private F. Moody
1219 Private J. Mooney
772 Acting Sergeant H. H. Moore
6012 Private J. J. Moore
6493 Private T. Moore
0982 Private W. Moore
6983 Private W. Moore
2554 Private J. Moran
4264 Private T. Moran
6409 Private W. Moreland
4918 Sergeant W.J. Morgan
6831 Private C. Morrell
1692 Q.M.S.W.A. Morris

6623 Private H. Morrison
3581 Private J. Morrison
6212 Private W. Morrow
2192 Lance/Sergeant J. Morton
2868 Private J. Morton
7114 Private S. Morton
4630 Sergeant W. Mudd
6117 Private F. Muldoon
6000 Private J. Muldoon
3385 Private H. Mulholland
3241 Private J. Mulholland
6496 Private J. Mullan
6385 Private M. Mullan
3558 Private R Mullaney
3097 Private G. Mullen
1352 Private J. Mullen
2751 Private J. Mullen
7146 Private W. Mullen
3573 Private J. Mulligan
5642 Private P. Mulraine
3588 Private J. Mulrine
3104 Private H. E. Mundy
2542 Private E. Murphy
2875 Private J. Murphy
3256 Private J. Murphy
6210 Private J. Murphy
6886 Private J. Murphy
7052 Private J. Murphy
1087 Private O. Murphy
3429 Private P. Murphy
5009 Private R. Murphy
6701 Private R.G. Murphy
6485 Private S. Murphy
2462 Private W. Murphy
4897 Private W. Murphy
3192 Private A. Murray
7102 Private A. Murray
5364 Private D. Murray
6161 Private D. Murray
6690 Private D. Murray
6737 Private D. Murray
1422 Private J. Murray
3318 Private J. Murray
6903 Private J. Murray
3004 Private P. Murray
6925 Private T. Murray

Mc

6830 Private R. McAdam
5935 Private W. McAfee
6667 Private J. McAllister
2579 Drummer R. McAllister
6720 Private R. McAllister
2950 Private P. McArdle
6306 Private J. McAuley
5701 Private F. McBarron
6137 Private A. McBrain
1043 Private E. McBrian
1186 Private P. McBrian
6394 Private D. McBride
5979 Private J. McBride
5093 Private M. McBride
2946 Private M. McBride
2731 Private P. McBride
4674 Private T. McBride
6373 Private T. McBride
6215 Private J. McBurney
1046 Private F. McCabe
6498 Private J. McCabe
6446 Private J. McCafferty
5096 Private W.J McCafferty
1550 Private W. McCaffrey
 589 Private C. McCallion
6718 Private J. McCallion
6232 Private W. McCallister
3266 Private A. McCallum
6689 Private D.McCandless
7174 Private J. McCandless
3115 Lance/Corporal F. McCann
3609 Private H. McCann
5788 Private D. McCarron
6262 Private J. McCarron
7072 Private P. McCarron
6107 Private A. McCarthy
6024 Private H. McCarthy
3338 Sergeant J. McCarthy
6025 Private W.J. McCarthy
6010 Private J. McCartney
6988 Private S. McCartney
1677 Private D. McCauley
6608 Private W. McCausland
3158 Private E. McClean

5989 Private P. McClean
6168 Private D. McClelland
752 Private J. McClelland
1394 Corporal W McClements
1377 Privater R. McClintock
3313 Private G. McClure
6827 Corporal D. McClurg
6680 Private H. McClurg
6287 Private A. McClusky
6429 Private B. McClusky
1109 Private C. McColgan
3227 Private T. McColgan
3391 Private J. McConkey
2034 Private J. McConnell
2770 Private J. McConnell
5514 Corporal T. McConnell
6389 Private D. McCoo
6765 Private T.D. McCoo
3585 Private G. McCool
3491 Private J. McCorkell
7060 Private A. McCormick
2943 Private J. McCourt
4152 Private N. McCourt
7054 Private P. McCourt
6586 Private P. McCoy
6563 Private T. McCracken
336 Private J. McCready
5993 Private J. McCreanor
6325 Corporal E. McCristall
2411 Private W. McCrory
2385 Private B. McCrossan
1220 Private J. McCrossan
5956 Private O. McCrossan
6874 Private J. McCrudden
1561 Private P. McCrudden
6411 Private A. McCrum
5486 Private J. McCullagh
2918 Private P. McCullagh
1106 Private G. McCurley
6246 Private P. McCusker
4377 Lance/Corporal J McCutcheon
6424 Private M. McDaid
6545 Private M. McDaid
1054 Private D. McDermott
6670 Private W. McDermott
702 Private J. McDonagh
3647 Private M. McDonagh

6415 Private C. McDonald
5802 Private G. McDonald
3482 Private H. McDonald
3124 Private J. McDonald
3200 Sergeant J. McDonald
6233 Private J. McDonald
6374 Private J. McDonald
5783 Private M. McDonald
1136 Private F. McDonnell
2338 Private W. McDonnell
1889 Private S. McDowell
2289 Sergeant P. McElhone
6405 Private D. McElroy
165 Private T. McElroy
7068 Private J. McEwan
3091 Private D. McFadden
889 Private R. McFarland
6749 Private W. McFarland
6887 Privater W. McFarland
1075 Sergeant H. McFarlane
7045 Sergeant J. McFarlane
1547 Sergeant R. McFarlane
1600 Private M. McGaghey
2748 Private F. McGahey
0074 Private M. McGarr
6719 Private T. McGettigan
1231 Private M. McGhee
7124 Private J. McGill
911 Private T. McGilly
2636 Private P. McGilton
7191 Private J. McGinley
3822 Private M. McGinley
7066 Private M. McGinley
1315 Private C. McGinty
6478 Private J. McGivern
1008 Private C. McGlinchey
3287 Private J. McGlinchey
5596 Private T. McGlinchey
3598 Private J. McGoldrick
6647 Private D. McGonigle
1003 Private J. McGonigle
6070 Private P. McGourty
6510 Private D. McGowan
7119 Private H. McGowan
2800 Sergeant P. McGrain
7154 Private E. McGrath
1730 Private T. McGrath

6020 Private T. McGrath
1815 Private J. McGuinness
6015 Private J. McGuinness
2755 Private M. McGuinness
1673 Private J. McGurk
6794 Private J. McHugh
4890 Private A. McIlree
5857 Private D. McIlree
6630 Private D. McIlroy
6569 Private H. McIlroy
457 Private C. McIntyre
3156 Private T. McIntyre
6879 Private A. McKay
3083 Sergeant M. McKee
2447 Private H. McKenna
1067 Private J. McKenna
6517 Private J. McKenna
496 Private O. McKenna
5659 Private F. McKeown
3144 Private M. McKeown
6360 Private F. McKernan
6497 Private E. McKerr
6104 Private D. McKillop
1281 Private J. McKillop
6950 Drummer G. McKimn
6573 Corporal J. McKinlay
6203 Private G. McKnight
6871 Private J. McLarin
6404 Private J. McLough
1520 Private H. McLoughlin
980 Private J. McLoughlin
1162 Private J. McLoughlin
3719 Private J. McLoughlin
6208 Private J.J. McLoughlin
1029 Private M. McLoughlin
6260 Private R. McLoughlin
1750 Private T. McLoughlin
3327 Private W. McLoughlin
5991 Private W. McLoughlin
1560 Private H. McMahon
835 Lance/Corporal A. McManus
4664 Sergeant J. McManus
3016 Private S. McManus
3125 Private S. McMenany
3514 Lance/Corporal. D. McMonigle
4772 Private J. McMorrow
6613 Private A. McMullen

7206 Private A. McMullen
3875 Private H. McMullen
815 Private J. McMullen
1034 Drummer J. McMullen
2394 Lance/Corporal J. McMullen
5840 Corporal J. McMullen
2568 Private E. McNamara
5200 Private C. McNamee
4016 Private D. McNicholl
6637 Private F. McNicholl
2206 Private E. McNulty
2156 Private F. McNulty
2086 Private P. McNulty
5985 Private D. McParland
3770 Corporal W. McPherson
76 Corporal J. McPhillips
5612 Private H. McPike
1186 Private P. McQuade
1610 Private P. McQuade
1153 Private W. McShane
4066 Private W. McTier
159 Private E. McVeigh
156 Private J. McVeighty
975 Private W. McVeighty
1833 Private F. McVicker
456 Private A. McVitty

N

6198 Private A. Nash
6786 Private M. Naughton
7202 Private P. Neelan
6926 Private D. Neill
1613 Private F. Neill
3136 Sergeant F. Neill
435 Private C. Nelis
3029 Private M. Nelis
6408 Private R. Nelson
6118 Private J. Nesbitt
6263 Private A. Niblock
6579 Private J. Niblock
921 Private A. Nixon
2583 Sergeant F. Nixon
6528 Private R. Nixon
6650 Private W. H. Nixon
7020 Lance/Corporal T. Noble
6891 Corporal W. Noble

6606 Private J. Noble
7141 Private J. Nolan
1523 Private W. Norris
5974 Private W. Nugent
1539 Private R. Nutall

O

418 Private A. Orr
5776 Private J. Orr
6119 Private J. Orr
0898 Private T. Orr
764 Private W. Orr
5607 Sergeant J. Osborough
3733 Sergeant E. Over
2931 Private W. Owens
3657 Private W. Owens

O'

6439 Private H. O'Brien
2377 Private J. O'Brien
1262 Private J. O'Connell
6708 Private B.E. O'Dare
6700 Private B.J. O'Dare
1505 Private C. O'Donnell
6403 Private E. O'Donnell
6126 Private J. O'Donnell
6345 Private P. O'Donnell
6207 Private S. O'Flaherty
1497 Private J. O'Hanlon
6110 Private B. O'Kane
6872 Private B. O'Kane
1886 Private J. O'Kane
6509 Private R. O'Malley
2453 Private C. O'Neill
780 Private H. O'Neill
2916 Private J. O'Neill
6684 Private J. O'Neill
1667 Private M. O'Neill

P

6123 Private F. Packenham
6395 Private A. Page
2133 Private H. Palmer

3594 Sergeant J. Park
6268 Corporal G. Parry
6534 Private T. Pattterson
2914 Private T. Patton
6241 Private J. Peden
7061 Lance/Corporal R.H. Pedlow
4604 Private F. Pell
4523 Sergeant R.G. Pemberton
1472 Private H. Pendelton
6722 Private J. Percy
2715 Private J. Perrin
6783 Private T. Perry
398 Private J. Phair
7207 Private A. Phillips
7164 Private D. Phillips
5966 Private G. Philpott
4403 Private H.H. Pike
4258 Private G. Pinwell
3137 Private W. Ponise
6948 Lance/corporal W. J. Poots
1693 Private C. Porter
6206 Private R. Porter
3500 Private A. E. Pothecary
5954 Private J. Powell
3663 Private G. Powers
4137 Private J. Power
2650 Sergeant W. Power
4676 Private T. Presley
6087 Sergeant W. Presley
6079 Private J. Prior
3400 Colour-Sergeant S. Prior
4872 Sergeant T. Prior
3921 Sergeant W.T. Prior
4518 Private J. Prunty
6487 Private P. Purcell
1483 Private J. Purdie

Q

6014 Private R. Quate
2125 Private J. Quigg
3497 Private B. Quigley
1020 Private E. Quigley
5878 Private D.F. Quigley
6580 Private H. Quinlan
1805 Private C. Quinn
5707 Corporal F. Quinn

6063 Private F. Quinn
642 Private J. Quinn
1182 Private J. Quinn
1897 Private J. Quinn
5655 Private M. Quinn
3326 Private P. Quinn
6558 Private P. Quinn
6693 Private P. Quinn
920 Private T. Quinn
1391 Sergeant T. Quinn
5946 Private T. Quinn

R

5747 Private G. Rafferty
6475 Private M. Raftice
1181 Private R. Rainbird
4902 Private R. Ravenscroft
5820 Private J. Raw
6044 Private J. Rearden
5597 Private J. Reay
5927 Lance/Corporal J. Redmond
3111 Drummer W.J. Reed
3635 Drummer E. Reegan
5938 Private E. Reid
6616 Private F. Reid
5812 Private F. Reilly
6034 Private F. Reilly
4121 Private J. Reilly
5431 Private P. Reilly
5770 Private P. Reilly
5847 Private P. Reilly
4952 Sergeant F. Le Restall
5775 Private T. Rice
6297 Private D. Richmond
1166 Private W. Riordan
3820 Private J. Roberts
2047 Colour-Sergeant C. Robinson
5799 Privater C.T. Robinson
3575 Private H. Robinson
490 Private J. Robinson
2390 Private J. Robinson
2774 Private J. Robinson
5996 Private J. Robinson
6193 Private J. Robinson
6308 Private W. Robinson
6675 Private W. Robinson

2585 Corporal J. Roche
3304 Private D. Rocks
6646 Private T. Rodden
6805 Private H. Rodgers
1686 Private J. Rodgers
5818 Private T. Rogan
1569 Private J. Ronan
3075 Sergeant J. Rooks
4371 Private F. Rose
5943 Private W. Rosemand
2853 Private D. Ross
3951 Sergeant J. Roulston
1374 Private J. Rourke
2600 Private J. Rourke
1609 Private A. Rush
845 Private J. Rutherford
1193 Private J. Rutherford
1215 Private J. Rutherford
7144 Lance/Corporal C. Ryan
2929 Private J. Ryan
6285 Private T. Ryan

S

6266 Private P. Salmon
3631 Private J. Saxon
4390 Private S.G. Sayers
6640 Private D. Scarlett
3212 Drummer J. Scott
4491 Private J. Scott
6909 Private J. Scott
5471 Private S. Scott
5508 Corporal L. Scrivener
3067 Private J. Scully
6659 Private W. Seary
5992 Private J. Semple
6481 Private T. Service
5917 Private J. Shanks
3232 Private R. Shanks
6060 Private J. Shannon
3344 Private G. Sharp
6607 Private H. Shaw
3365 Private R.F. Shaw
2923 Private J. Sheehan
1224 Private P. Sheehan
6159 Private J. Sheridan
7083 Private P. Sheridan

72 Private T. Sheridan
4315 Private T. Sheridan
2735 Private W. Sherry
5851 Private B. Shields
2491 Private H. Shirlow
3591 Private H. Shrubb
7205 Private J. Simms
748 Corporal W. Simmons
3492 Private C. Simpson
2718 Private J. Simpson
7131 Private J. Simpson
880 Private W. Simpson
4153 Private T. Singleton
6526 Private A. Skelton
1321 Private P. Slavin
1556 Private J. Slavin
5665 Private T. Sloan
4564 Sergeant A.E. Smith
548 Private E. Smith
2200 Lance/Corporal F. Smith
2582 Private G. Smith
932 Private H. Smith
4623 Private H. Smith
1005 Private J. Smith
2379 Private J. Smith
6425 Corporal J. Smith
7166 Private J. Smith
3240 Private P. Smith
6920 Private S. Smith
2881 Private W.J. Smith
7218 Private T. Smullen
4996 Corporal B. Smyth
6521 Private T. Smyth
6002 Private J. Smythe
6097 Private J. Smythe
2772 Private J. Snodden
1224 Private B. Somers
2447 Private L. Somers
6372 Private T. Somers
0302 Private J. Somerville
3401 Private J. Spears
2707 Private T. Speers
1200 Sergeant W. Speers
2375 Private W. Spence
6269 Private W.J. Spratt
2944 Private J. Stafford
7089 Private J. Stafford

2769 Private S. Stafford
1185 Private R.H. Starkey
5690 Corporal T. Stead
5029 Private G.J. Steele
6507 Private J. Steele
3207 Cpl. W.J. Steele
6489 Private C. Stenson
5267 Private J. Stenson
6129 Private J. Stenson
911 Private S. Stevens
3387 Private J. Stevenson
3707 Sergeant G.J. Stewart
5538 Private J. Stewart
6400 Private J. Stewart
6665 Private J. Stewart
1184 Private W. Stewart
6225 Private W. Stewart
6468 Private W. Stewart
1402 Private E. Sterling
2446 Private S. Stockwell
6250 Private J. Stokes
5821 Private J. Stone
6566 Boy J. Stone
5362 Corporal T. W. Stopford
6315 Private J. Strain
2987 Private H. Styles
2475 Private M. Sunderland
5990 Private H. Stutters
6982 Private A. Swann
5844 Private A. Sweeney
2394 Private G. Sweeney

T

2897 Private R. Taggart
816 Private W. Taggart
3458 Sergeant W. Tate
6194 Private D. Taylor
3763 Private J. Taylor
5846 Private J. Taylor
6449 Private J. Taylor
6916 Private R. Taylor
2440 Private W. Taylor
3987 Sergeant W. C. Taylor
5628 Private W. Teacey
5251 Private P. Teehan
6672 Private D. Telford

6685 Private A. Thompson
2365 Private G. Thompson
1704 Sergeant J. Thompson
2422 Private J. Thompson
3311 Private J. Thompson
3382 Sergeant J. Thompson
3673 Sergeant J. Thompson
1132 Private W. Thompson
2655 Private W. Thompson
2744 Private W. T. Thorpe
656 Private F. Tierney
677 Private W. Tierney
4549 Sergeant E.A. Tilly
5063 Sergeant H. Tilly
2371 Private R. Tilly
6175 Sergeant J. Todd
3831 Pte. W. H. Tombs
951 Private D. Toner
6458 Private T. Toner
6375 Private W. Totton
5736 Pte. H. Townsend
2358 Private A. Tracey
6488 Private J. Tracey
6495 Private W. Tracey
946 Private B. Travers
765 Private J. Travers
2609 Private J. Travers
6173 Private P. Travers
5643 Private C. Trussler
4468 Private F. Turner
3034 Private E. Tuthill
7128 Private W. Twaddell

U

5863 Private J. Upson

V

7179 Lance/Corporal J. Vallely
5792 Corporal S. Vanthal
6218 Private A. Venard
6318 Corporal D. Vincent

W

3333 Private G. Wainwright
3148 Private J. Waldron
964 Private C. Walker
5827 Private J. Walker
6775 Private J. Walker
6875 Private J. Walker
6192 Private W. Walker
4197 Private W. Walmsley
6604 Private A. Walsh
1528 Private J. Walsh
2346 Private J. Walsh
2017 Private P. Walsh
3260 Private P. Walsh
6185 Private P. Walsh
759 Private W. Walsh
2697 Private C. Warburton
2522 Private H. Ward
1646 Private J. Ward
6963 Private C. J. Warnock
1829 Private J. Wasson
3587 Private J. Watson
5452 Private J. Watson
6065 Private J. Watters
5135 Private T. Watters
5912 Sergeant J. Waugh
5939 Sergeant H. H. Waugh
4436 Private A.C. Wayre
5354 Private T. Webb
6432 Private H. Weir
6653 Private J. Weir
1401 Sergeant P. Weir
6332 Private P. Weir
954 Private T. Weir
3405 Private H. Welch
3366 Sergeant A. F. Welland
7050 Private A. Wetton
2560 Private E. Whelan
4288 Private J. Whelan
3054 Private J. Wherty
93 Drumer H. Whissard
6753 Private A. White
2631 Private J. White
2498 Private W. White

2486 Corporal S. Whitehead
3068 Corporal S. Whiteside
1160 Private A. Whittaker
3438 Private J. Wilkinson
6427 Private F. Williamson
6529 Private T. Williamson
5382 Drummer J.C. Willoughby
3568 Private G. Wilson
2086 Private J. Wilson
2763 Sergeant J. Wilson
6731 Private J. Wilson
5750 Sergeant R. Wilson
4560 Private W. Wilson
6444 Corporal W. Wilson
3560 Private S. Winters
4780 Private W. Woodside

3608 Colour-Sergeant H Woodward
 184 Corporal J. Wylie
5169 Private S. Wylie

Y

726 Sergeant A.E. Young
6216 Private D. Young
6438 Private J. Young
5666 Sergeant R. Young
3671 Private S. Young
6763 Private T. Young
2158 Private W. Young
4477 Private W. Young

Appendix V

Recipients of the Victoria Cross
Boer War 1899-1902

Of a total of 78 Victoria Crosses awarded to British and Empire forces engaged in the Boer War 1899-1902, the following are of particular interest to the Royal Inniskilling Fusiliers.

Lieutenant Edgar Thomas Inkson (Later Colonel)
RAMC...........Hart's Hill (Inniskilling Hill)..............24th February 1900
(attd. Royal Inniskilling Fusiliers)
Aged 27.
During the attack on Hart's Hill (Inniskilling Hill) Lieutenant. Inkson carried 2nd Lieutenant Devenish, Royal Inniskilling Fusiliers, who had been seriously wounded and unable to walk, for approximately 400 yards under extremely heavy fire, to safety. His VC is held by the Royal Army Medical Corps Museum in Aldershot, England. He was mentioned in Despatches during the Boer War. During World War I he was awarded the DSO in 1917 and Mentioned in Despatches in 1917 and 1919. He died on the 19th February 1947.

Captain Robert Johnstone
Imperial Light Horse.................Elandslaagte.............21st October, 1899
Aged 27.
Captain Johnstone and another fellow Irishman and officer of the Imperial Light Horse, Captain Mullins, rushed forward and rallied their men at a crucial point in the battle, the advance being halted temporarily by very heavy fire at almost point blank range. Such a display of gallantry enabled the advance to continue. Captain Mullins was wounded in the advance. Later in his military career he achieved the rank of Major.
Captain R. Johnstone previously served with the 5th Battalion the Royal Inniskilling Fusiliers, "Donegal's Own".

Notes

Details of military careers listed in this section relate to the individuals up to and including the Boer War 1899-1902.

Chapter I
Declaration of War, Mobilization-Transportation

1   The Great Trek or Groot Trek in Afrikaans is the name given to the journey the Boers made from Cape Colony to Natal, north of the Limpopo River, in their endeavour to break free of British political policies and escape the land shortage by settling new lands.

2   Outlanders or Uitlanders were largely foreign mineworker and business people but also foreign settlers whose numbers threatened to overwhelm the Afrikaners.

3   Kruger, Stephanus Johannes Paulus, (born 10 Oct. 1825 - died 14 Jul. 1904) President of the Transvaal (South African Republic) from 1883 until his flight to Holland in 1900 during the 2nd Boer War.

4   Photocopy of Natal Government Telegraph held by the Royal Inniskilling Fusilier Museum, Enniskillen Castle.

5   *With the Flag to Pretoria* p. 15. Alfred Milner was born in Würtemburg the son of Charles Milner, MD, Professor at Tübingen and of a daughter of Major-General Ready, Governor of the Isle of Man. He was educated in Germany and King's College, London and Balliol College, Oxford. He became a barrister in 1881 and worked as a journalist from 1882 until 1885. He was Private Secretary to Mr. Goschen, 1887-1889; Under Secretary for Finance in Egypt, 1889-1892; Chairman of the Board of Inland Revenue, 1892-1897; KCB, 1895; Appointed Governor of the Cape and High Commissioner of South Africa, 1897. He was raised to the peerage in 1901.

6   Ibid., p. 15. The Rt. Hon. Joseph Chamberlain was born in London in 1836 the son of a Birmingham screw manufacturer. He was elected Mayor of Birmingham 1874-5-6; MP for Birmingham in 1876; President o the Board of Trade,1880; President of the Local Government Board, 1886, in both instances under Mr. Gladstone.
He resigned over the question of Home Rule in 1886. In 1895 he became Secretary of State for the Colonies in Lord Salisbury's administration.

7   Majuba Hill (the Hill of Doves) 26 February 1881 was a crushing defeat for the British under Sir George Pomeroy-Colley, Commander of the Natal Field Force, during the first Boer War.

8   *With the Flag to Pretoria* p. 59.

9   Queenstown was the English name for *Cobh* in County Cork, Eire.

10 *With the Flag to Pretoria* op. cit. p. 2.

Field-Marshal Lord Roberts of Kandahar, KP, VC

Born at Cawnpore, India 1832; son of General Sir Abraham Roberts, GCB; educated at Eton, Sandhurst and Addiscombe; Second-Lieutenant (Bengal Artillery), 1851 Lieutenant 1857; Captain 1860; Brev. Major 1860; Brev. Lieutenant-Colonel 1868; Brev. Colonel 1875; Major-General 1878; Lieutenant-General 1883; General 1890; raised to the peerage 1892; Field-Marshal 1895. DAQMG throughout the Indian Mutiny; served in Abyssinia, 1867-8; commanded the Kurram Field Force, 1879, Kabul Field Force, 1879-80, Kabul-Kandahar Field Force, 1880; in Afghanistan, 1880; in Burma, 1886. Commander-in-Chief (Madras), 1881; Commander-in-Chief in India, 1885-93; Commander of the Forces in Ireland, 1895, and in South Africa, December,1899.

11 During the course of this book two spellings of the name Hart can be found. It also appears as Harte depending upon which diarist is speaking at the time. General Arthur Fitzroy Hart was born in 1844 and entered the Army in 1864 as an Ensign in the 31st Foot, later the East Surrey Regiment. During the Ashanti War of 1873-4 he saw action at Amoaful, Ordahsu and Coomassie; South African War of 1879-81 against the Zulu as Captain; promoted Brevet Major and served in Transvaal as Deputy-Assistant - Adjutant and Quarter-Master-General of the Natal Field Force; Egyptian Expedition of 1882; appointed DAA and QMG Intelligence Branch and was present at Kassassin and Tel-el-Kebir.

He received his seventh mention in Despatches and promoted Brevet Lieutenant-Colonel. Commanded the East Surrey Regiment in 1891 for four years before becoming Commander of the 1st Infantry Brigade at Aldershot in 1897. Commanded the 5th Irish Brigade during the Boer War 1899-1902.

Chapter II
Battle of Colenso

1 *With the Flag to Pretoria* op.cit., p. 77. General Sir Redvers Buller, VC KCMG, KCB. Born in 1839 he entered the 60th Rifles in 1858; served in China, 1860; Red River Expedition, 1870; Ashanti War, 1874; Kaffir War, 1878; Zulu War, 1878-9; Deputy Adjutant-General, 1885; Under Secretary for Ireland, 1887; Adjutant-General, 1890; Lieutenant-General, 1891; in command at Aldershot, 1898; appointed to command of Army Corps, South Africa 1899. Sir Redvers Buller arrived in Cape Town October 31; moved on to Natal, arriving on November 25. Commander-in-Chief of the forces in South Africa up to the arrival of Lord Roberts.

2 Ibid., p. 84. Major-General Henry John Thornton Hildyard, CB had command until the beginning of the war of the 3rd Infantry Brigade at Aldershot. Originally destined for the Navy in which he served from 1859 to 1864; three years later he entered the Army, and in 1876 became a Captain in the Highland Light Infantry. He served with Egyptian Expeditionary Force in 1882, and was present at Kassassin and Tel-el-Kebir. From 1893 until 1898 he was Commandant of the Staff College. He commanded the 2nd Brigade in South Africa.

3 Ibid., p. 84. Major-General Geoffry Barton, CB
He took part in the Ashanti War of 1873-4, and in the Zulu War of 1879 commanding the 4th Battalion of the Natal Native Contingent. He again saw active service in the Egyptian War of 1882 as DAQG, being present at the battles of Kassassin and Tel-el-Kebir. During the Sudan campaign of 1885 he was Assistant Military Secretary to Sir Gerald Graham before taking up the post of commander of the 6th Brigade, South African Field Force.

4 Ibid., p. 197. Major-General Hector McDonald, CB, DSO
Served in the Afghan War of 1879-80; accompanied Lord Roberts on his march to Kabul, and was present at the battle of Kandahar; served in the Boer War of 1881; he was Garrison- Adjutant at Assiout (Upper Egypt) in 1885, and was in the Sudan during the operations of 1888-91. In 1896 he took command of the 2nd Infantry Brigade under Lord H. Kitchener, and in 1897-8 commanded Egyptian Brigades, being present at the battles of the Atbara and Khartoum. He was appointed an aide-de-camp to Queen Victoria in 1898. While acting as Brigadier-General commanding at Umballa (India), he was summoned to take command of the Highland Brigade under Lord Methuen, in succession to General Wauchope. The appointment of "Fighting Mac" as he was called was greatly welcomed by the entire Brigade.

3   Ibid., p. 84.
    Major-General The Hon.NevilleGerald Lyttelton, CB
Was in command of the 2nd Infantry Brigade at Aldershot. He was born in 1845 and was educated at Eton. He joined the Rifle Brigade in 1865, and served with it in Canada and India, seeing a good deal of active service. ADC to Lord Spencer, Viceroy of Ireland, from 1868 to 1873, and Military Secretary to Sir John Adye, Governor of Gibraltar, and to Lord Reay, Governor of Bombay. He fought in the Egyptian Campaign of 1882 and commanded a brigade in the Nile Expedition of 1898, being present at the Battle of Khartoum. He was Assistant Military Secretary at the War Office during 1897 and 1898 and given the command of the 4th Brigade in South Africa in 1898.

4   Ibid., p. 108.
Colonel C. J. Long, RA obtained his Lieutenancy in 1870; served in the Afghan War of 1878-1880, and in the Sudan under Lord Kitchener in 1897-8 as commandant of the Egyptian artillery. He was present at the Battle of Khartoum and for his services on that occasion was mentioned in despatches. Colonel, September 1899; in command of the Royal Artillery at Colenso, where his anxiety to get within effective range of the enemy led to the loss of ten guns.

5   Lieutenant Roberts, only son of Field Marshal Lord Roberts, awarded VC for his attempt to save the guns at Colenso.

6   *With the Flag to Pretoria* op.cit., p. 20. General Sir George Stuart White.-Born 1835; son of J.R. White, of Whitehall, Co. Antrim. He was educated at Sandhurst; entered the Army, 1853; served in Indian Mutiny; Captain, 1863; Major, 1873; was in the Afghan War of 1878-80; and present at the occupation of Kabul, and in the exepedition to Maidan, Sharpur; Military Secretary to Viceroy of India; Lieutenant-Colonel, Gordon Highlanders, 1881; Colonel, 1885; Assistant Adjutant and Quartermaster General in Egypt; commanded a Brigade in Burma 1885-86 (for which service he was promoted Major-General) and an expedition into Zhob. He was Commander-in-Chief in India, 1893-98.

7   General De Villebois-Mareuil (Count) was a retired French Army officer whose assistance was sought by Dr. Leyds.

8   *With the Flag to Pretoria,* op.cit., p.125.
Paul Sanford, Lord Methuen, was born in 1845 and entered the Scots Guards in 1864. He was sent on special service to the Gold Coast in 1873, and in the following year became Brigade-Major at Ashanti and for the Home District. In 1876 he was appointed Assistant Military

Secretary to the Commander-in-Chief in Ireland. From 1877 to 1881 he was Military Attaché to the British Embassy in Berlin. He commanded Methuen's Horse and the Field Force during the Bechuanaland Expedition of 1884-5, and was Deputy Adjutant General in South Africa in 1888. From 1892 until 1897 he commanded the Home District and on the outbreak of the Boer War was given command of the First Division of the Army Corps taking over command on his arrival in Cape Town on 10 November 1899.

Chapter III
Spion Kop, Vaal Krantz

1   "Skins" a nickname for The Royal Inniskilling Fusiliers.
2   Heliograph was an apparatus for reflecting sunlight in flashes indicating letters and words. It was used extensively throughout the South African campaign e.g. it enabled General Buller to keep in contact with those besieged within Ladysmith.
3   *With the Flag to Pretoria* op. cit p.284. Born in 1859 Lieutenant-Colonel A. W. Thorneycroft was in command of Mounted Infantry during the South African campaign. He was originally in the Militia; joined the Royal Scots Fusiliers in 1879; fought in the Zulu campaign and in the 1st Boer War of 1881; was appointed Deputy Assistant Adjutant-General in Natal in September 1899 and formed his regiment, Thorneycroft's Mounted Infantry, which saw action at Colenso and Spion Kop.
4   Ibid., p. 215
Lieut.-General Sir Charles Warren, GCMG, KCB, RE.
Born in 1840 he joined the Army in 1857; conducted excavations in Palestine, 1867-70; Commissioner for delimiting Griqualand West, 1876-7; commanded the Diamond Fields Horse in the Kaffir War of 1877-8; served also in Griqualand, 1878. He commanded an expedition into Arabia Petraea for the punishment of the murderers of Professor Palmer, 1882; and the Bechuanaland Expedition in 1884-5; Commissioner of Metropolitan Police, 1886-8; commanded Straits Settlements, 1889-94, and Thames District, 1895-8; appointed to the command of the Fifth Division of the South Africa Field Force, 13 November, 1899.
5   Ibid., p. 293
Major-General John Talbot Coke was educated at Harrow; entered the Army as 2nd Lieutenant in the 21st Foot in 1859, and was transfered to the 25th Foot (King's Own Scottish Borders) in 1860; Captain, 1866; Major,

1879; Lieutenant-Colonel, 1885; Colonel, 1889; was put on half pay, 1898. He served with the Suakin Field Force in 1888 during the investment of Suakin; was present in the engagement of Gemaizeh; served in the operations on the Sudan frontier in 1889; was appointed senior officer at Mauritius in 1898, with the local rank of Major-General, and left there to command the 10th Brigade of the South African Field Force, 1899.

6   Ibid., p. 283

Major-General Woodgate, CB,

Edward Robert Prevost Woodgate was the son of the rector of Belbroughton, Worcestershire. Born 1845; entered the Army as ensign in the 4th (King's Own Royal Lancaster) Regiment in 1865; served with the Abyssinian Expedition against King Theodore, 1868; in the Ashanti War of 1873-4; on the staff in the Zulu War of 1878-9; when he obtained the Brevet of Major; served as staff officer in the West Indies,1880-5, and as a regimental officer in India, 1885-9; Lieutenant-Colonel, 1893; CB 1896; Colonel 1897; appointed to command the Regimental District of the King's Own at Lancaster, 1897; raised the West African Frontier Regiment in Sierra Leone 1898; invalided home and given command of Leicestershire District. Appointed commander of the 9th Brigade in South Africa, December 1899; killed at Spion Kop, January 24, 1900.

7   Ibid., p. 319.

Major-General Arthur Wynne.

Commanded the Eleventh Brigade in the South African Field Force. He was born in Ireland in 1846; joined the 51st Light Infantry in 1863;Adjutant 1868-71; Superintendent of Signalling in the Jowaki Expedition of 1877; served in the Afghan War of 1878-9; employed on special service in South Africa in 1881; commanded the 4th Battalion Egyptian Army, 1883-5; held appointments as Deputy or Assistant-Adjutant-General at the Curragh, at Malta and at Aldershot.

8   Ibid., p. 266.

Commandant General Louis Botha.

Born in Natal, Louis Botha settled in the Transvaal prior to hostilities. He did not come from fighting stock but was a successful farmer. In the early days of the war, however, he demonstrated such   conspicuous   military ability that he was, upon Joubert's death, and despite being only thirty-six years of age, elected Commandant General of   the   Boer   forces.   Well educated, his wife's maiden name was Emmet, a descendant of Thomas Addis Emmet, the United Irish leader of 1798,   and   Robert   Emmet executed for high treason in 1803.

9   Ibid., p. 79   Winston Leonard Spencer Churchill was the eldest son of Lord Randolph Churchill.   He was born on 30 November 1874 and educated at Harrow and the Military Academy at Sandhurst, entering the Army in 1895.   He served with the Spanish forces in Cuba in 1895, in India with the Malakand Field Force in 1897, was orderly officer to Sir William Lockhart and was attached to the 21st Lancers with the Nile Expeditionary Force in 1898 and present at the Battle of Khartoum.   The Boers took him prisoner on 15 November 1899 when the armoured train in which he was travelling was ambushed at Chieveley.   He was imprisoned in the State Model School Pretoria, until his escape on 14 January 1900.   He made his way to Delagoa Bay and rejoined his regiment.   The British press closely followed these actions.

10   Ibid., p.221
Major-General Lord Kitchener of Khartoum GCB, KCMG, late R.E. became Chief of Staff to Lord Roberts in South Africa on 23 December 1899.   Born in 1850, Horatio Herbert Kitchener was the son of Lieutenant-Colonel H. H. Kitchener, and was born in Kerry.   He was educated at the Military Academy at Woolwich, and entered the Royal Engineers in 1871.   He took part in the Palestine Survey, 1874-1878, and the Cyprus Survey, 1878-1882. He commanded the Egyptian Cavalry, 1882-1884; served in the Sudan Campaign, 1883-1885; Governor of Suakin, 1886-1888; promoted Colonel, 1888; Adjutant-General of the Egyptian Army, 1888-1892; promoted Major-General, 1896; commanded the Dongola Expeditionary Force, 1896 and the Khartoum Expedition, 1898, in which campaign the power of the Khalifa was finally overthrown.

Chapter IV
Inniskilling Hill, (Hart's Hill)
Relief of Ladysmith.

1   Kimberley, one of three towns besieged by the Boers, the others being Ladysmith and Mafeking. The siege was raised on th 15 Feb. 1900 by General French's relief column.
2   *With the Flag to Pretoria* op. cit. p. 157.Lieutenant-General Thomas Kelly-Kenny, CB.   In February 1900 he commanded the Sixth Division in the Colesberg District, proceeded to Modder River Camp, and with Lord Roberts' Army, advanced to the Relief of Kimberley.   He took part in the battles of Paardeberg, Osfontein and Driefontein and in the march to Bloemfontein, which the Sixth Division was left to garrison. Lord Roberts appointed him General Officer

3 Commanding the Orange River Colony.

4 General Piet Cronje commanded the Boer forces at the beginning of the siege of Kimberley and subsequently at Magersfontein and Paardeberg where he surrendered with approximately 4,000 men to Lord Roberts. A veteran of the First Boer War, he was a ruthless and bitter enemy of Britain, having led the siege of Potchefstroom in March 1881. It was to him that Dr Jameson surrendered on 1 Jan. 1896.

5 Modder River, Magersfontein, Colenso, Stormberg. These battles were disasters for the British Army. The events of Magersfontein, Colenso and Stormberg were to give rise to the phrase by the British press, Black Week.

6 Inniskilling Hill named after the Royal Inniskilling Fusiliers due to their heroic efforts to take it, also known as Hart's Hill, (and geographically incorrectly as Wagon Hill and Pieter's Hill).

7 *The Royal Inniskilling Fusiliers December 1688 to July 1914* op. cit. p. 619
Lieutenant-Colonel T. M. G. Thackeray, Commanding Officer (1st. Feb. 1897), Born, 23 June 1849, Commissioned in 16 Foot, Joined West India Regiment 5 Jan. 1881, Joined 27th Foot 23rd Mar. 1881 MID (30 March 1900), Boer War, Killed in Action, Inniskilling Hill, Relief of Ladysmith, Natal, Boer War, 23 Feb. 1900.

8 Dum-Dum, often referred to as soft nosed, expanding bullets, explosive or man-stopping bullets. The nickel coating of the bullet is filed away at the top to allow the lead to expand.

9 Kitchener defeated General Piet Cronje at Paardeberg on the 17 Feb 1900, the anniversary of Majuba Hill, Britain's greatest defeat of the First Boer War.

10 *With the Flag to Pretoria* op.cit., p. 113. Lieutenant-General Sir William Forbes Gatacre, KCB, DSO. Born in 1843 he entered the Army in 1862: was Instructor of Military Surveying at the Royal Military College between 1875 and 1879. He was Deputy-Adjutant and QMG with the Hazara Expedition in 1888. He saw service in Burma, 1889, Chitral, 1895, Sudan, 1898 and commanded the British Division at the Battle of Khartoum. He was in command of the South-Eastern District, 1898 and appointed to command the 3rd Division in South Africa with the rank of Lieutenant-General, October 1899.

11 Mauser was the rifle used by the Boers. Cartridges were carried in a clip by which they slotted in the rifle by means of pressure exerted by the thumb. Once loaded they were pressed upwards by a spring and forced one at a time into the chamber by the bolt.

12 The Muster Roll Call, a list of all those serving with the Regiment, was the method in which it was determined who had been killed, wounded or gone missing after a battle.

13 *The Royal Inniskilling Fusiliers December 1688 to July 1914* op. cit. pp 448-449

14 Lyddite shells were fired from the Naval Guns, comprised of a detonating pellet, weight, guncotton priming and lyddite, a high explosive chiefly composed of picric acid. Closely resembling melinite, it was used mostly in rocky terrain.

15 Shrapnel shells were filled with metal balls, which on the explosion of the charge of powder, scattered in all directions. The fuse to be set to explode on impact or after a period of time.

Chapter V
Ladysmith

1. Long Tom was the name given by the Boers to their 15cm guns to counteract the guns the Royal Navy improvised by removing 4.7 inch (12cm) guns from battleships and cruisers and placing them on limbers.

2. *Echoes from the Battlefields of South Africa.* op. cit. p. 131.

3. Ibid., pp 131-132.

4. *The Royal Inniskilling Fusiliers from December 1688 to July 1914* op. cit. p. 274.

5. *With the Flag to Pretoria*, op. cit. p. 30.

Major-General J.D.P. French

Born in 1852. Served in the Militia but joined the 8th Hussars as a Lieutenant in Feb. 1874, and changed to the 19th Hussars in March of that year. Promoted Captain 1880 and Major in 1883. Served in the Nile Expedition of 1884-5, and accompanied Sir H. Stewart's Column in the attempt to rescue General Gordon at Khartoum. Subsequently promoted Lieutenant-Colonel, 1885 and Colonel 1889. He commanded the Cavalry Division in South Africa with the rank of Lieutenant-General in 1899. He was in command of the forces which routed the Boers at Elandslaagte, and left Ladysmith by the last train which succeeded in getting out of the town before the Boers laid siege. He took over command of the British forces operating in and around Colesberg on 10 November 1899, and led the Cavalry division which effected the relief of Kimberley, under orders from Lord Roberts, 15 February, 1900 and helped surround Cronje and force his surrender on 27 February. For these actions he was promoted Major- General in 1900. He also was in command of the cavalry at Bloemfontein and Wepener. During World War I he attained the rank of Field-Marshal.

6. Ibid., p. 59.

Field-Marshal Viscount Wolseley, Commander- in-Chief of the Army. Born 4 June 1833 at Golden Bridge, County Dublin, Ireland, the son of Major Garnet Joseph Wolseley he entered the Army in 1852. Promoted Captain, 1855; Major, 1858; Lieutenant-Colonel, 1859; Colonel, 1863; Governor of Natal, 1875; Lieutenant-General and Governor of Cyprus, 1878; General 1882; Field-Marshal, 1894; Commander of Forces in Ireland, 1890 - 1895. He served in Burma, the Crimea, at Lucknow, in China and Canada; commanded the Red River Expedition, 1870, the Ashantee Expedition, 1873; the Egyptian Expedition, 1882, and the Gordon Relief Expedition, 1884. As Commander-in-Chief at home he shared with Lord Lansdowne the overall responsibility for troop mobilization and supply throughout the South African Campaign. He died at Mentone, France on 26 March 1913.

7. *The Royal Inniskilling Fusiliers from December 1688 to July 1914* op.cit Colonel R. Lloyd Payne, DSO. Commanding Officer 27 Apr. !900 on promotion from the Somerset Light Infantry. Born 24 May 1854, Commissioned in 105 Foot (Militia) 5 Jan 1876, joined 13th Foot 19 Jan. 1876, DSO, Boer War, MID (Twice) (13th September 1900 & 9th November 1900) Boer War. Promoted Brevet Colonel Boer War 29th Nov. 1900, Colonel of the 13th Foot 5 April 1914, Retired 23 July 1917, Died 20 Dec. 1921.

8. Mafeking. Relieved 17 May 1900.

Chapter VI
" Our Doings in the Transvaal."

1. *With the Flag to Pretoria* op. cit., p. 121. Major-General Francis Howard, CB, CMG was born in Berlin in 1848. Educated privately and at Sandhurst he joined the Rifle Brigade in 1866 and served in the Jowaki Expedition, 1878, in Afghanistan, 1878- 1879, and in Upper Burma, 1887-1889. He was promoted Captain, 1878; Major, 1882; Lieutenant-Colonel, 1889; Brevet-Colonel 1895; ADC to Queen Victoria, 1895. He served in the Sudan Campaign of 1898, and in Crete the same year. He retired on half-pay in December 1898 but in October 1899 was appointed to the command of 7th Brigade in South Africa with local rank of Major-General, and went through the siege of Ladysmith.

2. Ibid., p. 334. General Ralph Arthur Penrhyn Clements, DSO, ADC commanded the 12th Brigade, South African Field Force. He was the son of the Rev. J. Clements, sub-dean of Lincoln Cathedral. He was educated at Rossall; Lieutenant 24th Foot (South Wales Borderers), 1874; Captain 1880; Major 1886; Lieutenant-Colonel, 1887; Colonel 1896; Aide-de-Camp to Queen Victoria 1896; served in the Kaffir and Zulu wars, 1879, and in Burma, where he gained the DSO, 1885-1889.

3. Ibid., p. 134.   General Pole-Carew, CB entered the Coldstream Guards as a Ensign in 1869 and commanded the 2nd Battalion until 1898. During the Second Afghan War he acted as ADC to Lord Roberts; and to HRH the Duke of Connaught in the Expedition against Arabi Pasha. He went through the Burmese War of 1886 and was awarded the CB for gallant conduct.

4. *With the Flag to Pretoria Volume 3, After Pretoria: The Guerrilla War*, op. cit. p. 5.   Major-General Arthur Henry Paget was born in 1851, the son of General Lord A. H. Paget, CB. He joined the Scots Guards in 1869 and was promoted Captain in 1872, Lieutenant-Colonel 1882; Regimental Major.

5.   1891; Colonel, 1895; Lieut.-Colonel Scots Guards, 1899, Major-General commanding the 20th Brigade, South Africa, April 1900. He served in the Ashanti Expedition, 1873-1874, during the second phase of the war, attached to Captain Buller's command; in the Sudan Expedition in 1885; with the 2nd Battalion Scots Guards in Burma 1887-1888; in the Sudan, 1888-1889; in the Boer War, 1899-1900, in command of the 1st Battalion Scots Guards, and was present at Belmont, Enslin, Modder River and during the march on Bloemfontein.

Chapter VII
1901

1. *After Pretoria: The Guerilla War.* op. cit., p. 576.
Colonel E. H. H. Allenby. He was born in 1861   and   joined   the   6th (Inniskilling) Dragoons in 1882; promoted Captain   in   1888;   Adjutant 1889-1893; Major 1897; Adjutant, Cavalry Brigade,   1898-9;   Lieutenant-Colonel, January 1901; promoted Colonel, April 1901, while commanding the 6th Dragoons in South Africa. He served   with   the   Inniskilling Dragoons in the Bechuanaland Expedition under Sir C. Warren, 1884-5; in the operations in Zululand, 1888; and in the South African War, 1899-1902.

2. Blockhouses were the invention of Major Spring R. Rice who had entered the Royal Engineers in 1877, obtained his Captaincy in 1888 and was promoted Major in 1896. Known as the Rice blockhouse, they were inexpensive and comparatively portable, made of corrugated iron. Circular in design the walls were filled with shingle. Blockhouses played a vital role in bringing the Boer War to a close by effectively restricting the movements of the Boer commandos.

3. Ibid., p. 555. Lieutenant-Colonel A. G. Hunter-Weston joined the Royal Engineers in 1884 and was subsequently promoted Captain in 1892, Major 1895 and Lieutenant-Colonel in 1900. He served in the Miranzai Expedition, 1891; with the Waziristan Expedition 1894-5; with the Dongola Expeditionary Force 1896; in the South African war 1899-1901. He commanded the Royal Engineers in French's Column; took part in the operations round Colesberg; in the advance to Bloemfontein and Pretoria. DAAG, Cavalry Division in the advance to Middelburg. Joined General French as a Staff Officer from December 1900.

4. Ibid., p. 676. After the relief of Kimberley Lieutenant-Colonel R. G. Kekewich CB was promoted and after a spell of rest took over one of three columns under General Babington in January 1901, operating against De la Rey. On the 30 September 1901 he was wounded twice in defence of his camp at Moedwill, west of Magato Nek , Magaliesberg, repulsing a night attack by De la Rey.

Chapter VIII
1902

1. *With the Flag to Pretoria* op. cit., p. 555. Lieutenant-Colonel Henry De Beauvoir De Lisle DSO was born in Dublin in 1864 the son of Richard De Lisle of Guernsey and was educated in Jersey. He joined the 2nd Battalion the Durham Light Infantry at Gibraltar in 1883 and obtained his Captaincy in 1891. He served with the Sudan Frontier Field Force from 1885 until 1886 with the Mounted Infantry; local Lieutenant-Colonel in command of the 2nd Corps, 1st Brigade, mounted Infantry, South Africa, January 1900. He distinguished himself during the fighting at Colesberg, Doornkop and Pretoria where he turned the Boer southern position and dispatched a flag of truce to demand the surrender of the town. His Column, because of its strange formation of galloping to attack a position with men extended fifty paces apart, became known as the "galloping column".

2. *After Pretoria: The Guerilla War.* op. cit., p. 555.   Major-General Edward Locke Elliot, CB, DSO was born in 1850 and joined the 108th Foot (2nd Inniskillings) in 1868. He was promoted Captain in 1880; Major, Indian Staff Corps, 1888; Lieutenant-Colonel 1894; Colonel 1898; DAQMG Bombay 1880-5; Inspector -General of Cavalry in India 1898; temporary Major-General 1898.   He served in the Afghan War 1878-9; with the Burmese Expedition 1885-9; with the Dongola Expeditionary Force under Sir. H. Kitchener in 1896. He was awarded the DSO in 1887; the CB in 1896. Major-General on the Staff in South Africa, February 1901.

3.   Ibid., p. 492. Lieutenant-Colonel The Hon. Arthur H. Henniker, CB was born in London in 1855 and joined the Coldstream Guards from the Militia in 1875. He was promoted Captain, 1885; Major, 1894 and Lieut-Colonel in 1899.   He was Commandant, School of Musketry for Auxiliary Forces, Wellington Barracks, 1886; Assistant Private Secretary to the Secretary of State for War. 1888-91; DAAG, Headquarters of Army, 1898. He served in the Egyptian Expedition, 1882 and in the South African War, 1899-1901 and was present at the Battle of Belmont.

Bibliography

Army List.

Commonwealth War Graves Commission

http://yard.ccta.gov.uk/cwgc/regi…teservicedetails?openagent&855629

hhp://www.chapter-one.com/vc/awards/i/0617.html

Kidd, Dudley, *Echoes of the Battlefields of South Africa,* (Marshall Brothers, Keswick House, Paternoster Row, London. 1900)

Ladysmith Museum Services.

Regimental Diary Lieut. D. G. Auchinleck, Feb. 1900 - Oct. 1901.

Regimental Diary 4445 Pte L. J. Bryant.

Regimental Diary Capt. A. C. Jeffcoat DSO.

Regimental Historical Records Committee,

The Royal Inniskilling Fusiliers from December 1688 to July 1914 (Constable & Company Ltd., London ,1934).

Robinson, C. N., Commander Royal Navy, *Celebrities of the Army* (G. Newnet, London, 1900.)

Roll of Honour of Ireland

Sprig of Sheelagh1897: A monthly Journal of the 27th Inniskillings.

Sprig of Sheelagh1898: A monthly Journal of the 27th Inniskillings

The Donegals' Own Journal No. 42, Vol. III Ballyshannon, April, 1903: A monthly Magazine for the 5th Battalion Royal Inniskilling Fusiliers,

The Standard Illustrated History of the Boer War,

With the Flag to Pretoria,

The Standard Illustrated History of the Boer War,

After Pretoria, the Guerrilla War.

The Times History of the War in South Africa Vol II.

Trimble, *Inniskilling Fusiliers at the Battle of Inniskilling Hill,* (Printed & published at the "Impartial Observer" Office, Enniskillen)

Index